D0132382

Abstracting Craft

Abstracting Craft

The Practiced Digital Hand

Malcolm McCullough

The MIT Press
Cambridge, Massachusetts
London, England

First MIT Press paperback edition, 1998
©1996 Massachusetts Institute of Technology
All Rights Reserved. No part of this book may be reproduced in any form by any electronic or mechanical means (including photocopying, recording, or information storage and retrieval) without permission in writing from the publisher.

This book was set in Garamond 3 and Meta by Graphic Composition, Inc.

Printed and bound in the United States of America.

Library of Congress Cataloging-in-Publication Data

McCullough, Malcolm.
Abstracting craft : the practiced digital hand / Malcolm McCullough.
p. cm.
Includes bibliographical references and index.
ISBN 0-262-13326-1 (hc: alk. paper), 0-262-63189-X (pb)
1. Digital computer simulation. 2. Virtual reality. I. Title.
QA76.9.C65M393 1996
004′.01′9—dc20 96-28356
CIP

AutoCAD is a trademark of Autodesk, Inc.
Director and Freehand are trademarks of Macromedia, Inc.
MacDraw is a trademark of Apple Computer, Inc.
Myst is a trademark of Broderbund, Inc.
Painter is a trademark of Fractal Design, Inc.
Photoshop is a trademark of Adobe Systems, Inc.
Pro-Engineer is a trademark of Parametric Technologies, Inc.

"On Craft, Creativity, and Surprise" reprinted by permission of Jerome Bruner.

In memory of Dorothy Humason, my grandmother, a painter

Contents

The true workman must put his individual intelligence and enthusiasm into the goods which he fashions. He must have a natural attitude for his work so strong that no education can force him away from his special bent. He must be allowed to think of what he is doing, and to vary his work as the circumstances of it vary, and his own moods. He must forever be stirring to make the piece at which he is at work better than the last. He must refuse at anybody's bidding to turn out—I won't say a bad—but even an indifferent piece of work, whatever the public wants, or thinks it wants.

—William Morris

Preface

Unless the distinction vanishes in some cyborg future, people will always be more interesting than technology. People have talents and intentions that technology may serve. People also have much more immediate requirements, such as for food, clothing, and transportation, which modern technology has provided quite effectively. But when these material needs are mostly met, continued industrial production increasingly depends on invented needs and induced demands, which are neither satisfying nor sustainable. People cannot endure as "consumers," but must actively practice at something, however humble. This means that the ultimate significance of postindustrial technology has to be in serving the need to work well—and not in automation. Here at the close of this very technological century, even the most hard-nosed technologists have begun to admit this. For example, the computer industry now advertises not computers, but human-computer partnerships: it matters less what the technology can do alone than what you want to do with it.

This is especially true in design. Consider how antiquated the philosophy of automatic design computing has become. Back in the space-age

1960s, high modern thinking actually sought to expunge any recourse to personal or habitual knowledge in design, and as recently as the headstrong 1980s many researchers seemed to believe in a completely formalized artificial intelligence. But by now such positivistic endeavors have achieved the quality of self-caricature. By now it is absurd to ignore the role of talent, of inarticulable knowledge, of contextual understanding, and of dedicated practice. Of course, these are some of the most interesting qualities of people.

Nevertheless, technology has become more intriguing than ever. As computers have expanded their roles from business automation into personal communication and visual arts, and as the internet has suddenly connected so many of us into a veritable ecology of talents, clearly the experience of technology has improved. Clearly we have escaped that industrial age in which technology and talent were so directly opposed. In the process, we are reuniting skill and intellect.

Early in the 1990s, I began hearing references to some of my skillful intellectual colleagues as craftsmen. This seemed quite odd because these people worked in the abstract realm of computers. Yet somehow this linguistic turn made sense, as if it filled a gap in our understanding. It was a big gap—one worth a book. Now the book is complete and the word "craft" has come into widespread usage in a great range of contexts, from beer to business memos to biomorphic spline surface modeling.

Virtual craft still seems like an oxymoron; any fool can tell you that a craftsperson needs to touch his or her work. This touch can be indirect—indeed no glassblower lays a hand on molten material—but it must be physical and continual, and it must provide control of whole processes. Although more abstract endeavors such as conducting an orchestra or composing elegant software have often been referred to as crafts, this has always been in a more distant sense of the word. Relative to these notational crafts, our nascent digital practices seem more akin to traditional handicrafts, where a master continuously coaxes a material. This new work is increasingly continuous, visual, and productive of singular form; yet it has no material.

In attempting to unwrap this contradiction, I have taken some unconventional approaches. I have tried to avoid the twin academic traps of scientific overspecialization and literary deconstruction and yet come away with something more than just palliative folk psychology. I have pursued comprehensiveness over certainty, as if lateral resonance and interdisciplinary insight are now too important to neglect just because they evade empirical proof. So in the spirit of inclusion, may you find enough unanticipated juxtapositions and fortunate discoveries to offset any assumptions and oversimplifications necessitated by the book's range. May you find some resonance with practices of your own. Finally, may you also share some joy in a variety of humane viewpoints, as if that alone can make scholarship worthwhile.

Acknowledgments

This work reflects contributions and suggestions by quite a number of colleagues and friends, many of them somehow associated with the Harvard University Graduate School of Design. Thanks mostly to the patient readers of progress manuscripts: Michael Benedikt, Carole Bolsey, Richard Dodge, Stephen Ervin, Kimo Griggs, Kit Krankel, Alex McCullough, Noam Maitless, Scott Minneman, William Mitchell, Daniel Schodek, Hinda Sklar, Andrew Szanton, and Warren Wake. In sum they brought a great range of expertise and interest to the project, reflected in the diversity of their very helpful comments. Surely the single most essential contribution came from Debra Edelstein, who edited the first complete draft so rigorously that I was quickly able to focus the project into its basically final form. Warren Wake's dissertation was maybe the earliest inspiration, and it left little unsaid on the topic of tools. William Mitchell has been a perennial source of guidance, and his many writings are often echoed quite directly here. Thanks also to those who contributed illustrations: Martha Mahard dug through slide libraries, Wade Hokoda created pieces expressly, and Noam Maitless offered a set of collages that became chapter frontispieces. Many others (cited elsewhere) granted use of recent work or rights to include previously published images. Apologetic thanks to Steve Harrison, who arranged my sabbatical at Xerox PARC, and then patiently watched the completion of this project absorb so much of my time there. Thanks, finally, to Melissa Vaughn and Yasuyo Iguchi, who so knowingly edited and designed this book.

Introduction

How might you read this book? In what manner is it intended to be received? How is it organized? How much does it expect you to know already? For whom has it been written?

In the unusual event that a master takes time out to articulate a craft, the result seldom takes a well-established literary form. If a scholar attempts to connect divergent aspects of a fundamental human activity, the result may not adhere to established standards of academic rigor. When such aspects range from the poetic to the technical, the social, and the theoretical, there may be no level at which all of the writing can work for every reader.

This book has been written and edited with four particular audiences in mind. The first of these groups is quite general: those urbane individuals who have decided only recently that computing has become a worthwhile topic. Many of these people might want a book that is neither about how to accomplish some particular process, nor how to assess what so much technology means—and most computer-related books seem to be one or the other of these. Instead, a literate person anticipating some computer experience might want to hear from a veteran about what using the technology is *like,* and which among the infinity of technical issues might still matter tomorrow, and how creative computing fits within a larger intellectual history. Such a person should enjoy this book without any prior knowledge of the subject matter. If the technical material is to make any sense, however, the general reader should have had at least enough rudimentary exposure to computer usage that elementary pieces of jargon such as "window" or "pointing" seem normal. The general reader is invited to skip over parts of the middle, more technical section if those seem too dry. The heart of the argument lies in the final third of the book, so get there!

The second audience should consist of technology specialists. Experts in human-computer interaction, software designers, and various other specialists may enjoy hearing from a seasoned if occasionally naive "user" what kind of anthropological and psychological issues seem to matter. Computer scientists in particular may uncover aesthetic terminologies and arguments pertinent to their own endeavors.

The third audience is academic. Orthodox researchers in computation should find an eccentric reminder of the peril that lies in ignoring whatever fails to fit one's theories or show up on one's instruments. Critical theorists and media arts critics should find a few jabs but also a neostructuralist case for digital aesthetics. Others such as cognitive neuroscientists, behavioral psychologists, and ethnographers of work might skim for interesting connections to their own conceptual structures.

The fourth anticipated audience could become the largest. It is all the digital craftsmen and craftswomen out there. Admittedly most people are not artists, and most computer usage experts are not philosophers, but there could be countless postindustrial artisans waiting for someone to acknowledge their artistry and humanity in a literate way. These are not the unfortunate legions consigned to tedious, injurious, back-office data-entry work, nor the also numerous dumb-it-down office automation managers, nor the high-end Hollywood special-effects gurus, but a growing class of everyday digital artifact producers. Anyone who makes a living on his mastery of a suite of software media applied to a particular discipline, who knows he is something far better than an industrial equipment attendant, (e.g., a "CAD operator"), who wants greater recognition or even license for artistry in very practical work, and who yet takes time to read anthro-techno-psychological books, might enjoy what he finds here. Such a person need not read every word, for much content should sound familiar. Again, for those who skip around, the heart of the argument lies in the final section.

The organization of the book is essentially as follows. Part I explores the fundamental humanity of handicraft, design vision, and tool usage, and introduces the potential impact of computing on each of these. In a way, the whole section is an Introduction. Because the book is inclusive and sometimes divergent by nature, it needs introduction from a variety of points on the intellectual compass. Indeed, chapter 1 is five separate introductions—a suite of prologues. In reading this part of the book it is not as important to keep track of a thread, which would be difficult to do in any case, as to develop scope.

Part II reviews the technical and theoretical foundations for the proposition of the computer as a medium. As technical exposition it is presumably less entertaining than the other parts of the book. As a work for a broad audience having such a range of technical backgrounds, it invites detailed attention in some places and cursory review in others. Beginners might jump out where experts might jump in. Be aware that these three chapters change scope from the most general to the very specific. Chapter 4, on symbols, is quite necessary to the overall book structure, but is sometimes quite cursory. Conversely, chapter 6, on constructions, is less essential to the overall argument except as a representative study based on the author's main area of depth. It is therefore the least necessary for the generalist to grasp, but at the same time perhaps the most credible for the specialist who is looking for cases of experience. But despite this invitation to jump around, these chapters have been laid out so that anyone should be able to follow their development in sequence.

Part III presents the experience of craft in the world of digital media.

In comparison to the other sections, which draw heavily on established sources to establish general intellectual context, this section offers a response to that context. Its three chapters make respective cases for computer as medium, the necessity of playful production, and the necessity of involved practice. These chapters do not necessarily draw a firm conclusion on where we are and how we got here, for we are in too many states and places to say, but they should express one clear voice on the personal worth of work.

Throughout the book, illustrations and examples have been drawn from a variety of disciplines. Due to this wide scope, certain sources have been taken as representative guides, at times to the exclusion of others, through wide areas of the literature. Graphical illustrations have often been taken from more traditional disciplines, such as architecture, but that selection should not suggest that this is a book only for members of those disciplines. Anyone who builds or practices software for giving form to things, whether in painting, animating, modeling, simulating, or manufacturing could take interest. May a broad range of people find relevance here.

I Human Context

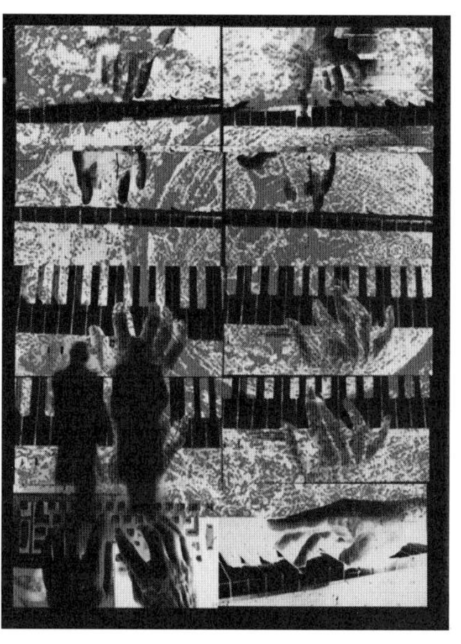

1 Hands

Five Prologues

1 Hands Are Underrated

Hands are underrated. Eyes are in charge, mind gets all the study, and heads do all the talking. Hands type letters, push mice around, and grip steering wheels, so they are not idle, just underemployed.

This is a sorry state of affairs, for hands can contribute much to working and knowing. By pointing, by pushing and pulling, by picking up tools, hands act as conduits through which we extend our will to the world. They serve also as conduits in the other direction: hands bring us knowledge of the world. Hands feel. They probe. They practice. They give us sense, as in good common sense, which otherwise seems to be missing lately.

Take a look at your hands. Right now they are holding this book. That alone makes the book more intimate than television. The two hands are working together, but sometimes one might take over the holding, by putting a thumb on the opposite leaf, while the other reaches out to adjust a lamp or raise a drink to your lips. When that hand comes back, the

1.1 Hands enjoying direct contact with material, from the documentary *In Praise of Hands*

two may find their old positions or assume new ones: the variations seem endless. Even amid this simple activity, hands seem to have a life of their own.[1]

Hands show life most when at work. They don't just hold: they grasp, they pinch, they press, they guide. To pick up a coin, to turn a key, to lift a handle: each uses a fundamentally different grip. Work that applies force takes a different form than work that exercises precision. Moreover, all this work is fast: the hand is quicker than the eye. Hands are versatile, too: they give and take pressure, heat, and texture, and maybe other energy fields. (Try a foot massage with the hands just above the skin.) And for working hands, taking may be as important as giving: hands get shaped. They may get callused or stained. They pick up experience.

Much life of the hands is a form of knowledge: not a linguistic or symbolic knowledge such as you might use to read this book or write a computer program, but something based more on concrete action, such as sculpting plaster or clay. The knowledge is not only physical, but also experiential. The way of hands is personal, contextual, indescribable. Little can surpass the hands in showing that we know more than we can say. Psychologists and social scientists have studied this inarticulable knowledge extensively, and they have many names for it: operative, action-centered, enactive, reflection-in-action, know-how. The most common word is *skill.*

You might be skillful at anything from a plainly mechanical task to a subtle lifelong practice. For example, perhaps you can type quickly, or have mastered wood joinery. Maybe you draw quite well. You probably understand skill in terms of your own abilities, whatever their level and application, and for this reason the word has as many meanings as there are different talents. However, we might generalize: skill is the learned ability to do a useful process well.

Some forms of this ability bear detailed study; others do not. For example, among cognitive psychologists there is substantial literature on a form of hand-eye coordination known as tracking. Technically, tracking is the use of continuous compensatory feedback to keep a tool on target, as in driving a car, or catching a ball. Similarly, there has been much study of skill in executing long sequences of discrete events, as for data entry or parts assembly. By contrast, there seems to be less documentation of skills that are not so purely behavioral, for example, skills of recognition, of appraisal, of knowing the limits of material. For example, although any experienced mechanic knows the feel of a well-tightened nut and bolt—he or she can recognize the point where the elasticity of the threads has been fully taken up—there is no easy way to test this skill except by indirect means, such as statistically sampling the results of skilled work. Although productivity is perhaps a measure of such a skill, the skill is not mere productivity.

Skill also differs from talent, and from conceptual grasp, even if it may reflect them. Talent seems native, and concepts come from schooling, but skill is learned by doing. It is acquired by demonstration and sharpened by practice. Although it comes from habitual activity, it is not purely mechanical. This is evident not only in the fact that some skills are

1.2 The versatile hand: various grips and grasps

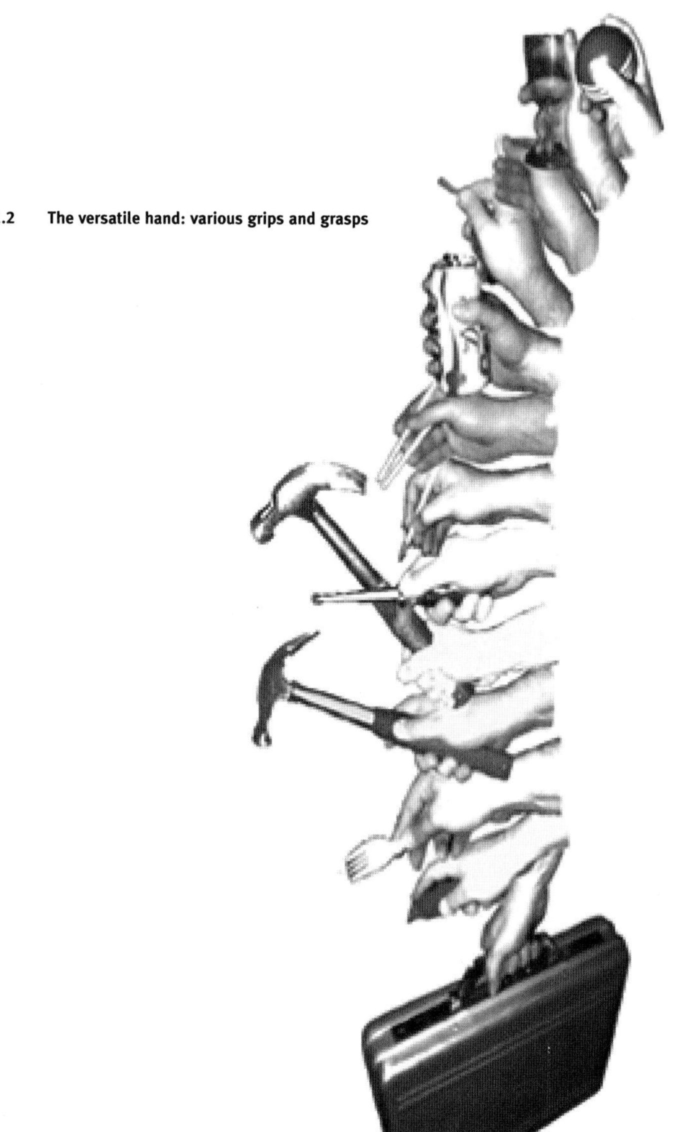

difficult to measure, but also in that skill can become the basis of an avocation. Commitment to skillful practice lies at the heart of traditional work, and although we cannot always explain how, we sense that the most refined practices belong to the hands.

Hands are underrated because they are poorly understood. Artists have seldom been able to simultaneously exercise and scrutinize their manual talents. Traditional artisans have seldom been inclined to articulate their expertise. Academics, despite a growing faction interested in "body criticism," generally ignore the hands in their epistemologies of the mind. There are exceptions, as in medicine. For example, kinesiologists can construct prehension for artificial hands. Psychologists can prescribe sensory-motor learning to rehabilitate wounded hands. Surgeons can use remote-control technologies that support some aspects of their delicate manual skill. Even in medicine, however, researchers seem unable to formulate much beyond the mechanical aspects of manual behavior.[2] Science has trouble explaining a caress.

Maybe the best defense of skill to appear in modern philosophical writing occurs within the philosopher/chemist Michael Polanyi's study of scientific learning, *Personal Knowledge* (1958). Polanyi aimed to show that even factual knowledge is acquired through personal commitment. His main argument concerns the subjective act of affirming objective scientific methods. Whatever it is that drives a researcher to pursue particular sorts of findings is inarticulable and personal. Polanyi's study probes tacit knowledge in a variety of nonscientific settings as well. For example, his most striking (and oft-cited) image portrays the hands playing a piano: "Musicians regard it as a glaringly obvious fact that the sounding of a note can be done in different ways, depending on the 'touch' of the pianist. To acquire the right touch is the endeavor of every learner, and the mature artist counts its possession among his chief accomplishments. The pianist's touch is prized alike by the public and by his pupils: it has a great value in money. Yet when the process of sounding a note is analyzed, it appears difficult to account for the existence of touch."[3]

Not surprisingly, many advances in touch technology that have occurred since Polanyi's time have come from digital musicians. The standard code for the musical instrument digital interface (MIDI) has effectively allowed many musicians to become instrument designers. Besides encoding sound waveforms, and supporting sequencers, MIDI controls interpretation of input actions such as keyboard strokes. Thus, for example, it can program a specific relation of touch to timbre, or it can program a pressure-sensitive device to transform an existing audio stream.[4] Yet this electro-mechanical virtuosity has not necessarily demystified traditional instruments. Nor has it carried nearly so far into other art forms, such as drawing or sculpture, let alone into everyday business.

By and large, everyday computing involves very little touch technology. Most ordinary tools and technologies, and most understandings of skillful process, exist without explicit formulations for the role of the hands. Nonmechanical aspects of touch elude practical engineering; some elude scientific description.

Often it is difficult to simultaneously apply and study a skill. Note that effectively maintained skill tends to hold a subsidiary relation to the focus of the action. Even if rules exist, we are not conscious of following them. It is emblematic, as Polanyi notes, that: "If a pianist shifts his attention from the piece he is playing to the observation of what he is doing with his fingers while playing it, he gets confused and may have to stop."[5]

Hands are not the sole locus of this kind of personal knowledge. The entire body may "know," as in dance. In such cases, knowledge is all the more likely to be physically inscribed, without an overtly intellectual component. What, for example, are the rules for swimming? Henri Bergson described this condition quite pleasingly: "Thousands and thousands of variations on the theme of walking will never yield a rule for swimming: come, enter the water, and when you know how to swim, you will understand how the mechanism of swimming is connected to that of walking. Swimming is an extension of walking, but walking would never have pushed you on to swimming."[6]

The work of hands, however, intrigues us more than most other forms of action. The hands can lend an interest to full bodily exertion, as in sport, but they can also act as guides or outlets for intellectual endeavor, as in art. Their learning can be subtle and practiced, more like piano playing and less like swimming. Hands, more than any other part of the body, become quite skilled.

If manual ability has a way of defying explanation, that is because it is based not in language but in action. Skill is participatory. This same basis makes it durable: any teacher knows that active participation is the way to retainable knowledge. In this regard skill has intrinsic, personal worth. It is an achievement. Almost any practiced person values her skill above and beyond what it is good for producing, as though there were psychological benefits to mastery itself.

For example, the circumstances of practice are often themselves a source of satisfaction. This is because skill is sentient: it involves cognitive cues and affective intent. It is also very habitual. In particular, it develops an intimate relation with certain contexts or tools, which makes it individual. No two people will be skilled alike; no machine will be skilled at all. Of course the latter is debatable if we accept simple mechanical or deductive capacity as skill—but we are maintaining that there is a sentient component too. One way our sentient activity differs from the action of machines is play. We putter about in our studios. We *enjoy* being skilled. We experiment to grow more so. Skills beget more skills.

In sum, hands are the best source of tacit personal knowledge because of all the extensions of the body, they are the most subtle, the most sensitive, the most probing, the most differentiated, and the most closely connected to the mind. They deserve to be admired.

2 The Phenomenon of Handicraft

"In Praise of Hands" is the name of two celebrated works of criticism worth recalling during these early days of abstract computational media. The first of these is the final chapter of Henri Focillon's classic aesthetic treatise, *The Life of Forms in Art* (1934). The second is a documentary film, *In Praise of Hands* (1974), with a narrative by poet laureate Octavio Paz.

Focillon addresses the dynamics of creativity, for which he argues that art must be tangible.[7] Object form, he asserts, is the one way to record the flux of forms that occurs in space, in matter, and especially in the mind. The apprehension and giving of form is a dynamic process, rather than a static code; giving form gives works their meaning. Of course the givers of form are the hands. Focillon writes: "When one realizes that the quality of a tone or of a value depends not only on the way in which it is made, but also on the way in which it is set down, then one understands that the god in five persons manifests himself everywhere."[8] Through the hand, authorship involves execution, and expression involves workmanship.

The quality of being set down may be understood as being what we might call "thrown," that is, executed at a particular moment, with a particular degree of skill, and with particular idiosyncrasy to the result. This suggests a focused action, at which moment the focused skill of the hands becomes critical, interrupting a more usual state during which time the hands quietly probe. The most essential point to Focillon's argument is that form giving is a two-way process. "The hand knows that an object has physical bulk, that it is smooth or rough, that it is not soldered to heaven or earth from which it appears to be inseparable. The hand's action defines the cavity of space and the fullness of the objects which occupy it. Surface, volume, density, and weight are not optical phenomena. Man first learned about them between his fingers and in the hollow of his palm."[9] Whereas the eyes stay fixed on the outer surface of things, hands have a way of getting inside, and so they contribute more to our belief in the reality of the world.

Hands also discover. They have a life of their own that leads them into explorations. For example, a sculptor's feel for a material will suggest actions to try, and places to cut. Learning through the hands shapes creativity itself. "The hand is not the mind's docile slave. It searches and experiments for its master's benefit; it has all sorts of adventures; it tries its chance."[10]

Focillon's position is all about sensate presence—it is pure phenomenology. The object is a manifestation and a gathering. This object presence is a product of a tool, and the tool used in form giving both fashions and is fashioned by the hand. The work is a daily form of communion. The practice of work maintains a necessary psychological connection to a dim archaic past. The impressions conveyed by the hands complement those expressed by speech, and both are necessary.

Focillon is ambivalent about industry, however, for he dislikes its artlessness. For example, he protests the loss of "even the most modest and uniform execution [that] betrays the artist's touch—that decisive contact between man and object."[11] In one place he accuses industry of being "a beast without hands, whose dull and monotonous products remain only at the threshold of art."[12] But he usually praises hands without any explicit critique of industrialization, and celebrates tools as a way of probing the world. "I do not know if there is a break between the manual and the mechanical orders—I am not very sure of it—but the implement at the end of his arm does not refute man's existence."[13] This is to say that tool usage, even when machine powered, can remain very much humane.

Focillon's argument survives quite well outside his own intellectual context, and it has enjoyed a recent revival for the counterpoint it offers to poststructuralist discourses. Current readers may recognize that Focillon's concern was mainly for high aesthetics, and that phenomenology was simply his form of opposition to the dematerialism of dada and schematism of the early moderns, but they may find that his lasting lesson centers on the unity of working and learning.

Another name for the same lesson might be "Use and Contemplation," which is the title of the Octavio Paz narrative accompanying the film, exhibition, and catalogue entitled *In Praise of Hands.* In this essay, Paz compares the wholeness of traditional craft with the modern separation of use and beauty: "In the work of handcraftsmen there is a constant shifting back and forth between usefulness and beauty. This continual interchange has a name: pleasure. Things are pleasing because they are useful and beautiful. This copulative conjunction defines craftwork, just as the disjunctive conjunction defines art and technology: usefulness *or* beauty."[14]

This is a remarkably clear invocation of the spirit that motivates craft. These themes of continuity, practicality, simple beauty, and play will keep coming back to us. We should take them to heart.

Paz constructs both art and industry as surrogate religions, each seeking a communion lost through this separation. Art consecrates objects that have no other function than to be. "In modern works of art meaning dissolves into the sheer emanation of being. Jackson Pollock's paintings do not mean, they are." We might say that art became separated from utility at the time of industrialization, from representation after the rise of the camera, and from symbolic interpretation in the era of television and cinema—and after two centuries at last achieved complete independence from workmanship. (Each of these was once considered a source of meaning.) In the generation that elapsed between Focillon and Paz, art became fully intertextual—that is, self-referential.

Industry, meanwhile, worships objects that have no being but their function—that are *nothing but* useful. Industry's creed is efficiency. According to Paz, "The industrial object tends to disappear as a form and to become indistinguishable from its function. Its being is its meaning and its meaning is to be useful. It is the diametrical opposite of the work of art. . . . The destination of the work of art is the air-conditioned eternity of the museum; the destiny of the industrial object is the trash barrel. The handcrafted object ordinarily escapes both of these."

The handcrafted object reflects not only an informal economy of energy (as opposed to one of process efficiency), but also pleasure. Its production involves some play, some waste, and above all a kind of communion. Its long life continues to enhance its qualities through use and contemplation—to invoke the title chosen by Paz. As an object it represents and serves its culture; its daily handling is a humble act of participation in that culture. Paz the poet evoked a metaphorical communion with archaic pasts:

> Since the thing is made by human hands, the craft object preserves the fingerprints—be they real or metaphorical—of the artisan who fashioned it. These imprints are not the signature of the artist; they are not a name. Nor are they a trademark. Rather, they are a sign: the scarcely visible, faded scar commemorating the original brotherhood of men and their separation. Being made by human hands; the

craft is made for human hands: we can not only see it but caress it with our fingers.

It has many tongues: it speaks the language of clay and minerals, or air currents flowing between canyon walls, of washerwomen as they scrub, of angry skies, of rain. A vessel of baked clay: do not put it in a glass case alongside rare precious objects. It would look quite out of place.[15]

3 A Short History of Craft

To wax poetic on a humble water jug is an act of which only the modern era could be capable—this kind of appreciation arises only against the threat of extinction. (Appreciation was indeed the purpose of the film *In Praise of Hands,* which was one of the earliest instances of the "trade, not aid" policies by which the developed world now tries to sustain the indigenous craftspeople it contacts.) As a way to define terms, and to generalize the idea of abstraction set forth in the introduction, consider some history of craft.[16]

The Ancients produced solely by craft—that is, without organized industry. Everything was craft, especially utilitarian production, which often involved slavery. Relatively little is known about these conditions, because the learned disdained handwork, and the artisans kept no lasting records other than their products. It is clear, however, that the decline of the ancient world was accompanied by a decline in production, and with it the loss of many expertises that ancient practices had supported. If for no other reason than this, the centuries of scarcity that followed gave craft objects greater value.

In the European early Middle Ages artisans gained rank, for as free men they took refuge in the monasteries—where it was appreciated that indeed, Jesus Christ was a craftsman's son. Later, amid expanding urbanization and trade, high Medieval guilds diversified and regulated the supply and demand for a great many crafts. The essential distinction reflected by guilds was the making of goods not for local use: towns created guilds—

and guilds made towns—in order to instigate commerce.[17] For this reason it is doubtful that this period was the apex of an innocent craftsmanship, dedicated to the glory of God, later romanticized by the Victorians. Commerce was its own reward, and work was not all whole: certainly, guild members' work contained many tedious elements, which were usually carried out by the apprentices, and even master artisans had responsibilities of toil and business outside their nominal area of endeavor.[18]

By the fifteenth century, although the prospering guilds had elevated the *Ars Mechanicae* to further respectability, the fine arts began to have a distinct identity, in which Man and Nature had emerged as muses in their own right. Meanwhile, mercantilism steadily surpassed artisanry as the basis of middle-class wealth. Economic historian Fernand Braudel has described the *Jeux d'Echange* as the economic engine of Western Europe. His classic thesis is that more than production itself, and since long before capitalized industry, elaborate structures of practice have been the main source of bourgeois prosperity. Braudel described a web of diversified production, laboring organizations, and trade patterns. Artisans and merchants alike were caught up in this net.[19]

At least in Europe, the Renaissance introduced an intellectual separation of practical craft and fine art. Art came to be held in higher esteem. The transition took a long time, but slowly the word "artisan" was coopted to distinguish the skilled manual worker from the intellectual, imaginative, or creative artist, and artists emerged as a very special category of cultural workers, producing a rare and marginal commodity: works of art.[20]

Meanwhile the artisans often organized their labors to the point where their workshops became factory-like. By the eighteenth century, this proto-industrialization made Medieval practices of craft something no longer to be taken for granted, and further degraded the stature of the artisan. The following entry from Diderot's vast *Encyclopédie* (1751–80) is still one of the best definitions available.

> CRAFT. This name is given to any profession that requires the use of the hands, and is limited to a certain number of mechanical operations to produce the same piece of work, made over and over again. I

1.3 Some of the hundreds of traditional craftsmen depicted in Diderot's *Encyclopédie*

do not know why people have a low opinion of what this word implies; for we depend on the crafts for all the necessary things of life. Anyone who has taken the trouble to visit casually the workshops will see in all places utility applied with the greatest evidence of intelligence: antiquity made gods of those who invented the crafts; the following centuries threw into the mud those who perfected the same work. I leave to those who have some principal of equity to judge if it is reason or prejudice that makes us look with such a disdainful eye on such indispensable men. The poet, the philosopher, the orator, the minister, the warrior, the hero would all be nude, and lack bread without this craftsman, the object of their cruel scorn.[21]

By the nineteenth century, industrialism was in full swing. Industrial technology had consequences from the political to the aesthetic, the assessment of which remains at the foundations of many academic disciplines today. The engines of industry established new social relations, and gave force to the intellectual discipline of political economy. Amid this broad sweep, artisanry entered full decline in the face of machine-powered industry. Skills became less important, and design disciplines became distinct from handicrafts. Indeed the machine established an adverse relation between hands and mechanized production methods, one that most people still experience. This happened recently enough that many oppositional records remain. Some of the most vehement of these criticisms came from gentleman critic and historian John Ruskin, initially in *The Seven Lamps of Architecture* (1849):

> The last form of fallacy which it will be remembered we had to deprecate was the substitution of cast or machine work for that of the hand, generally expressible as Operative Deceit . . . There are two reasons, both weighty, against this practice: one, that all cast and machine work is bad, as work; the other, that it is dishonest.

Ruskin was especially attentive to the role of hands:

> For it is not the material, but the absence of the human labour, which makes the thing worthless; a piece of terra cotta, or of plaster of Paris, which has been wrought be the human hand, is worth all the stone in Carrara, cut by machinery. It is, indeed, possible, and even usual, for men to sink into machines themselves, so that even hand-work has all the characters of mechanism.[22]

Opposite Ruskin's eloquent reactionary prose, the Republican technologists of the emerging American nation saw technology as the way to realize the latent promise of a great continent. Ralph Waldo Emerson, in particular, translated this vision into a lasting national creed, as expressed in his famous aphorism that "Railroad iron is a magician's rod in its power to evoke the sleeping energies of land and water."[23] Emerson was able to reconcile unrestrained advocacies from early industrialists such as Edward Everett or Francis Cabot Lowell with emerging cautions over the ills of factory work as well as romanticisms of nature.[24] Unlike Ruskin's, this was a measured position. The image of the machine in the garden represents an unwelcome intrusion of railroad iron into the classic pastoral landscape, but also a union between liberating technology and the developing nation. This distinctly American justification of technology though democracy has endured for nearly two centuries—from woolen mill to World Wide Web.

Industrialism also bred a socialist response. If we are to judge by the sheer number of academic citations, there has yet to be a more influential scholar on the topic of work than Karl Marx, who was emblematic of the view that modern production harmed its workers. The problem as identified by Marx was twofold: serial manufacturing based on semiskilled processes denied this new form of laborers any control over quality, and specialized production still based on highly skilled processes denied artisans their previous range of other activities.[25] Avoiding such harm required conscientious resistance. Even after Marxist political economies were to have run their course, not without abuses of technological authority themselves, this oppositional stance would still inform critical theory in the electronic age.

Also of the nineteenth century we must observe more utopian forms of socialized production, such as those practiced by the Shakers in America or William Morris and his followers in Britain—great craftsmen the lot of them. The Arts and Crafts movement, whose start was signalled by Morris, became one of the more significant responses to industrialism. Its concern for the aesthetic consequences of hasty profiteering may have been socialist in its origins, but its appeal to amateur creativity and taste was ultimately quite democratic. Its emphasis on functional integrity and material economy was an important correction in the course of modern aesthetics. Its claim that art had a place outside the galleries is one we can renew today.

The fact is that by the early twentieth century, artisanry had fallen not only out of industry, but also out of art. The Arts and Crafts movement began as a valiant response to industrial aesthetic deficiencies, but a few decades after its gentlemanly start it had become burdened with the stigma of amateurism. At best, craft was the mere execution of preconceived ends; more often, it was a mere hobby.[26] Art—which was the true search—became increasingly independent of technique.[27] Early modern art expunged personal touch. A generation later, pop art, found art, minimal art, and conceptual art would deny the need for any artisanry at all. Seen against the accelerating pursuit of the latest ironic pose, particularly the appropriation of broadcast and industrial debris, any emphasis on execution would appear positively banal. Crafts, like astrology, would be left to the soft of mind.

Meanwhile, mechanized industry had become much more refined. Electrification lit the workplace and moved the heat and noise of the furnaces elsewhere. Conversely, it made it possible for small electric motors to go many places where clumsy mechanical drive belts could not—for example, away from the water mill. Electrification enabled assembly lines, switching and control signals, and hand-held power tools. It also affected materials, for example, by making aluminum and stainless steel more practical.[28]

Largely as a result of these changes, manufacturing matured to the point where its products were now art forms in themselves. This art was not of *works,* however, but of *products.* As industrialization shifted attention from piecewise execution to generative design, processes such as production planning, material optimization, and product analysis became essential. Industrial design emerged as the darling of the self-proclaimed "machine age," and a new breed of industrial craftsmen emerged as mediators between design and the machine. Herbert Read, the great advocate of industrial design as a high and abstract art, stated in 1936: "The real problem is not to adapt machine production to the aesthetics of handicraft, but to think out new aesthetic standards for new methods of production."[29] Read identified a secondary problem arising from the first: "If we decide that the product of the machine can be a work of art, then what is to become of the artist who is displaced by the machine? Has he any function in a machine-age society, or must he reconcile himself to a purely dilettante role—must he become, as most contemporary artists have become, merely a society entertainer?"[30]

Workmanship in a factory setting became less a matter of putting oneself into the job and more of getting the most out of the machines. It shifted care from individual pieces to composite processes. Certainly this was no place for the hands. In his seminal design book *Mechanization Takes Command* (1948), Sigfried Giedion wrote: "In its very way of performing movement, the hand is ill-fitted to work with mathematical precision and without pause. . . It cannot continue a movement in endless rotation. That is precisely what mechanization entails: endless rotation."[31]

At the apex of industrialism, on the eve of the digital age, the economist E. F. Schumacher observed in *Small Is Beautiful* (1973):

> The type of work which modern technology is most successful in reducing or even eliminating is skillful, productive work of human hands, in touch with real materials of one kind or another. In an advanced industrial society, such work has become exceedingly rare, and to make a living by doing such work has become virtually impossible. A great part of the modern neurosis may be due to this very fact; for the human being, defined by Thomas Aquinas as a being with brains and hands, enjoys nothing more than to be creatively, usefully, productively engaged with both his hands and his brains.[32]

Today, the electronic information machine is a new chapter in the story. As the slogans put it, the computer or communications device is inherently a tool for the *mind*—not the hands. Its essential action is to process and transmit not power but symbols. Its products are not mechanical artifacts but abstract information.

The immediate reaction to the arrival of information technology was to imagine its use in terms of furthering existing modernist agendas. By projection, trends such as managerial command and control, productive efficiency regardless of the social cost, deliberate deskilling, replacing people with machines, and so on, were now given just the leverage they needed to deliver the final blow to any humane aspects of work. The circumstances of working with the technology itself would be harmful in their own right: new class divisions, concessions to the technology providers, antisocial working arrangements, worker surveillance, endless mind-numbing technical detail, and overall sensory deprivation. For the hands, the only prospect would be painful repetitive motion disorders.

Today for an unfortunate class of data-entry workers, who perhaps outnumber any other kind of computer-based workers, these fears have proved altogether too prescient. We can easily despair. As in the time of Ruskin, we could yearn romantically—and in vain—for a more innocent way of work. Or we can strive for a future with more appealing technology more justly applied.

For example, maybe the 1990s will be remembered as the decade where technology escaped authoritarian control. It was then that the modernist masters, like Pynchonesque villains, proved unable to deliver that final blow, and an antiheroic counterforce of digital Prairies and Slothrops unwittingly seized the postmodern day by default. There in the decade of recombinant businesses, ad hoc marketplaces, digital artists, hackers and phreaks, web architects, avatars, agents, and overall online anarchy, there when nobody was looking, the modernist technological project collapsed like communism. Maybe. Other storytellers imagine more holistic and silicon-centric outcomes.

Yet surely some change will be for the better. Much as industrialists used the prosperity they so incontestably produced to remedy some of the adverse conditions their activities created, so too the disciplines of computing shall compensate for their crude and inhumane origins. Today we may deplore our personal technology for its unnatural keyboards, irradiating screens, and tedious forms of instruction, but at least we can value it for being at personal scale. We must not forget that twenty years ago personal computing did not exist at all: there were only institutionalized, air-conditioned behemoths attended by technicians in white lab coats. We cannot know what to expect twenty years from now. If computers continue to become smaller and more numerous at the same mind-boggling pace, they may conceivably pervade everything we own and operate, from office doors to garage workbenches. When it accommodates not only touch but also sound, physical context, social community, and accumulated experience, this ubiquitous technology may actually seem quite pleasant—especially to the more skillful or sensitive person.

One thing is clear. We have reached a point in the history of technology where it is especially important to take pride in human abilities. We must not only defend against further deskilling, but also direct inevitable technological change in a more human-centric direction. Just because much of the world is being spoonfed a particular form of technology (the one based on mouse, keyboard, and screen) does not mean that we know what computing is or will be just a few years from now. And if and when any chaotic fantasy and fugue comes true, and the conditions of work grow more post-whatever, there are likely to be unwitting digital artisans on the scene, making fairly good use of their hands.

4 What Is Craft?

Tools and technologies have both assisted and opposed the hand throughout history; the relation is not necessarily adversarial. Although we find no recourse to traditional production—no more than there was in the time of Ruskin—nevertheless we must look very closely at craft. As a part of developing more engaging technology, as well as developing a more receptive attitude toward new opportunites raised by technology, we must understand what matters in traditional notions of practical, form-giving work. This will take some study of tools, some study of human-computer interaction, and some study of practicing the digital medium. But it will not require us to identify what (if anything) is truly made by hand. Nor does our praise of hands necessarily mean condemnation of technology.

As a point of departure, consider the example of a skilled computer graphics artisan—if we may use this word. His or her hands are performing a sophisticated and unprecedented set of actions. These motions are quick, small, and repetitive, as in much traditional handwork, but somehow they differ. For one thing, they are faster—in fact, their rates matter quite a bit. They do not rely on pressure so much as position, velocity, or acceleration. The artisan's eye is not on the hand but elsewhere, on a screen. The actions have a practical component, and the skill may be practiced for a livelihood and a trade identity. If we test a description of this work against Diderot's description of craft, almost every word fits.

According to Webster, the word "craft" derives from the Middle English *craeft,* which simply meant strength or power. We must remember that because such forces were regarded with suspicion, the word retains some residual meaning of arcane intellectual skill, or even deceitful cunning (e.g., a crafty fox). In later meanings the word referred to a more specific power, namely specialized skill or dexterity in the manual arts. It also referred to a calling or occupation, or the members of a trade who share that skill.

Artisanry can be defined as the practice of a craft for a livelihood. Traditionally this implied a certain economy of means, particularly with respect to getting the most out of a limited medium. Of course very few people still practice a material craft for a livelihood. According to our current proposition, however, aspects of craft in practical computational work may lead to habitual practices that we could understand as artisanry.

Different from artisanry there is artistry, which is the role of art in other processes. There may be an element of art in craft, or an element of craft in art. Pure art has endless definitions. For example, Paul Klee said the purpose of art is to awaken reality. But relative to craft, we can say that art is the creation of artifacts for indescribable, not preconceived, and possibly impractical ends: to search, to reveal, to release.

Industry is defined in distinction to art or craft as the application of technology to practical production. (This is to ignore the word's archaic meaning of personal diligence.) Engine-powered, continuous-process mechanical reproduction works consistently without the intervention of any particular person.

Industrial design seeks to establish aesthetics for mechanized production. It seeks variation not in the individual objects, but in the kinds of standardized objects that become available. It brings artistry to the precision, detail, and material quality of work generally impossible to achieve at any cost by hand.

Technology is—literally in the Greek—the study of skill. It is order imposed on skill, and it is also the apparatus derived from applying the results of study. Technique is a method of doing something, possibly skilled, possibly using technology. Tools, machines, computers, materials, and media all will be explored in greater detail later on; but it should be safe to say that given ubiquitous technical examples such as oil painting or motion pictures, technology can become a medium, or at least the basis of a medium.

Now there is reason to explore the possibility of craft in the emerging realm of information technology—with the computer as a medium. This hardly fits the conventional usage of the word "craft," for the usual meaning opposes high-technology processes in which the hand plays a diminished role. Thus the proposal of craft in the electronic medium is something of a paradox. But can we, here in the computer age, with fully optimistic and benevolent intent, suggest that the word needs a more inclusive definition?

This seems to be happening anyway. The word has resurfaced in popular usage—but as a verb. People "craft" everything from business memos to good stout beer. In digital production, craft refers to the condition where people apply standard technological means to unanticipated or indescribable ends. Works of computer animation, geometric modeling, and spatial databases get "crafted" when experts use limited software capacities resourcefully, imaginatively, and in compensation for the inadequacies of prepackaged, hard-coded operations. As a verb, "to craft" seemingly means to participate skillfully in some small-scale process. This implies several things. First, it affirms that the results of involved work still surpass the results of detached work. To craft is to care. Second, it suggests that partnerships with technology are better than autonomous technology. For example, personal mastery of open-ended software can take computers places that deterministic software code cannot. Third, to craft implies working at a personal scale—acting locally in reaction to anonymous, globalized, industrial production—hence its appeal in describing phenomena such as microbreweries. Finally, the usage of "craft" as a verb evades the persistent stigma that has attached itself to the noun. The noun suggests class differences and amateurism. For example, craft still recalls the provincial dilution of the Arts and Crafts movement into what now consists of folk art at best, and rustic shops full of tourist trinkets at worst. Craft is seldom any longer practical trade, but it is not yet often art. It is outside of academic consideration: ever since mechanization has taken command, craft has been stranded in bourgeois territory where few self-respecting aestheticians would dare to tread. But new usage may change this situation. Based on observations of a linguistic tendency, and with a desire to explore an academically belittled area, this book is a meditation on the seeming paradox of intangible craft.

Craft remains skilled work applied toward practical ends. It is indescribable talent with describable aims. It is habitual skilled practice with particular tools, materials, or media, for the purpose of making increasingly well executed artifacts. Craft is the application of personal knowledge to the giving of form. It is the condition in which the inherent qualities and economies of the media are encouraged to shape both process and products. It is not about standardized artifacts, however. It is not industrial design. It remains about the individually prepared artifact, which is newly practical due to digital computing. Craft is certainly an application of skill, and it may yet involve the skilled hand.

Thus the defense of skill may no longer remain a losing philosophical position. If previously it was usual to assume that computation would only worsen the hand-mind splits engendered by industrialism, now we might reconsider this problem. We might observe how software usage is restoring some respect for mastery. We might also note the invention of technologies that support the subtleties of the hand. Although most people have failed to perceive in the technology's fledgling states any capacities for new kinds of active skill, perhaps it is still early in the game, and many of these views may well shift.

The question is largely generational: younger people, for whom computing is normal, may shape the most change. As the columnist and MIT Media Lab founder Nicholas Negroponte has noted, "All that seems to count, like learning French in France, is being a child." Within computing, "The haves and have-nots are now the young and the old."[33] Anyone on the edge of this generational change—say between the ages of thirty and forty—should be keenly aware of this distinction.

5 Direct Manipulation

The first glimmer of digital craft, and the main breakthrough to popular computation as we know it, was the introduction of pointing. "Direct manipulation" is a term coined in 1983 by software designer Ben Shneiderman to describe a principle that we now take for granted: pointing at our work with a mouse. More specifically, the expression referred to the combination of three fundamental activities: (1) continuous visibility of the object of interest; (2) rapid, incremental, reversible, physical actions on the object; and (3) immediately visible results.[34] The slogan "What you see is what you get" popularized the essence of this technical combination, but hand-eye coordination meant more than just visual fidelity.

The Macintosh popularized the direct manipulation strategy in the mid-1980s, and MacPaint and MacDraw became the first commercially successful direct manipulation programs. Here were the first uses of tool icons, modified cursors, and realtime pixel coloration (well, black and white at least). Here the graphical objects first developed grips and intrinsic operations, such as selecting, stretching, and replicating. Here, at last, you could draw without typing in numbers on a keyboard.

This early Macintosh was commonly referred to as the first human-computer interface good enough to criticize. By now it is a familiar and storied lineage: Xerox PARC in the late 1970s, then Apple, today Microsoft. Soon the Macintosh's direct manipulation format was imitated by most of its competitors. Some expanded it into three dimensions, as with

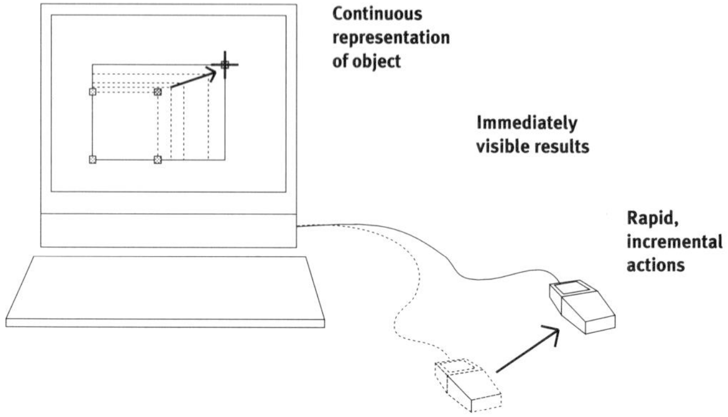

1.4 Basic principle of direct manipulation

the specialized Silicon Graphics machines of the late 1980s. And when Microsoft promoted it to the mainstream millions in the form of Windows, direct manipulation based on graphical user interfaces became the unquestioned norm.

The best measure of direct manipulation as a basis for digital craft is its capacity for continuous actions. Direct manipulation's continuity depends on having enough computing speed to calculate realtime graphical feedback, so this capacity improves almost as fast as the power of the chips themselves. It may have let us start by manipulating lines and squares in MacDraw, but there is no reason why direct manipulation cannot also be applied to gestures, three-dimensional renderings, tactile textures, complex multimodal structures, or abstracted architectures of information. In research settings, and in some specialized commercial products, it already does so.

Touch technology nonetheless remains far behind other aspects of human-computer interaction. Most interaction technology has emphasized output, not input; foreground tasks, not background contexts; and visualization, not a more fully rounded sensory balance that one might call "perceptualization." So far, the much ballyhooed "look and feel" of contemporary computing is almost all look and hardly any feel.[35] For one thing, the sense of touch is relatively difficult to engineer. This is partly because it does not rely on a particular organ like the eye or ear—unless that is the hand. Pressure feedback is relatively straightforward to engineer—some arcade games do this—but temperature, texture, and wide-area contact prove more difficult. If there is something common to much research on tactile computing, that might be an emphasis on action. Researchers often use the term *haptic,* which means the exploratory and manipulative aspects of touch, as opposed to passive sensation. Some fields such as music and medicine have been advancing pressure components of touch quite rapidly, and specialized research in haptic computing is fairly easy to find within them. For example, many remote surgical operations conduct delicate touch by means of computer technology.

Haptic skill should play an equally important role in the fields of design and fabrication; but these fields have not come as far in realizing their potential. Nor have the findings of research in better-funded fields yet found their way into much merchandised software for designers. No, the two-dimensional mouse, point-and-click form of direct manipulation has prevailed for a strangely prolonged period of time. And although there is every indication that human-computer interaction is evolving toward much more satisfactory haptic engagement (among other perceptual dimensions), there is also evidence that this just might take a while.[36]

Without touch, in the meantime, perhaps we are stretching to call direct manipulation craft. There is a natural objection: What good are computers, except perhaps for mundane documentation, if you cannot even touch your work? The fact that traditional craft endures at all is because it satisfies some deep need for direct experience—and most computers are not yet providing that experience.

However, other developments are at least partially compensating for the limited role of the hands. For example, sophisticated motion tracking can incorporate gesture, and large flat-panel displays can unite the computer's metaphorical "desktop" with a real physical desktop, so as to escape the limits of screen pointing. Multimodal activities, such as coupling actions to sounds, are beginning to emerge. These many techniques first appear on the market in computer video games, for multisensory activities awaken the intuition and heighten the sense of drama, but this suggests much capacity for talent in other applications as well. As some of these interaction developments disseminate into practice, it may seem that we do not need to wait for the arrival of haptic interfaces before we raise the possibility of craft. Rather, we can begin to develop a provisional sensibility based on what we have, and wait for eventual developments in touch technology to remove our remaining reservations.

Already plenty of skills have emerged amid the application of ordinary commercial software. This is difficult to generalize because people work in so many different contexts, but obviously a lot of computer usage involves a good deal more than coded memorization of routines. Learning involves more than operational training, for practice and outlook also contribute to expertise.

If you use a computer, you might observe several aspects of inarticulable skill in your everyday work. You might feel that this begins from manual dexterity. You have probably learned to find mouse positions and control key combinations by reflex. Your hands and eyes become closely coordinated despite being focused on different objects. You may recognize the importance of sequence: motions usually last only fractions of a second, but they occur in a constant stream, where their rate matters. With practice you become able to execute tightly synchronized combinations, as if you were playing an instrument.

Besides manual dexterity, you may feel some intellectual agility. You will learn to build mental models, and to switch frames of reference when necessary. You alertly monitor feedback from a variety of sources, and recognize and recover from errors before they compound themselves. You benefit from the habit of identifying patterns—and using them to work at a higher level. You learn to read system states in multiple ways, and this versatility lets you go about operations in whatever manner is currently most convenient. Your hands too, may work together in complementary modes, and each may move quickly between modes.

At times you may think that computer work mainly just tests your patience. It is incremental, like chiseling away at a piece of stone. It involves unexplained roadblocks and glitches. It is monotonous, fatiguing, and yet full of interruptions on a whole spectrum of time scales—some a couple of minutes, some a couple of seconds, some just subliminal fractions of a second. Unlike the soothing quality of continuous process in traditional work, this staccato pace is irritating. Fortunately you can compensate. For example, you may know how to slow down to match the pace of near realtime processes. You learn to cut down on unnecessary motions or state changes. You know when to put aside direct manipulations and resort to command languages or delegated agents. You *work around* problems: when one approach is blocked, you quickly find another that is open.

Meanwhile you experience new kinds of continuous actions. As computers become faster, and interfaces improve, more processes become operable by continuous strokes instead of discrete selections. This switch from discrete to continuous distinguishes digital craft from mere mechanical machine operation. When some continuous pointer motions become more precise than all but those required for the finest traditional tool applications, you might discover them quite satisfying.

Above all, you develop a contextual awareness. Like a good pianist you improve your ability to push what you have learned into a subconscious background, so that you don't have to keep so much in mind at any one time. Instead of thinking the actions, you feel the actions—and actions stir your memory, and give you a better sense of inhabiting your work. As an expert you sense what to try when; how far a medium can be pushed; when to check up on a process; which tool to use for what job. If you have used computers much you know this kind of judgment, or know that you want to learn.

Something very important is happening, and it has to do with the growing capacity of electronic symbol-processing technology for a range of skillful practices. There are three essential components to this sea change. First, the tools have become much more affordable. This reverses perhaps the greatest blow against the artisan two centuries ago, namely the establishment of means of production too large and complex for any individual to afford. As a result, industrial-age stereotypes about the complicity of technology with authoritarian or institutional agendas may soon be irrelevant. Second, human-computer interface technology has improved, and is now beginning to diversify. This means we are on the verge of much greater capacity for talent. As computers balance a greater breadth of input with their current emphasis on output (and so relieve us of too much burden of instruction), we should find it easier to work skillfully. Better gestures, more sensory combinations, and improved three-dimensional frameworks should open up many new niches of practice. Finally, there is a growing appreciation of new abstractions. Increasingly, computers let us treat abstract relations as visible, workable things. As a result, new kinds and levels of work become viable. This is partly due to better support for active skills, and partly due to better abstractions of background contextual awareness.

Histories of technology reveal the increasing abstraction of work. Successive levels of invention have freed us from hunting down our next meal, breaking our backs in the fields, sweating over the forge, and numbing our minds with accounting. Each level forms a layer over the old, rather than casting it aside, as in the stages of a natural growth. This means that even if new abstractions eventually become the most prominent methods, they do not replace existing activities so much as transform or complement them.

Because the move to electronic means of production is now in full swing, we must carefully consider potential losses and gains at a highly abstract order. Although computers are useful, are they good? But this question may be too broad and unanswerable, so let us inform it with a simpler question: Does further abstraction necessitate further decline of human skill, particularly of the hand? Let us direct our curiosities and practices in the high-tech realm toward one of the most humane of ends: craftsmanship.

If the beginnings of computing ultimately appear to future historians as the most significant outward expression of our time, they are not likely to do so on the basis of functional utility alone. Social and aesthetic concerns will matter too. The artifacts and practices that computing produces will demand—and reward—more refined interpretations. Note that traditionally it is in interpretation that we have used the word "craft" most broadly: the writer's craft, the actor's craft, and the conductor's craft join those of the cobbler and carpenter. What all such crafts share is not just technique, or hard work on form, but also a probing of their medium's capacity, a passion for practice, and moral value as an activity independent of what is produced. Is there any reason to expect these in the electronic realm? We must make them our goal.

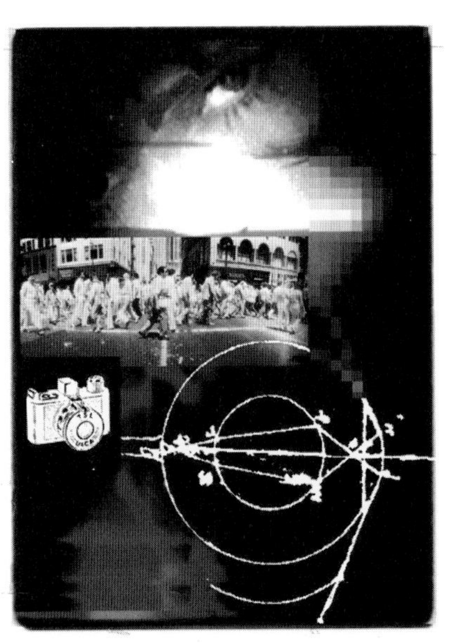

2 Eyes

Eyes are in charge. What you see is what you get. Seeing objectifies the world, and for this reason no other act of perception is so closely connected to working and thinking. Eyes guide tools, read notations, appraise designs. Whereas hands feel their way one piece at a time, eyes see wholes, and compare many objects simultaneously. They recognize images and understand pictures. Signs and symbols *appear* more than they taste, feel, smell, or sound. Even in spoken language, we often say "I see" to mean "I understand." We have "insights." Seeing is believing. No wonder the eyes have been called "the great monopolists of the senses."[1]

Biologically, our paired eyes are made for searching through the depth of the natural field for anything we must catch (or avoid) to survive. We see far beyond the grasp of the hands or the range of our strides; we gaze upon a lot that we cannot or need not act upon. Contrast the sense of touch, which always elicits a response.

At close range our powers of focus improve. Eyes activate the hands, and hands direct the eyes. To examine something, we prefer to have it within reach. We walk over to it; where possible, we pick it up. Held in our hand, scrutinized by our eyes, the object comes to life. We not only study it, we modify it. We envision variations and alternatives, and we then proceed to give those form.

Hand-eye coordination distinguishes humanity as the maker of things: *homo faber.* It is our talent to bring a mass of raw material into conformity with a vision. We fashion tools and coax materials. Under visual guidance, what would otherwise be brute grasp grows into specialized skill. Hands acquire some independence through training, but they still turn to the eyes for purposes. When in action, a skillful touch remains subsidiary to focal vision. Because this kind of coordination satisfies, we pursue it in play, too: sports, musical performance, building projects, and traditional handicrafts give pleasure though coordination. Reflection finds harmony in the steady flow of hand, eye, tool, and material.

The craft artifact, always the traditional object of coordinated efforts, is therefore as much a product of the eye as of the hand. Vision appreciates its qualities of proportion, material economy, and workmanship—recorded harmony. In the process of production, the artisan's eye for detail continually assesses the artifact's condition. For example, the eye can watch for material stress through visual cues such as dents or deformations. The eye can follow the imperfections and eccentricities of the material, such as the cracks in fine leather, and make those into assets. The eye can find quality in such workmanship by others, and this is an important basis for appreciation. Vision finds cultural identity, too, as form and ornamentation bear tradition. Much that we appreciate in craft, the eyes understand.

Literate notation is different. In a way it is more visual still—indeed it lets the eyes take over. In doing so it opens abstractions, invites organization, and administers invention. But visual literacy requires education, whereas handicraft can be learned doing or simple training, and this has separated professions from trades. Moreover, the literacy needed for scripted notations such as writing or programming often comes at the expense of a more general visual literacy practiced in reading images. It

2.1 **Holistic vision is integral to traditional craft**

has also overspecialized the hand. Although manual control of position is sometimes refined in writing, the hand's role is diminished overall: exertions of force become quite monotonous, and the capacity to probe goes almost entirely unused. And although for some people the writing pen, or particularly the drawing instrument, remains an object of considerable skill, for most others the act of writing, or just simply reading, does not entail much physical ability.

Today we no longer even need hold much of our reading matter, for instead we stare at screens. The two-dimensional object of vision has become cinema, television, or especially the computer, which has become a visual medium itself and has permeated many older visual technologies as well. Computer graphics now mediate enough activities to suggest that computing's preeminence and visuality are somehow related. Even text production becomes more visual: most developed writing is now done on a screen rather than on paper, at least when authors have a choice. Similarly, drafting now is almost universally computer-assisted line processing, at least in professional settings. Photography is going digital quite rapidly. Manufacturing increasingly relies on computer-aided design and manufacturing (CAD/CAM) and related process control systems. Entertainment promises to unite television and computing. Each of these technologies contributes to an image culture, which we may expect to generate still further forms of visual production.

The onscreen image moves. In comparison to paper, screens can not only mix writing and images more easily, but also can change their contents more rapidly. In comparison to objects or texts, photographs reach a much wider audience, and moving images get more attention. With as few as a dozen images per second we can construct depth and movement as if peering through the screen into a natural space, and we can assume that just about everyone will be able to read this as a movie.

The screen, however, is hardly the ultimate condition. As has been the focus of much recent hype, appropriately engineered stereo images—for example, those achieved with headsets or goggles—can let us read "through the looking glass" into an immersive representation of artificial

2.2 Eyes take command: the introduction of television, 1939 New York World's Fair

worlds.[2] That this optical artifice is so commonly referred to as virtual "reality" demonstrates our willingness to give the eyes a monopoly.

Under present conditions of computer usage, hand-eye coordination changes. Traditionally, hand, eye, and tool converged in one place: when the hand worked a material, the eye followed it continuously; or the hand held a paper, while the eye read. Now the hand moves a mouse while the eyes look at a screen. Hand-eye separation may be normal among some sorts of processes, such as playing from a musical score, drawing from the human figure, catching a baseball, and driving a car. But for processes that work a material, hand-eye union has always been essential.

Without the guiding eye, the hand performs fewer continuous strokes, like drawing a bead of watercolor across a sheet of fine paper, and more quick, discontinuous actions, like clicking on lots of boxes. For most people, this reduction of hand-eye coordination is a source of regret. The hand was not made to twitch—or to click boxes all day. Yet for some people, especially those who never had the traditional skills, computing is a source of new opportunities for coordinated action. This is particularly true where direct manipulation software makes the repetitious work more tolerable. Recall that direct manipulation is defined by the continuous *visibility* of the object being modified. Many people understand only those computer operations that produce a visible result—whereas working on an abstract mental model without visual identity or graphical acknowledgment is much more difficult. Nevertheless, relatively few graphical operations are truly direct manipulations: pointing at commands on menus, and filling in forms in dialogue boxes, do not satisfy our instinct for tools.

But mechanical actions like pointing are easily improved. Recent technologies such as digital notepads and video-conference whiteboards may restore a more normal hand-eye union. In general, more computing power means more continuous representation, and more complex objects and worlds. Maturing software frameworks support more psychologically coherent operations. Better hardware support allows for bettor sensory coordination. This need not mimic traditional actions, but may invent new techniques. As an example of how engaging some of these may become, note that gaming enthusiasts (who tend to be the first to gain access to emerging human-computer interaction technologies) already find some new forms of coordination outright addictive.

Better sensory frameworks, not limited to vision, make for better computing. Better software to orchestrate our skills and senses, and to structure our mental models, makes for more satisfactory work. In this regard, provision for richer hand-eye coordination is only the beginning—the ultimate goal might be described as a multisensory grasp of sophisticated intellectual structures. Whole-body expression and kinetic memory could perhaps find a role. Audio dimensions, too, can and should be considered. Nevertheless, principles of abstraction, literacy, and symbolic communication—as well as artisanry and other ways of form giving—have traditionally been the province of the eye.

Thoughts on Visual Thinking

Vision abstracts. In his influential work on visual thinking, Rudolf Arnheim observed:

> We need and want to rebuild the bridge between perception and thinking. I have tried to show that perception consists in the grasping of relevant generic features of the object. Inversely, thinking, in order to have something to think about, must be based on images of the world in which we live. The thought elements in perception and perceptual elements in thought are complementary. They make human cognition a unitary process, which leads without break from the elementary acquisition of sensory information to the most generic theoretical ideas. The essential trait of this unitary cognitive process is that at every level it involves abstraction. Therefore the nature and meaning of abstraction must be examined with care.
>
> There is no getting around the fact that an abstractive grasp of structural features is the very basis of perception and the beginning of all cognition.[3]

Abstraction means that vision is not just sight. Vision goes beyond simply recording arbitrary samples to formulate identities and recognize patterns. Yet this abstraction is not the opposite of concreteness, or unrelated to tangible things, but may have its origins in those very phenomena. Nor is abstraction just a token by which one thing, image, or symbol represents others, but rather it is a higher-level schematization. It is more than a classification, too, or more than generalization by induction, by either of which methods a higher order is inferred from what is perceived.[4] The difference is that visual abstraction is active, imaginative, adaptable—and above all else, *generative.*

This impetus toward abstraction is of course most pronounced among great artists, but it is something that all of us do, even when we are just walking around. Perhaps nobody can equal the visual drive and agility of Picasso, whose particular three-year body of work shown together at Antibes, for example, supremely demonstrates the abstractive visual impetus. But each of us has an abstractive imagination: we can identify essential similarities amid superficial differences, and we have a tendency for what we have been looking at to shape what we are inclined to notice next. For most anyone, generative vision is evident in evolving visual preferences, sensibilities, or fashions. And for creative people visual speculations assist inventions, and visual tokens most effectively represent ideas.

Normally these tokens are images. We might then define visual thinking as the use of images to generate ideas and knowledge, plus the use of abstractive grasp to detect patterns and identities in images. Note, however, that images may be perceptual or conceptual, pictorial or topological (spatial). Note also that images are not very formal. Visual thinking occurs in enough contexts to suggest that it is largely independent of formal symbolic reasoning. Like text, mathematics, or software code, but independent of them, images produce ideas too. Visual thinking creates recollections, recognitions, correlations, comparisons—especially when the mind works with a stream of fleeting, freely associated images.[5]

Not everyone agrees with this principle. Psychologists, art critics, cognitive scientists, computer scientists, and software designers have debated about visual thought for decades. The intellectual context for these inquiries encompasses the most general findings of the last half-century. For example, postmodern physics has established that the observer influences the observed. Literary criticism holds that any piece of authorship is selective and rhetorical, as is any reading. Vision becomes relative, and aesthetic theorists contend that any form may represent anything. Unconscious imagery gains respect, and psychologists suggest that we pay a high cost for keeping a schism between this latent imaginative power and the greater focus of symbolic reasoning.[6] Many educators observe that, for better or worse, images compete powerfully against text. Traditions based on *logos,* or the authority of the word, are challenged by the *tekne,* or masterful manipulation, of the image. If television has numbed many minds, perhaps interactive simulations have opened at least a few others. In some cases, visual computing has provided a few children with a newer window on knowledge.[7]

This debate may continue perpetually because vision takes so many forms, some difficult to document. A behavioralist might study external stimuli, a semioticist might observe cultural contexts, and a cognitive scientist might focus on the physio-neurological basis for syntactic structures. An artist, however, might simply seek a receptive condition, and a philosopher could posit a platonic mind's eye not measurable by scientific instruments. In any case, we should be comfortable in saying that vision is many things: part sight, part significance, part structure, part state, and part intent. Anthropologist Ken Wilber has formulated a useful classification whereby men and women possess at least three modes of knowing: the eye of the flesh, which discloses the material, concrete, and sensual world—the world of sensibilia; the eye of mind, which discloses the symbolic, conceptual, and linguistic world—the world of intelligibilia; and the eye of contemplation, which discloses the spiritual, transcendent, and transpersonal world—the world of transcendelia.[8]

A substantive work of art may encompass all of these forms of vision, and of course the fine arts are particularly rich in theories of the image. Consider one standard: the work of art historian Ernst Gombrich. Gombrich regularly argued that seeing and representation are anything but literal, unfeeling acts. "The eye is not a camera," he wrote. "One thing can be taken as established. There is no fixed correlation between the optical world and the world of our visual experience." Subjective visuality pivots between recognition and recall, for while the former depends on what we have previously learned to see as well as what we have presently chosen to focus upon, the latter depends on our ability to associate the many things we have seen. As evidence that these two processes mix, Gombrich notes that otherwise, "oculists who wish to test our eyesight would not have to use random letters rather than coherent texts." Moreover, not only symbolic systems such as text, but many more general aspects of the visual world are significantly coded and afford each of us a visual disposition.[9]

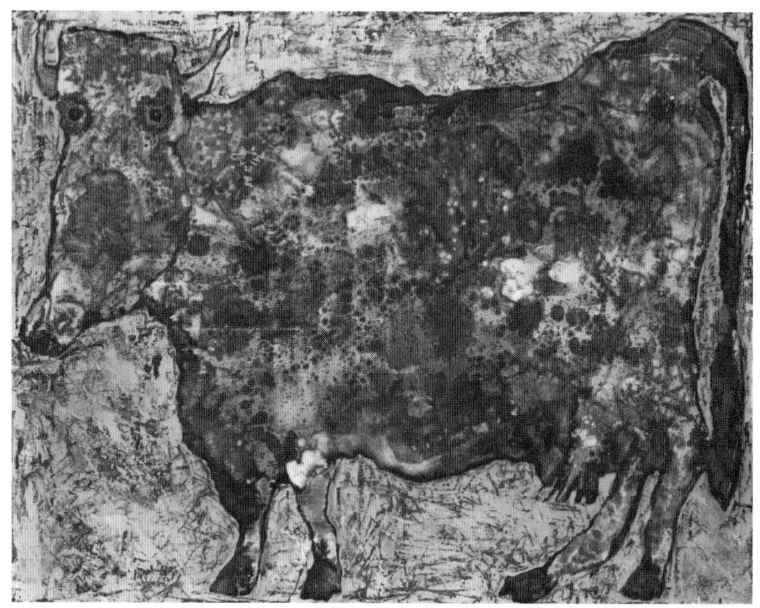

2.3 Gombrich's example of subjective vision: Jean Dubuffet, *Cow with Subtile Nose*

Practical graphic design employs more or less the same principles. Visual communication must establish context for its content and appeal to the disposition of its intended audience. It presents rhetorically, and is read by cues, such as hierarchy, differentiation, or identification. Effective graphic design therefore uses structure and selection not only to transmit but also to reinforce and explain content. In this way, mere data can become useful information. Nobody has demonstrated this better than Edward Tufte, whose books *The Visual Display of Quantitative Information* (1983) and *Envisioning Information* (1990) have become standard references among graphic designers. Tufte insisted that format could reinforce content, that all data reporting was selective if only by format, and that most formatting was negligent. That Tufte was turned away by publishers and had to resort to his own production indicates the degree to which the communication of "hard data" had been misunderstood. The need for a visual, digital form of rhetoric had been unrecognized. Thus for those designers who do appreciate the distinction between raw data and effective communication, these books stand as landmarks at the arrival of visual computing.

Naturally the role of visual thinking varies by discipline: design is certainly more visual than law. Not only graphic designers but also architects, engineering designers, and even many eminent theoretical scientists have been documented to rely on visual thinking.[10] For example, atmospheric scientists benefit by visualizing trends that are neither especially perceptible first-hand nor very intelligible in complex systems of equations.

Software designers are influenced by all of these considerations. Their quest might sound like this: Can the visual representation of tools, media, and artifacts become sufficiently intuitive to allow us to use the full spectrum of our abilities and imagination? Can the visual codes and metaphors themselves become objects of craft? Can they become three-dimensional, dynamic, expressive, full of workmanship? Just as important, can the overwhelmingly visual world of the computer accommodate nonvisual actions and perceptions? The answers to these questions will be a long time coming, but the general course of inquiry should be clear. Vision is key: its mechanisms can inform technology design, and its cognitive power can make sense of symbolic orders. Both vision and computation are very prone to abstraction, and the trick is to get them to coincide.

Image Culture

There is no denying the power of visual thinking, for it is everywhere. In the course of a single day, you will see more artificially constructed images than a seventeenth-century Englishman would have seen in his entire lifetime.[11] Between the morning news and your bedtime reading there will be road signs, billboards, computer screens, junk mail, posters, photo prints, presentation slides, pictures on people's shirts, snippets of television shows, maybe a movie, a computer game, maybe a couple of downloads from the internet, a videotape—thousands of images in all. There has been an explosion of image production. The 1989 Biennial at New York's Whitney Museum charted some data.[12] Despite the electronic age, Americans in 1989 produced 15 billion conventional photographs—triple the number taken twenty years before. They continued to spend billions of dollars on going to the movies. They upgraded millions of computers to begin using graphical user interfaces. Their overall domestic advertising expenditures cleared $118 billion. This was up by a factor of six from twenty years before, and came to nearly $500 per capita. As a result Americans were subjected to 1,600 advertisements per person per day. Many of these ads appeared on the nation's 160 million televisions.[13] The total image flow over television alone is staggering. If it is on for just one hour, and the camera shot changes about once every two seconds (a very conservative estimate these days, especially given the popularity of channel surfing), television transmits 1,800 images. More aggressive content, as might be encountered in a nightclub or arcade, can have hundreds of edits not per hour but per minute. Of course, statistics routinely indicate that the average American household runs a television for more like six or seven hours a day, which if anyone is watching, comes to many thousands of images.

Now as the critical theorists are so fond of telling us, those thousands of images are neither literal nor free. Consider the latter. The usual argument goes that images have replaced tangible things as essential economic commodities.[14] In postmodern culture, aesthetics and consumerism fuse, and even basic physical commodities get overlaid with images. Consider the plight of an ordinary cotton shirt. The overlay can happen directly: the shirt could be imprinted with an image. But the indirect method is more significant: a plain cotton shirt might be marketed in mail-order catalogues that represent several different ways of life. Consumers would then make a selection guided by these images—more than by any inherent distinctions in the style or workmanship of the actual shirts—and the product they receive would include a logo indicating which lifestyle image they have bought. This insignia can double the retail value of a shirt, and indeed there have been lawsuits over counterfeit shirts.[15]

Of course image culture goes beyond simple commodities. For instance, politicians cultivate images by staging photo opportunities. Business managers manipulate statistics with animated charts. Market analysts use automated graphs to detect feedback loops in investment patterns—and thus to oil the wheels of runaway finance. Television news editors broadcast sponsored simulations as events. Cinematic merchandise (especially computer games) competes with merchandised cinema for leisure-time attention. Electronic reproduction and transmission now confer legitimacy—they make reality. For example, on the streets of Los Angeles, crowds gather around anything at which TV cameras are pointed, because people want to see what other people are going to see, because that alone is most real. Conversely, forms not onscreen tend to fade from consideration. For example, in a research library, those books cited in the computer database enjoy much more circulation than those listed only in the old card catalogue. Visual media determine what gets noticed, what gets demanded, what gets admired. In the marketplace, visual identities such as the controversial cigarette-smoking Joe Camel are carefully cultivated to generate demand for products, events, and services. To be viable, then, is to be visible. The safest way for work to be sustainable is for it to be presented though the image.

Meanwhile the image itself is transformed. Now made of bits, it is increasingly malleable. The same image can appear in a growing range of media: produced on conventional film, or in a digital camera, a photo CD-ROM, a file moving about the internet, or as pixels on your screen. And so we get "memes"—ideas, usually images, that proliferate like viruses. These are not just mechanically reproduced, but come in versions, with content altered almost as easily as format. Some of these versions and recombinations capitalize on the presumed veracity of the camera to present altered instances as photographic reality. And more generally artists of all kinds appropriate and invert famous images, whose fame consists anyway in copious reproduction, or more accurately, transformation. The origin of a meme is of far less concern than its proliferation. Electrified culture produces a flux of images for which there is no original, and all of us can just sit back and enjoy the free play of signifiers, much as we would admire a good sunset.

Dematerialization

The pertinence of these conceits to our question of digital craft is essentially twofold. On the one hand, the image culture reduces the importance of physical objects; on the other, it generates many new forms of individual knowledge and production.

Dematerialization is not new, for in a sense it began with mechanization. We can recite from Walter Benjamin's celebrated essay, "The Work of Art in the Age of Mechanical Reproduction" (1934), which stands sixty years later as one of the perennial favorites of aesthetic theory—the essay itself mechanically reproduced everywhere on college copy machines. Benjamin's argument certainly pertains to our question of craft, for it refers to an archaic condition, similar to the one evoked by Paz, which Benjamin calls "aura":

> The presence of the original is the prerequisite to the concept of authority . . . Confronted with its manual reproduction, which was usually branded as a forgery, the original preserved all its authority; not so vis-à-vis technical reproduction. The reason is twofold. First, process reproduction is more independent of the original than manual reproduction. For example, in photography, process reproduction can bring out those aspects of the original that are unattainable to the naked eye and yet accessible to the lens . . . Secondly, technical reproduction can put the copy of the original into situations which would be out of reach for the original itself . . . One might subsume the eliminated element in the term "aura" and go on to say: that which withers in the age of mechanical reproduction is the aura of the work

2.4 The work of art in the age of mechanical reproduction: Roy Lichtenstein, *Image Duplicator* (courtesy of Lichtenstein studios)

of art . . . One might generalize by saying: the technique of reproduction detaches the reproduced object from the domain of tradition.[16]

As we know, none of this bodes well for traditional craft. When its aura fades, an artifact loses its authenticity—that is, its history, its cultural identity, or its autographic, personal stamp. It becomes a merely useful thing. Moreover, if people see the copy before the original, or never see the original at all, they become more likely to accept the image for the thing. The material aspects of the object lose any importance except with regard to appearance. This in turn means that things get made expressly for the images they shed, indeed in some cases just for how they appear from a particular vantage point, like a movie set. Conversely, artifacts about which there are no images, or which were never intended to be experienced as images, seem destined for obscurity. Whether a noble "last" craft like the bark canoe or a mundane folk commodity like *huaraches* being replaced by Tevas®, artifacts not merchandised or loaded with a marketing image tend to disappear in the image culture.

At the same time, common sense becomes visual sense. Innate sensibilities—always the blessing of the artisan—become increasingly visual, and other skills slowly vanish. The experience in which most people become most practiced is no longer the workings of nature or the use of hand-held tools, but rather the reading of images—staggering numbers of images.[17] We get the picture, or, more accurately in the era of target marketing, the picture gets us.

Much the same trend was prophesied long ago by Oliver Wendell Holmes, who in 1859, just twenty years after the invention of photography, exclaimed: "Matter in large masses must always be fixed and dear; form is cheap and transportable. We have got the fruit of creation now, and need not trouble ourselves with the core. Every conceivable object of art and nature will soon scale off its surface for us. Men will hunt all curious, beautiful, grand objects, as they hunt cattle in South America, for their skins, and leave the carcasses as of little worth."[18]

The camera was an appropriate metaphor of modernity for other reasons as well. Its power to chemically fix light and shadow came out of, and effectively represented, the overall project of an innocent scientific realism.[19] Its product, the photographic print or film, was celebrated by the moderns for its immediacy, its objectivity, its closure, and its freedom from codified interpretation.[20]

Now a digital image culture separates practical production from traditional artisanry by a second order of magnitude. Bits replace atoms, and digital signal processing undermines the very physicality of reproduction. Where industrialism diminished the role of the hand, now postmodernism diminishes the role of the physical artifact.

Painting, for example, is now twice removed: if the camera succeeded painting (at least for practical representation), the digital computer in turn now succeeds the chemical camera. One of the first to explore this idea was William J. Mitchell in *The Reconfigured Eye* (1992). Much as in 1839, after seeing the new Daguerreotype, critic Paul Delaroche announced "From this day on painting is dead," Mitchell updates, "From the moment of its sesquicentennial in 1989 photography was dead—or, more precisely, radically and permanently displaced—as was painting 150 years before."[21]

Where a photographic print requires little more work to make many identical images, a computer image requires little more work to make many, no two of which are exactly alike. The digital image file is synthetic, multivalent, fragmented, sampled, appropriated, independent of output format—every version the original, without degradation, no matter how many transmissions, no matter how many transformations. Filters, geometric transformations, tone scale adjustments, synthesized textures and lighting, plus incredible powers of layered adjustable cutting and pasting are all provided in everyday image-processing software capable of transforming a computer into a digital darkroom for just a few hundred dollars. So where the mass-produced photograph was the characteristic metaphor of the modern, today the digitally generated image, in its place, has become the effective metaphor of the postmodern.

Of course such abstract manipulation is hardly limited to the production of images. Designers do it with three-dimensional form. Industrial engineers do essentially the same thing with flexible production. Business planners do it with site selection and product distribution scenarios. Unfortunately, some such abstractions contribute to a growing rift between high-tech factories without many workers and low-tech third-world sweatshops. People become operands in optimized numerical models. Organizations become virtual and recombinant. This may be getting ahead of the narrative, but we can see that Henry Ford-style manufacturing, too, is being radically and permanently displaced—as was artisanry 150 years before.

It follows that artisanry, like painting, now becomes twice removed. For purposes of practical production, hand-eye-tool work must now compete not only with the leverage of standard mechanized production, but also with the leverage of process models and design computation. Hence any return to traditional artisanry becomes all the more unlikely. A century ago, in the time of Ruskin and Morris, hand work may have seemed only recently displaced—and perhaps recoverable. But today the separation is so great that traditional methods seldom survive as anything more than a personal recreation or a form of protest. Truly practical craft, practiced as a livelihood, is reserved for esoteric production, where cost is no object or where the main impetus is not the product, but the process. In most other forms of work and play, the hand is no longer any match for the eye.

Visual Production

Although physical objects may decline in importance, that loss could be offset by gaining new forms of abstract visual knowledge and production. The latter is certain: to work in a technologized image culture is to produce and deliver all manner of visual information. Our products are electronic graphs, charts, maps, plans, diagrams, pictures, movies, hypertexts. Much as industrial goods formed a "second nature" that supplanted the "first nature" of agricultural production, so now has postindustrial visual information established a "third nature." We work this nature, and make these dematerialized artifacts, using computers—which are increasingly necessary in a world already shaped by computers. To produce is to employ a range of digital media, against which analog media are increasingly hard pressed to compete. New media have upset old distinctions of trade and profession, especially where work has become equated with information delivery alone. For example, architects might occasionally imagine that they are in the business of producing sets of drawings, except now those drawings have become just reports on databases, which themselves have become a matter of professional service and responsibility to administer. Organization itself, and not only the document delivery it structures, increasingly relies on digital media. But at the same time new practices have revealed that the real basis of professions remains to administrate knowledge.

Many other givers of form encounter similar circumstances. There are few exceptions to this change in the means of production. Three-dimensional designs are produced in geometric models, process models, machined part parameterizations, global illumination models for renderings, scores for animations. All these various representations are constantly mediated through images. All this abstract work is monitored on a computer screen. Even physically formed artifacts can be mainly visual. For example, the product of a rapid prototyping system, such as a laser-sintered model of an airplane part (made by incrementally fusing metal flakes and resin) lacks the structural, inertial, or thermal properties of the manufactured thing it represents. It is only for testing form fit or appearance.

Although image production comes first, new forms of visual knowledge should follow, and this is the second side of our interest in image culture. New forms of production invite corresponding changes to outlook, artifacts, and methods.

The computer has already reshaped many forms of thoughtful work. Writing, the traditional medium of focused thought, is itself influenced by the technology of word processing. Design, which is especially visual work, is especially transformed. Composition and printing of two-dimensional images benefit from the instantaneous verification provided by graphical computing. Projection and construction of three-dimensional models may employ the rigors of operations formerly practical only in two dimensions, as well as a flexibility similar to that of word processing. This might become understood as "form processing." In the fourth dimension of time, digital apparatus enables the orchestration of forms, images, and text into compelling visual presentations.

In these many different facets and guises, the computer has become a visual medium. It has subsumed many older visual technologies such as photography and video as well. Throughout these endeavors, computing has not so often introduced the strict formal methodologies for which it was initially notorious as it has opened up possibilities—for involvement, for expression, and for individual talent. Visual computing has provided a new form of hand-guided, continuous processes. Its dynamic representations invite incremental refinement of artifacts. So far both the conduct of process and the presentation of artifact are purely visual, and the artifacts are what we might call virtual, but even this state suggests aspects of a workable medium. Increasingly computing shows promise of becoming the medium that could reunite visual thinking with manual dexterity and practiced knowledge.

This reunion lies at the heart of any proposition for a digital craft. New approaches to the likes of continuous process, refined artifact, workability, and the application of individual talent all relate to traditional notions of craft. This is the point. Reuniting hand, eye, tools, and mind, at the level of visual (and otherwise sensory) abstraction, may be the way toward more satisfying and more incisive work.

One distinct advantage comes from the way the computer couples graphic representations with symbolic notations. Consider the spreadsheet, the application that drove the initial spread of the personal computer. In essence, the spreadsheet takes the most fundamental abstract data construct (the variable) and makes it into the most fundamental visual element (a location) that can be pointed to. The first popular spreadsheet was thus named *VisiCalc* (1980). Given this fundamental relation, the spreadsheet can then include the names of locations (cells) in expressions held in other cells, and include those cells in others still, and so on. As a result, we can point to a single location, enter a single number, and see the consequences that ripple though an entire ledger of calculations. And this is what first made personal computers popular—*seeing* the results of quantitative propositions.

Similarly, one can couple graphics with physical activities. For example, manufacturing engineering software lets us visualize, study, and correct machine tool paths before implementing them in physical production. It also permits fabrication of complex physical forms, such as curved surfaces, directly from abstract geometric models. (Today's sleek car parts are a common example.) And conversely, it supports the development of geometric models from found physical artifacts—that is, reverse engineering. Graphical-kinetic couplings support digitizing processes such as the three-dimensional motion capture used by game animators.

Computer-aided design and manufacturing recasts relations between images and things. It models and manipulates not only objects, but also the processes by which they are made. By converting geometric models into machining instructions, and conversely basing those models on machining variables, CAD/CAM closely couples design geometry and process models in a feedback loop. For example, a parametric model of an injection-molded ski boot makes it easier for designers to identify and explore the design variables most inherent to the process by which the boot is made. This is superior to simply drawing up a design and tooling up production because manufacturing processes become more easily visualized and more quickly adaptable, and design becomes more easily executed as physical things. Thus, conversely to the widespread condition noted by the cultural critics, wherein things become images, here there occurs an inversion: thanks to CAD/CAM, and more controllably than ever before, images can become things.

In like manner, general organization has become more visual. Desktop environments let us see—and graphically organize—the structure of our workplaces. Image databases, clickable image maps, navigable virtual spaces, and other such access structures give us access to information by means of visual devices and appearances. Graphical access popularized the World Wide Web, for example—where before one had to know the name and location of remote data, now one can simply point and click at labels and images of data elements without any concern for their actual address. Instead of having to know in advance what one was looking for, one can see possibilities presented visually onscreen.

Let us generalize. Work has begun on making our data constructions coincide with our abstractive powers of visual thinking. Visual computing has expanded our capacity to visualize abstract symbolic structures as physical images. It lets ideas become things. Many high-level abstractions, some now as common as the evening weather forecast, are made visual and dynamic by computing. At the same time, many of these structures are coupled to continuous manual operations. For example, a mouse stroke might give us a tracking shot in viewing a three-dimensional model, or slowly change the proportions of a shape, or adjust the contrast in a photograph, or alter the composition of a set of forms. Visual production demands, and visual computing increasingly supports, a cultivated practice of abstraction based on direct manipulation of graphical symbols. Computing has taken its first steps toward our senses. Our work involves a limited role of the hand, empowered by a very particular mode of the eye.

Personal Vision

Who could doubt that the quality of work is somehow in the balance? Yet too little is said about what it is *like* to use computers. For example, what would it be like to have an abstract craft? How does it feel to assimilate the skilled hand, the contemplative eye, and the technology for manipulating abstract structure? The underemployed hand has been noted, and the capacities of symbolic structure will be explored later on; consider here the place of vision.

Imagine a design and fabrication technology that lets us explore a continuum of formal possibilities by means of rapid, continuous transformations between related versions (as opposed to executing individual pieces by trial and error). Imagine that we have the means to productively and playfully navigate that continuum—by reversible operations on bits as opposed to irreversible operations on atoms. Assume that we still care to produce physical artifacts, which we might then use and contemplate without need for the apparatus by which they were made. In this case no skill should remain more important than design vision, that is, the capacity both for envisioning what to try and for recognizing desirable form amid the flux of possibilities.

Where a discrete trial-and-error process, such as drawing successive iterations of a design on layers of tracing paper, involves some preconception, or some explicit quantitative specification, a continuous exploratory process such as realtime sculpting a spline-controlled curved surface depends much more on qualitative recognition and discovery. Note that although vision's technological context becomes thoroughly externalized, its arresting capacity remains internal (and this is exactly the power described by Focillon). This ability to develop an image in the mind's eye from which to give form to artifacts in the outer world, by means of discovering appropriate states of continuously manipulated materials, should be a far better acknowledged aspect of electronic art, digital craft, and computer-aided design.

Unfortunately, electronic image technology presents a compound challenge to the mind's eye. First, it pummels people into passivity with its ever-intensifying barrage of external stimulation. Visions are furnished, and attention spans are eroded, until the result is "couch potatoes"—people lacking the discernment by which one book read, piece finished, or argument reasoned can dictate the next. Personal agenda, which is required for craft, seems to have become merely optional for leisure.[22]

Second, interactive computing invites a reflex-based kind of activity often difficult to reconcile with thoughtfully planned work. Computers fragment our thinking by substituting discrete events for continuous actions, and by requiring us to learn and manage a bewildering multiplicity of processes. They provide the temptation toward proliferation, rather than

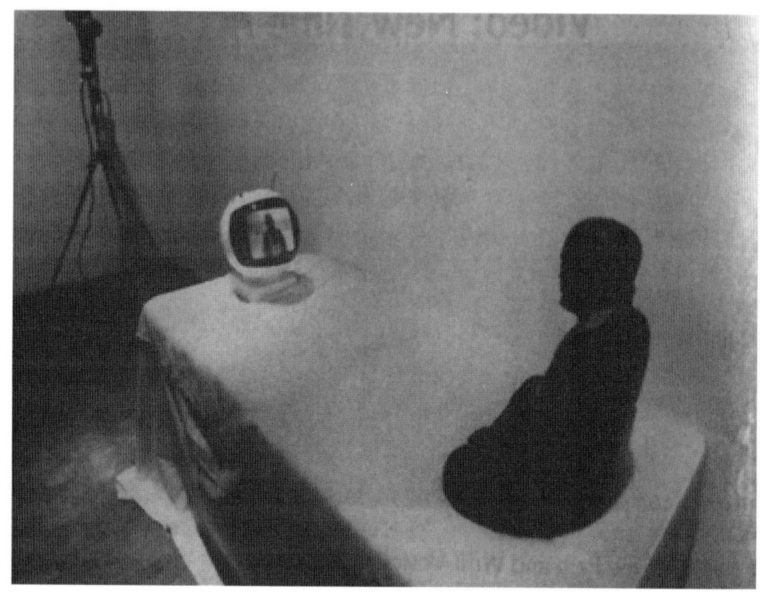

2.5 The contradiction of quiescence: Nam June Paik, *TV Buddha* (courtesy of Stedilijk Museum)

unity and refinement of pieces of work. They invite a certain myopia by denying any opportunity to step back and study the big picture. Moreover, they too can erode concentration—or at least calmness—by a spectrum of interruptions from nanoseconds to days, especially the endless quarter-second to ten-second delays typical of today's software operations. At the same time computers are a bit too rewarding to the short reflexive response: too much of what they ask of us takes just a second, gives an instantaneous reward, and requires something more the next second. Instead of thinking, we are just pointing and clicking, and the result is "mouse potatoes"—people content to keep working a computer without pauses for reflection or quiescence.

Third, computation encourages evaluation to take the form of analysis rather than contemplation. Note for example that engineering began as a visual discipline, but then evolved into a numerical one in which visual thinking has relatively low status. Although there are some recent trends toward social and conceptual approaches to problem solving, engineering schools of today seldom teach design directly. The overwhelming science of numerical analysis, fueled by computer-based calculations, has obscured the role of judgment and created fewer engineers capable of understanding the accuracy or validity of precise numerical models.[23] The same thing is happening in visualization, even for artistic rendering: calculations of lighting intensity models yield "photorealistic" images that despite the precision of their textures and lighting intensities may be inaccurate, incoherent, or rhetorically inappropriate. We might learn from such examples that in general, any detection, reporting, or validation of data, however exact and objective, also needs to incorporate some personal participation and vision. Polanyi argued this for scientific research; Tufte said as much for reporting.

Personal vision and personal computing are hardly incompatible: reconciling them just takes the right attitude. Benjamin wrote this of cinematic apparatus, arguing that "The thoroughgoing permeation of reality with mechanical equipment [offers] an aspect of reality which is free of all equipment."[24] To pursue this reality with digital equipment, first we must master the technology to the point where it becomes more transparent (and without our becoming mouse potatoes along the way). Then we must use this paradoxical freedom more effectively. We must recall that the mind works perfectly well without any external action or apparatus. We must assert that behavior is not the mind's only manifestation: awareness and intent may occur without any corresponding measurable action. Next we must admit that Paz is correct in suggesting that what we are missing in our work, in both the making and the employment of physical artifacts, is contemplation—the playful shifting back and forth between use and beauty. Therefore we must find ways to cultivate vision and play amid the transparency of ubiquitous technology. We must combine our personal vision with our perpetual desire to make something. We must develop good habits about letting our current piece of work dictate the next, nurture our hope that the next piece will somehow be a bit better, and mix our meditative play with ongoing work. Then we can talk about craftsmanship.

To realize the proposition of craft, we must also acknowledge that visual computing is far from mature, and that future software design must go deeper and strike better balances. For example, software designers should do more about reconciling direct with indirect actions, structure with improvisation, work with play, use with beauty. These combinations are worth pursuing, but to reach them will require going places where explicit software code cannot. Any better-balanced medium should approach our intelligence not only through formal logic, which computers perform better than humans, but also through visual insight, which humans perform better than computers. For whatever technical advances may come our way, one thing is unlikely to change. Computers are very good as calculators, constructors, and transmitters of visual information, but we're the ones who can see.

3 Tools

You probably think of a tool as something to hold in your hand. It is something to extend your powers: a piece of technology, or applied intelligence, for overcoming the limitations of the body. The hand-held tool comes to mind because more than any other it demands an especially active sort of skill. It requires your participation, and for that reason it engages your imagination.

A tool directs your attention. Its function becomes your focus: as the saying goes, when you hold a hammer, all the world looks like nails. Its function extends some powers of your hand, and prevents the use of others. In other words, it serves a specialization.

A tool usually belongs to a set, which implies a hierarchy of specializations. A toolkit provides every function needed for a single specialization by means of its members' many different specializations. Its effectiveness for a single purpose emerges from the combined or alternative effects of its differentiated members. Multiple tools may provide alternatives of scale, like a set of socket wrenches, or incremental differences of hardness or weight, like a set of pencils. Multiple tools may work in

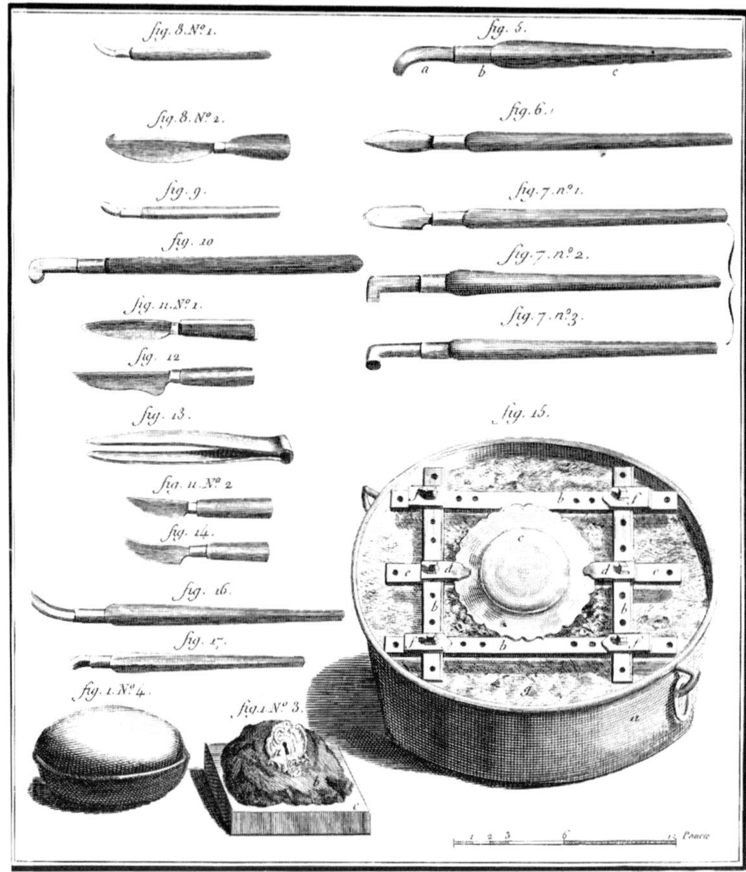

Vol. I, Argenteur, Pl. I.

3.1 Silversmith's tool set from Diderot's *Encyclopédie*

specific combinations, like a knife and a fork. Instruments for measuring complement implements for forming, and tools for clamping and guiding complement tools for action.

A tool or toolkit normally benefits from the context of a studio or shop. For example, surfaces and lighting support particular tasks. Multiple collections of tools and kits for a variety of related purposes distinguish a practice. A shop supports and gives place to that practice.

Above all else, tools take practice. You must learn how to bring skills and intentions together. You must learn how each tool works, how one tool works with another, and how all are maintained. You must know what tools are for. A well-equipped woodshop might make you feel like building something, but only if you are so inclined—only if you are in practice.

If you feel satisfaction in using a well-practiced tool, you probably do so on several levels. Tool usage simultaneously involves direct sensation, provides a channel for creative will, and affirms a commitment to practice. The latter is quite important: only practice produces the most lasting and satisfying form of knowing. Practiced mastery is something we crave in itself. Aquinas said that we cannot live well without working well.[1] Most anthropologists would affirm a fundamental relation between tools and humanity. Deep in our very nature, we are tool users.

A tool may not only perform some action, but may also come to represent that action.[2] A tool is inscribed in your imagination not only as an activity, but also as a symbol. An oar, if you are a skilled boatsman, is not just for plying the water, it is *about* plying the water. It may evoke memories, it may have romance. This is important to us, as reflected in the way we prize our favorite tools. Furthermore, a particular tool may represent not only an action but also an approach. In this manner, a French kitchen knife is quite different from a Japanese kitchen knife, even if both are used to cut fresh vegetables. Such implicit differences in approach are especially evident in toolkits, which more effectively represent whole structures of tasks. For example, the cookware in a fine restaurant differs from the cookware in an institutional cafeteria. The tools come to stand for the processes. This symbolic aspect of tools may help you clarify your work. Choosing the right tool is not only about completing a task, but also about establishing and focusing that task. Holding a tool helps you inhabit a task.

Tools may also work *upon* symbols. A clock, for example, although a piece of power machinery, produces abstract measure of hours, minutes, and seconds.[3] A book is hand-held, but is mainly the object of symbolic skills. A computer, part clock and part book, thus far allows insufficient physical control: although it involves a lot of pointing, computer usage is mainly mental. That is, not all tools are prosthetic. These various tools that introduce abstractions do not so much extend the powers of the body as those of the mind. They are for processing symbols. We use these tools of abstraction every bit as much as any others, because deep in our nature we are also symbol users.

History has taught that we might do well to divide our tools into those that transmit power and those that transform information. This division is fundamental enough to have formed a basis for social classes. Although humankind has used both of these classes of tools from the very outset, historically the information tool users—scholars, statesmen, and clergy—have dominated the mechanical tool users—the farmers, traders, and craftsmen. New thinking and new tools have often shifted the roles, but seldom the balance. But today the information tools take on a physical dimension, and may begin to unite skill and intellect in new ways. To understand how this potential might develop, we need to understand the symbolic processor not only as a form of tool, but also as a medium.

Tool and Medium

We have noted that the hand works in two directions: part effector and part probe. When enhanced by a tool, the hand remains such a two-way conductor, but its powers become narrowed and intensified. That is, when using a tool we can sense some things better, and we can alter some things better, but others not at all.

Normally this specialization occurs in terms of a medium. Tools are means for working a medium. A particular tool may indeed be the only way to work a particular medium, and it may only be for working that medium. Thus a medium is likely to distinguish a particular class of tools. For example, a material that is workable by chipping it away incrementally gives rise to chisels. The nature of that material will determine the nature of the tools: thus a carpenter's wood chisels are different from a stonemason's chisels.

Sometimes a medium implies such a unique set of tools that the whole is referred to without differentiation. Painting is a medium, but it is also the use of specific tools and the resulting artifact: a painting. The artifact, more than the medium in which or tools by which it is produced, becomes the object of our work. The presence of an artifact is more important than any clear-cut distinction between tool and medium. Artifact, tool, and medium are just different ways of focusing our attention on the process of giving form.

Many tools, especially tools that operate on symbols, do not work a medium so much as they assist observations, make measurements, or interpret scores. We usually refer to such tools as instruments. Although there may be a craft of scientific measurement or musical performance, let us focus on tools that work a medium to produce a lasting artifact. As mentioned earlier, it is the craft that involves continuous operations on a workable medium which is most compelling. But this does not rule out our consideration of an abstract medium: our scope includes abstract artifacts produced by means of continuous operations (e.g., direct manipulation) in symbolic media. Nor does it eliminate consideration of instruments, for many form-giving tools that demand highly refined practices are understood as instruments. We are simply limiting the focus to the interplay of the effecting tool and the workable medium.

In many refined practices, the perception of a medium surpasses any perception of tools. If a medium is a realm of possibilities for a set of tools, then any immediate awareness of the tools may become subsidiary to a more abstract awareness of the medium. Although a tool focuses your work, it should also let you focus on your work—in this sense it should go largely unnoticed. Cognitive psychologists agree that some sensory-motor activities can be learned to the point that they become automatic. This normally takes practice. Even for a known process, it may also require some adjustment of a tool's performance and to its subtleties—breaking it in. But with practice you should be able subconsciously to handle your tools without interfering with your active intent.

In this case, the tool may be said to have become transparent. When you use a hammer, you focus on the hammer striking the nail, and remain only secondarily aware of the feeling of its handle meeting your hand.[4] Indeed you think you feel the hammer striking the nail itself. Interestingly, tools far more sophisticated or abstract can be just as transparent as a simple hammer. When painting in watercolor, for example, you should mostly be looking at the light bathing your subject; you should be able to subjugate any awareness of your control of paint streaming off your brush; and the fact that you are holding a brush at all should be completely transparent.

Tool, Machine, and Technology

The experience of transparency is hardly limited to unitary, hand-held tools. Adjustable tools fit better than monolithic tools under a greater variety of conditions. Mechanical tools extend the possibilities of the hand to a far greater range of applications than can monolithic tools. Even machines can behave as tools under the appropriate circumstances. In the loose sense that a tool is a human extension as means to an end, all machines are tools, and all tools are a kind of technology, even if in the case of an ancient device such as an ax, it is difficult to think of them as engineering.

Given the abundance of mechanical tools, some definitions are in order. A mechanism is a device with multiple moving parts for the transfer of motion. For example, a pair of gears is a mechanism for the transfer of rotation from one axis to another. A machine is a mechanism for the transfer of power. Power may be the force of the hand or the body, or it may come from outside sources. For example, an engine is a machine powered by combustion. Motive power may assist or replace human guidance, and this is an important distinction.

Transparency depends on the effectiveness of an extension as a conductor. Like the hand itself, this extension may be two-way: part effector, part probe. So long as it is driven by the hand, this extension may be a crude implement, an elegant machine, or a complex, baroque world of technology—what makes it a tool is the hand. Although no tool will be as rich a conductor as the bare hand, it may compensate by working under a greater range of conditions. For example, it may overcome the interference of one undesirable sensation to provide a clearer perception of another, just as a fork in a skillet bypasses overwhelming heat to let you test the firmness of cooking food. It may translate the scale or reach of the hand so that it may work in tight spots, or at very large scales. Such magnifications, large or small, are accomplished with mechanisms. Well-fitted mechanisms, and mechanisms augmented with high-resolution sensors, may be more than adequately transparent. Or at least the surgeons doing teleoperations think so.

To this way of thinking it seems fairly meaningless to ask what, if anything, is truly made by hand.[5] Only in a few exceptionally simple cases such as pottery or basketweaving do the hands work in direct contact with a material. The word "medium" intrinsically suggests the mediating action of tools. Beside tools mediating the hand, guides such as jigs and templates mediate the tools; wheels or clamps handle the material; and motors assist in providing power. A *machine tool,* such as a lathe, couples mechanical precision and motive power with direct manual operation. Does it matter whether an expert machinist is truly doing hand work? In his study of workmanship, Thorstein Veblen observed:

> But in these more primitive industrial systems—as also in the days of handicraft—the workman is forever in constant control of his tools and materials; the movements made use of in the work are essentially of the nature of manipulation, in which the workman adroitly coerces the materials into shapes and relations that will answer his purpose, and in which also nothing (typically) takes place

beyond the manual reach of the workman as extended by the tools which his hands make use of. Under these conditions it is a matter of relatively slight effect whether the workman does or does not rate the objects which he uses as tools and material in quasi-personal terms or imputes to them a degree of self-direction, since they are at no point allowed to escape his manual reach and are by direct communication of his force, dexterity, and judgment coerced into the forms, motions, and spatial dispositions aimed at by him . . .

The matter lies differently in machine industry . . . [where] the operative's work supplements the machine process, rather than makes use of it. On the contrary the machine process makes use of the workman.[6]

The matter is mainly an issue of impetus. Continuous control of process is at the heart of tool usage and craft practice. Processes may be indirect, and mechanical and powered, so long as they are under manual guidance. Furthermore some operations that reduce the role of the hand (substituting motorized power for brute-force activity) may contribute to an overall process that increases human impetus. Master craftsman Gustav Stickley raised this same point:

> An expert carpenter or cabinet-maker will save much time that can be used to better advantage, and will lose nothing of artistic quality in his work, if he makes use of all the modern machines, for sawing, planing, boring, mortising, scraping, sandpapering, and otherwise preparing his material for use, instead of insisting that all these things be done by hand.[7]

Or to take a more recent example, master stonecarvers at New York's Cathedral of St. John the Divine use CAD/CAM machining to do their rough cuts, plywood templates to frame their initial carving, and power grinders to polish up their finished chisel work. Is the result handmade? A lot depends on your attitude toward technology.

Technology has a Promethean quality, like the mastering of fire, for study renders skills more powerful than the societal forces that harness them. Technology in its more usual modern usage means the applied results of such study: powered mechanisms, sophisticated capital equipment—hardly traditional tools. But let us adopt a hybrid meaning. The important thing is that technology has both intellectual and physical elements. Let us use the word "technology" to refer to the *means* of engineering: both study and implementation. If to engineer is to design and to economize as a system, then to accomplish this takes not only equipment but principles. In other words, technology is hardly limited to machines—it is a philosophy.

"Technique has taken over all of man's activities, not just his productive activity," warned the sociologist Jacques Ellul in 1964.[8] The more sophisticated the techniques, the more people become intrigued by them, and the less anyone cares to focus on other aspects of the human condition less conveniently subject to exactitude and method. Ellul seems to have anticipated computing very well in this regard. The majority of books about computers are simply technical instruction manuals. The more time people spend learning about and tinkering with computers, the less time they spend setting goals or applying existing skills. And at a most general level, the more we learn *how* to do, the less we know *what* to do.

Like Ellul, many people feel that the tyranny of technique is wrong, yet they are unclear on how much technology to accept. Few seem happy without electricity, for instance, and most still want to drive cars. Few people benefit from having categorical opinions for or against a largely undifferentiated Technology. There is certainly no advantage in blurring light switches and Walkmans and jumbo jets into one big wrong turn in human history.[9] Despite the examples set by many well-meaning people such as Ellul, there is no point in uncritically accepting or categorially rejecting Computers. Nor does imagining handwork fundamentally as a rejection of Technology lead one very far.

Here then is the pivotal importance of studying tools. A right approach to tools may help lead us toward more measured positions on

Perception

Coarse, Discrete			Fine, Continuous
Detecting events	Watching	*Drawing* · *Directing traffic*	Deciding
Sorting items · *Monitoring processes*		*Playing tactics* · *Playing music*	
Typing codes · Tapping	*Forcing objects*	*Guiding motions* · Tracking	*Dancing* · *Doing tricks*

Action

3.2 Hand-eye guidance: a chart of tracking skills

technology. There may be not always be a clear cutoff between tool and medium, between manual and mechanized, or between traditional and digital. We are likely to explore this middle ground.

So here is an inclusive definition: *A tool is a moving entity whose use is initiated and actively guided by a human being, for whom it acts as an extension, toward a specific purpose.* This definition is explicitly kinetic, yet it is open to abstraction: the entity may be physical or conceptual; the motion may be manual or machine powered; the guidance may be manual or by indirect control.[10] It reflects that condition that tools may suggest new uses for themselves, but unlike some other technologies, they remain subject to our intent. A tool depends on us to control the scope, the pace, and the focus of its work; merely attended machinery does not.

It clarifies a distinction very useful to discussions of craft, namely: *The degree of personal participation, more than any degree of independence from machine technology, influences perceptions of craft in work.*

The Abstraction of Work

Individual guidance of process participation in outcomes of work was of course the very condition upended by industrialization. Today amid increasing technology we may naturally despair of the prospects for such work. Yet the symbolic tools, abstract media, and intellectual technologies of our time are not necessarily direct projections of what has gone before. Rapid industrialization did have such an impact on working and thinking that even today, as much as two centuries later in some places, we cannot escape its influence. Theories on the relation of technology and work remain heavily weighted by the industrial age. As a result, we must constantly struggle to rethink production, and we often draw parallels from the past to help us do so—hence all the pronouncements about a revolution.

There is no question that technology accompanies social change, but there is much question about which comes first. As an example of change, consider just a few details from one of the clearest transformations, namely a fifty-year span in England culminating in the Great Exhibition of 1851. Remarkably, having been reasonably stable for three hundred years, the country's population proceeded to double; in several new industrial cities such as Manchester it quadrupled. But economic growth was greater still: between 1800 and 1850 iron production grew by a factor of 100 (or 10,000 percent), and cotton imports to feed the textile mills grew by a factor of close to 150. Moreover, these patterns of economic growth were indicators of general social structural change. Although industry grew fastest, commercial and professional activities also rose dramatically. Agriculture thus declined relatively over this period; later it would decline absolutely, and land ceased to be the main source of wealth. Thus by 1851, for the first time in the modern world, the majority of the population lived in the cities. There, at the site of machine-powered industry, the nature of work itself was transformed, particularly in its tools.[11]

It is pertinent to recite this old story, for among the changes wrought by industrialization, none seems more significant than the abstraction of craft. From a technical standpoint the change was a twofold transformation in tools. First, the tools' motion became machine powered; their control became indirect; and they incorporated a greater conceptual component, which often surpassed the scale of the individual. Next the tools' very pace and position became governed by independent mechanisms (at which point they no longer fit our definition of tools). From a social standpoint, however, the change was more singular: the means of production had become too elaborate, too extensive, and too centralized to be owned and operated by an independent craftsman. This too was a consequence of abstraction: if time was money, then work was labor. This famous abstraction was a near-fatal blow to artisanry, for it quickly moved power from the traditional tool users to the innovative symbol users—financiers, engineers, and factory managers. This situation has been at the crux of critical theory ever since. Marx insisted that the replacement of human skill was more significant than the application of motive power.[12] Veblen noted later that "Producer" had come to mean the owner of the industrial plant, rather than the workmen or the apparatus.[13] Productivity became best measured in capital infrastructure per worker, as opposed to the skill of the individual worker. Under these conditions semiskilled workers were good enough. So in the face of new abstraction, traditional skills waned.

As we know, technical change was accompanied by aesthetic and intellectual change. Declining skills led to a loss of innate design sense and a deprival of workmanship. Machine production led to a proliferation of cheap objects, which were marketed to precisely those classes whose self-sufficiency (and natural sense of design) had been debased by the new division of labor.[14] "Our work has constantly the look of money's worth," decried Ruskin.[15] Victorian households became cluttered with things needlessly ornate and expensive. This situation eventually led to aesthetic reactions and counterreactions such as the movements known as Craftsman and Bauhaus.

But also during this time, abstract scientific thinking about visual things accelerated. More systematic understanding led to more functional invention, and therefore unprecedented possibilities, some of which had long-term innovative consequences. Consider just four: the camera, as we have seen, transformed visual communication; telecommunications freed communication from transportation; powered machinery expanded the range of practical fabrications; and descriptive geometry increased the capacity and predictability of design. Note that each of these four is a germ of what by now has become an element of the contemporary CAD/CAM system—a new technology with old roots.

As technology and aesthetics entwined, design changed accordingly. Consider the case of architecture, where mechanization led to new materials, new economies of scale, and many unprecedented practicalities. New kinds of buildings began to incorporate steel and glass, large complex functional programs, and a range of specific inventions from elevators to balloon-frame construction. As a result of technological change, architecture emerged as a distinct profession. Engineering, and many other disciplines, followed a similar trajectory. At least as many creative practices arose as declined, the roles changing with the technology.

But from the artisan's perspective, any control over the pace and scope of practical work had been lost irrevocably. Powered factories took away the artisan's freedom to own the necessary tools and hire oneself out by the job. Organized labor such as piecework also removed the opportunity to work continuously, at one's own rate, with oversight of the process. This in turn discouraged practice, involvement, and care. And here technology struck right at the personal nature of work.

Today the abstraction is information. In our lifetime, symbolic processing has been tooled up very seriously. "Industrial Revolution" is a coinage attributed to the historian Arnold Toynbee, who toward the end of the nineteenth century had the hindsight to comprehend the many economic, social, and intellectual changes accompanying the rise of machine-powered industry as a major historical divide.[16] Today, as we are constantly assured, the growth and change associated with electronic information technology constitute a "Second Industrial Revolution," as Norbert Wiener called this one as early as 1948.[17]

This state of technological change began about fifty years ago, when the challenges of organizing a war effort had strained traditional notations, calculations, and transmittals to their limits. Not only military command-and-control practices, but also large-scale manufacturing, New Deal social record keeping, and with the end of the war, burgeoning capital trading each faced catastrophe unless abetted by new tools and methods. In this same decade, Claude Shannon's work at Bell Labs showed how to quantify information and how signals carry that information, and John Von Neuman's work at MIT showed how to store and process information—how to implement Turing machines. Norbert Wiener's work, also at MIT, suggested the social consequences. Wiener expressed the difference of the dawning era quite concisely: "*The preoccupation of modern engineering is not the economy of energy but the accurate reproduction of a signal.*"[18]

Technology for the abstract processes of computing and global telecommunication took only a few decades to materialize: technical change was at least as explosive as English industrialization. For example, in the mid-1950s, a then-young IBM estimated there would be a market for as many as 100 computers in the world; less than forty years later there were well over 100 million—without counting the ones in everybody's automobiles, microwaves, and watches, in which case it has been estimated that microprocessors now outnumber people. Compared to the first transatlantic cable of 1866, recently installed fiber-optic ones have increased communications capacity by a factor of 2 billion. The explosive growth of processing power has been greater still: as processing technology has evolved from tubes to transistors to integrated circuits to microprocessors, its power, measured in bits per second per dollar, has increased by an order of magnitude approximately once every three years for the last thirty, or by a factor of at least a trillion.

By the 1970s, sociologists had begun to proclaim an information economy, two of the more notable documents being Daniel Bell's *The Coming of Post-Industrial Society* (1973), and Marc Porat's *The Information Economy* (1976–78). By the 1980s, the practicality of tools was accelerating fast enough that the value added by the computer industry surpassed even that of the darling of the machine age—the automobile industry. The potential of the technology (artificial intelligence in particular) seemed especially boundless then. Today in the 1990s, the concept of an information economy is the norm: the media hype, the fashion accessory, the government policy, the way to work. The tool on every desk, in many homes, in almost every hand, is a computer. If we describe information according to Gregory Bateson's criterion of "any difference that makes a difference,"[19] then information has value, *by definition.*

Of course, this fact has major consequences for skilled work. Where two centuries ago the middle-class worker lost first-hand artisanry, now he or she is losing first-hand subjectivity. Norbert Wiener cautioned: "The machine plays no favorites between manual labor and white collar labor. Thus the possible fields into which the new industrial revolution is likely to penetrate are very extensive, and include all labor performing judgements of a low level, in much the same way as the displaced labor of the earlier industrial revolution included every aspect of human power."[20]

This is to say that deskilling is now mental. The relief the computer provides from tedious thinking corresponds to the relief machine power provided from strenuous work. Besides reduced physical exertion, we now have reduced mental exertion. Regrettably, just as artisans had become laborers, now citizens became mere consumers. The allegation is that thanks to the pervasiveness of media and the complexity of issues, people are losing the tendency to form their own opinions.[21] We might say that postmodern consumers are ceasing to spin their own yarns, figuratively, every bit as much as the artisans of industrializing Britain stopped spinning their own yarns, literally.

But there is a positive side. Consider the situation in anthropological terms. It appears that the species whose specialization (brain) happens to best coincide with the direction of evolution (consciousness) has finally used its particular habits (tool making) to support its strength (thought). A generation ago, the biologist and theologian Teilhard de Chardin, from whom the above is paraphrased, expressed a vision for a *noosphere* (literally, thought-sphere) supplementing lithosphere, atmosphere, biosphere, etc., as a new skin of the living earth.[22]

So we will undoubtedly think globally; the question is, what does it mean to act locally? How do we uphold subjectivity and personal skill? In comparison to the situation wrought by earlier industrialization, the possibilities are a bit more difficult to grasp this time.

Cultural Lag

There exists a tendency to label an era by its most advanced technologies, whatever their pervasiveness. We know very well, however, that not everyone in a new technological age lives by its advances. For example, most people don't even understand their own computer, much less planetary networks. Most people don't even have a computer. From a technological perspective, then, we might refer to this condition as cultural lag.

Consider a parable. Say "books" and "inventions" and most people will say "Gutenberg": the printing press is the oldest cliché on the power of new technology to propagate knowledge and reshape civilization. Part of the fame of this example is that the printed page was the first completely standardized product—it faithfully reproduced typographers' errors, even. More specifically, what Gutenberg invented was a method for casting movable type blocks. Although the Chinese had mastered the printing press five hundred years earlier, the alphabetic languages of the West were ultimately better suited to the economies and precision of practical, large-scale printing. A pictographic language such as Chinese might allow printers to cut blocks for frequently used words, but it would always require the addition of further symbols. By contrast, an alphabet's finite number of simple characters could all be punched and cut once, after which great numbers of pieces could be cast from the resulting forms as needed. Note that the letter forms of the Roman alphabet, designed for carving in stone, would have been the most sensible for being cut in these dies, but early applications of the technology attempted to mimic the current Gothic alphabets whose forms were shaped by the strokes of the monastic calligrapher. To appearances, then, the new technology did not change the presentation or purpose of the book, only the production. What Gutenberg really did with the printing press was essentially what people did before, which was to produce commissioned, monumental bibles—he just did it more efficiently.

To a Medieval way of thinking, a book was a huge undertaking—about on the scale of putting up a building today. By the end of the Renaissance, all this had changed, but only after quite a bit of delay between the arrival of the altogether new tool and the practice of the altogether new task. Technology hardly drove the change; other factors came into play. Mercantile wealth challenged the power of the scholastic clergy. Levantine trade and teaching made paper cheap and plentiful where it had been unknown for centuries. The conquest of Constantinople sent precious texts from classical antiquity westward to Venice. It was there that Erasmus, who translated many of these works, and his employer Aldus Manutius, became the first to understand new potentials of typography for publishing an inexpensive, portable book. Together they were the first modern editors. Acting in this altogether new role they soon had the surviving work of every major known classical Greek author circulating about the streets of Europe.[23] Aldus is the new cliché: compared to automating commissioned books, redefining the audience for text was more the revolution.

New thinking and new tools may go together, but only rarely are an altogether new tool and an altogether new task invented simultaneously. More often a cultural lag occurs. Usually a new tool is used to do things pretty much as they always had been done; usually a new task is done for quite some time by means of adapting existing tools. Thus invention and innovation are most often gradual.

Given enough cultural lag—or advance—the very idea of industrial revolutions falls into question. Much recent scholarship supports the position that technological change is hardly revolutionary, or even the primary

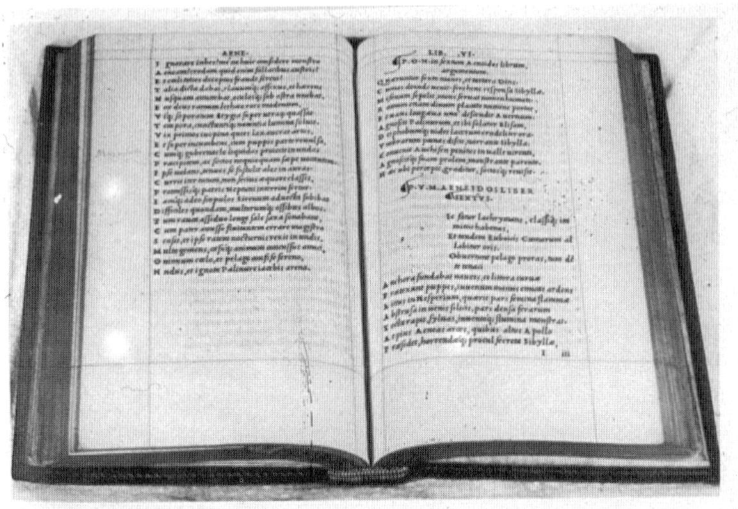

3.3 Redefining the role of information technology: Aldus Manutius, a portable book of Virgil

social force. Even British industrial history gets revised. Economists note considerable organizational change—proto-industrialization—preceding overt technological change by as much as a century: early eighteenth-century wares were produced and marketed in a distinctly modern manner. Sociologists note that capitalized factory methods may have reached their zenith alongside mechanical technology, but they predated the rise of power machinery and assembly lines, which came much later, after electrification. Where temporary social injustices arose, often they were mitigated later with infrastructures built on the new prosperity. The same went for aesthetic problems: for example, the Arts and Crafts movement shifted tastes away from the crude objects of new industry. Manufactured objects improved in any case, as a new breed of industrial craftsmen emerged as mediators between design and the machine.[24]

Developments in our time may not be so technology-driven themselves. Scholars have identified how theoretical shifts predate technical development in our century, following the familiar pattern. More than ever, contemporary technologies depend on increasingly complex needs and the establishment of sophisticated theoretical underpinnings. Thus cultural lag is evident. Too often computers are pervasive in businesses, factories, and schools without changing what the businesses, factories, and schools actually do. Television too may be so pervasive because it has made efforts to comfort popular culture, rather than challenge or threaten it. The deep convictions that universal adoption of information technology will produce universal access to information and a better world for all seem confined to those who have a stake in the technology.[25]

To its critics, the new technology is actually a conservative force. In some regard, social change has equally often been said to be technology-obstructed. Dissenting computer scientist Joseph Weizenbaum wrote: "The computer saved societal institutions which were otherwise threatened with collapse under the weight of a rapidly growing population; computers were only necessary to a world already shaped by computers."[26] Lewis Mumford once said that "too often information technology appears employed in the service of institutions and values belonging to an earlier and more selfish era."[27] The intellectual left essentially accused the enormous electronic marketing-consumerist-entertainment-newsmaking apparatus of the Reagan era of being a public opinion factory—straightforward distraction engineering. It has also been said that: "Only a very small part of any ordinary person's knowledge has been the produce of his own observation and reflection, all the rest has been purchased in the same manner as his shoes or his stockings, from those whose business it is to make up and prepare for the market that particular species of goods . . . (including) religion, morals, philosophy, science, and art."[28] But this was Adam Smith two centuries ago; information economics is not so new.

Whatever their outlook, each of these critics suggests more gradual transitions and prolonged coexistence of conditions than the term "revolution" implies. Predictions about the impact of new technologies have known fallacies: that new technologies totally replace earlier ones; that technologies alone will change the world; that limiting our work to only whatever shows up on our instruments is at all appropriate. Toynbee's progressivist expression does seem outmoded. Our own time carries a fundamentally different idea of progress, limited by experiences of technology's destructiveness. We understand better that societies and their technologies reconstruct one another constantly, and that one set of freedoms just gets exchanged for another. Thus at the scope of individual practice we should acknowledge that if indeed such exchange must occur, the best response is to not to jettison the old freedoms, but to calmly, conscientiously explore the new ones.

Computer as Tool

It is with some healthy skepticism and amid considerable dissension, then, that most people approach computer technology. Although some people advocate change based on new possibilities, others actively resist it; if some advance their work, others retreat; even if the majority accepts new technology, only a minority truly adopts new practices. We see this today in that "computer ownership doesn't guarantee computer literacy."[29]

If there is a middle-of-the-road stance, it is that the computer is "just a tool." We are now in a position to explore what this means. In the legacy of industrialism we see an immediate source of the tool mentality in the psychological desire for containment, the wish for comprehensibility and control. A tool is for serving intent, whereas a medium might create intent, and a machine might work on its own. A tool does only what you tell it to do; it is never out of control. This is a reassuring viewpoint to those concerned about runaway technology.

In addition, even advanced industrial technologies such as assembly lines have been easier to understand as tools of a sort than as a medium. Because of their cost and rigidity, industrial technologies generally have been applied only to known problems and processes with foreseeable outcomes. For example, the way industrial engineers have had to "tool up" production lines has prevented much use of machine tools in any improvisatory or exploratory manner. Furthermore, the rigidity of production lines has caused use of the technology to become equated with unimaginative, semiskilled labor such as attending machines.

These same outlooks about industrial automation have been carried over to computer technology—a clear-cut case of cultural lag. In essence, the computer has been treated as a mere machine, in the mechanical sense of a device that determines its own scope and pace once set in motion by a programmer/attendant. This mindset tends to regard the whole computer as a single tool.

Yet computing is not at all monolithic: information tools are multiple. In hardware alone there is a spectrum of tools from institutional mainframes to office computers to wireless personal organizers to home entertainment equipment to incredible varieties of input and output peripherals. In software, tool metaphors are usually the main interaction strategy, and toolkits the main organizational schema. Even the data are increasingly tools of a sort: object-oriented data structures incorporate information about what operations are meaningful to conduct on them. Altogether, it would be more accurate to say that the computer is not a tool so much as hundreds of tools.

This single-tool mentality is especially pervasive with respect to the use of personal computers in large organizations, where it takes the form of a management practice known as task automation. Task automation is the use of computers to perform known processes more efficiently—as opposed to replacing those with different, higher-level processes. One good indictor of this familiar state is the use of just one piece of application software per computer—using the computer to do just one thing all day long. One prevalent case is drafting systems. For example, architecture and engineering firms have been prone to regard CAD as equipment, which they then hire paraprofessionals to "operate," work that consists in putting sketches already completed by hand onto the computer. Such drafting automation is a natural outgrowth of leftover industrial-era attitudes about technology.

There is a more accurate current source of the tool mentality, and that is the representation of individual software processes as tools.[30] Many programmers tend to refer to any independent module of code created for a particular purpose as a tool, but this is not very helpful. Let us stick to our kinetic definition. A software tool gives visible form and physical action to a logical operation. Like a physical tool, it modifies the effect of your hand, which it accomplishes by modifying the function of the nonphysical but visible cursor that you operate with the physical pointing device (i.e., the mouse). For example, a paint system offers pencils, brushes, airbrushes, etc., for applying color to a surface. This plays on the fact that a tool can be conceptual, and indirectly controlled. Whether direct or indirect, what matters is manipulation. Note also that like a physical tool, software becomes a symbol for the operations it performs. To employ any particular tool, you have to look around for it, pick it up, and move it into relation with the objects to which it will be applied. Its use is initiated and guided by your intentions—and by your hand.

Software tools introduce great power. It is the singular advantage of the software tool to give visible form and physical action to a logical operation otherwise lacking any physical correspondence, let alone traditional counterparts. To accomplish this, software designers rely on our skills by analogy. Human-computer interaction methods use tools as a metaphor for developing some comprehension of abstractly conceived activities.

Many software designers believe that the tool metaphor appeals not only to ingrained outlooks about work, but also to deeper fundamentals of human psychology. Research proceedings on human-computer interaction include numerous works on cognition, mental mapping, psychological loads, and psychomotor skills.[31] Representing particular abstract operations as tools is the best way yet developed for engaging the kinds of actions and intents that have traditionally motivated the craftsman. All this suggests that software tool makers would do well to place more value on tacit knowledge: the best tools will account for levels of mastery and psychology of participation, and conversely tool users should get more leverage from software's formal constructions.

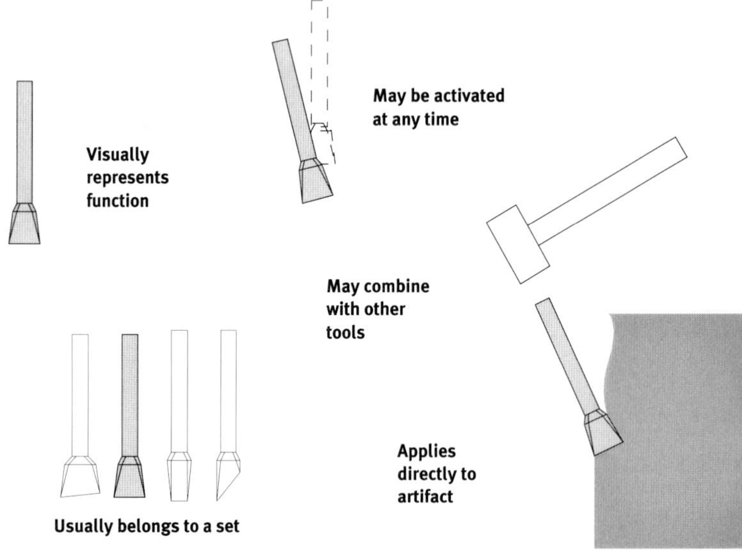

3.4 Properties of a software tool

Ultimately the computer is a means for combining the skillful hand with the reasoning mind. We never had such a tool. If designed and used properly, this already lets us apply something about what we know of symbolic processing to using tools, and this alone should become more enjoyable than industrial automation. But at the same time computers let us turn the tables—to apply something of what we know about using tools to achieve richer symbolic processing. Metaphorically, they let us get a hold of our ideas. Concepts become things. We can't touch them yet, but already we can look at them, point at them, and work on them as though with hand-held tools. All this is ultimately more interesting than automation. Our use of computers ought not be so much for automating tasks as for abstracting craft.

II Technological Context

4 Symbols

Consider the Renaissance algebrist Franciscus Vieta, who demonstrated the power of symbols as well as anyone. Vieta's contribution merits a brief explanation for the nonmathematician.[1] The story begins with the fact that Medieval mathematicians contented themselves with the use of natural numbers. Recall that the natural numbers are positive whole quantities—phenomena found in nature—for example, seventeen sheep. This usage may seem normal enough, until we note that even the most basic operations of arithmetic are not closed under natural numbers: that is, the outcome of the simplest operations may fall outside the set of natural numbers. For example, although six minus four yields a natural number, four minus six does not; similarly eight divided by two yields a natural number, but seven divided by two does not. The traditional solution to this problem was straightforward: Medieval mathematicians declared expressions of the latter sort to be "impossible." One simply *could not* subtract six from four.

Vieta proposed a better solution. In his *Logistica Speciosa* (1577) Vieta introduced a letter notation by which given magnitudes, to be represented by consonants, were distinguished from those that were unknown or sought, to be represented by vowels. This might be recognizable as the precursor to the Cartesian notation, such as $ax + by = c$, where letters to represent givens are taken from the beginning of the alphabet, and those for unknowns from the end. (This adaptation of Vieta's system has survived to this day, so let us use it here.) This might seem trivial to us, but in the sixteenth century it was a turning point in the history of algebra, much as the Arabic invention of zero had been the turning point for simple arithmetic. Here is the logic. Under this system, six minus four, and four minus six, both become simply $x = a - b$. Similarly both eight divided by two, and seven divided by two, become simply $x = a / b$. Using letter equations for simple operations creates a *symbolic* solution. Using this notation it becomes difficult to hold that the expression $a - b$ has meaning only if a is greater than b, or that a / b is meaningless when a is not a multiple of b. Moreover it also becomes impossible to tell from the face of the symbols whether an arbitrary expression $c - d$ brought before us is legitimate or not.[2]

Sooner or later, these conditions might suggest that there is no contradiction involved in operating on these symbolic beings as if they were legitimate numbers. Possibility and impossibility are not intrinsic to the operation, but rather are simply restrictions that arbitrary tradition had placed on the field of the operands. Remove these artificial barriers, and it becomes a simple step to recognize those symbolic beings a and b as numbers *in extenso*. This generalized set of numbers providing closure on simple arithmetic then needs a theory.[3] Thus the use of symbols introduced by Vieta led to a powerful abstraction known as the rational numbers, and so to modern Cartesian algebra, and the rest is history.

The point should be clear: in symbols we have the ultimate tools of abstraction. Not everyone may care to explore what this means, but it is important at least to recognize. Clearly the source of the symbol's power is that the symbol is not the signified. Symbols differ from that for which they stand, and they are presumably easier to use: easier to reproduce, easier to transmit, easier to transform. Else, like the Sages of Lagado in *Gulliver's Travels,* we should carry about the subjects of our conversations and hold them up before one another to save speech. Furthermore, besides standing elegantly for more cumbersome things, symbols may represent concepts, conditions, or qualities lacking in embodiment or measure—things we could not carry about at all.

In processed symbols we have a basis for formal reasoning. This power comes from the fact that, when replaced by a symbol, an object becomes a mere operand. As an operand, it may be manipulated in an abstract manner, such that the syntax of forming consistent expressions, rather than any representational significance of the symbols, governs the formation of new expressions. And as shown in the example, an operand used in such a formal system may be transformed to suggest a new meaning for which there is no object—no previous external significance. The rigor of the formal syntax suggests constructing an indicated meaning: a new representational significance emerges from syntactical operations alone. This is how symbolic processing yields abstract results.

In symbolic structures we have notations for formal reasoning in a variety of disciplines. Symbolic structures apply the principles of formal reasoning to many more kinds of operands: not just magnitudes or quantities, but coordinates and fields of numbers; not just algebraic numbers, but musical sounds, chemical compounds, logical assertions.

It follows that a technology for processing symbolic structures should be a very powerful means of abstraction. Using computers we perform not only calculations, but also communications, visualizations, and abstract structural transformations; and we perform these not only in the fields of traditional notations, but also on attributes of people and places, all variety of documents, millions of colors, shapes, three-dimensional forms, industrial processes, and global communications networks. Today computers dominate information storage and formal reasoning. Tomorrow, as we are often assured, they will become the province of many new forms of thought processing.[4]

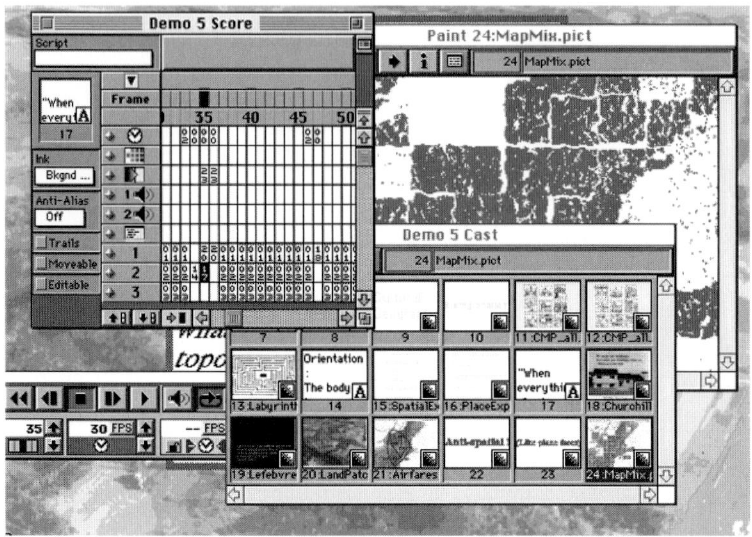

4.1 Many nontextual processes now have notations, such as this multimedia orchestration in *Director*

Symbolic Context

Symbolic notation has taken many forms. Probably the first writing was less like word processing and more like a spreadsheet: tables and formulas for accounting purposes, presumably for taxation. (Note the parallel with early applications of computing.) Only later did there arise a need or desire to inscribe the spoken word. Tallies required only a few symbols, and tools for pressing on clay tablets favored pictographs. Pictographic writing existed for over three thousand years before the invention of a phonetic alphabet. But once developed, linear sequences of phonetic characters slowly and steadily became the dominant means of learning and recorded communication, at least in the West, and have so remained for six thousand years. Only in our century did information tasks finally become too much for writing. New technologies arose in the form of pictorial telecommunication and computers, which now are uniting.

In a sense, any markings made for explicit purposes of representation, record keeping, or transmittal could be understood as notation. Pictures, numbers, and text have been the usual formats (and today these are being united by their underlying representation in bits). Of these, pictures have been around the longest, and still reach the widest audience. Images feed the imagination especially well, and as discussed earlier, images speak to the greatest range of people. They are the stock-in-trade of contemporary culture. However, as also noted, while images are very easy for electronic media to record and transmit, they are very difficult for computers to interpret. If we wish to understand notation as an unambiguous symbolic code, images are the least manageable format. Neither images nor their readings are based on distinct elements or syntactic conventions. Furthermore, any given image may have many implicit meanings. For example, classical painting relies on conventional identities rather that overt expressions. This is a matter of affinity: the symbol suggests a meaning but does not express it literally. For example, a lion may be taken as a symbol of strength, but a lion is not strength itself—it is a lion.[5]

More often, context and structure shape the use of symbols. For example, three sides of a triangle do correspond with the three persons of the Trinity, but a triune God has many attributes not possessed by a triangle, and the same triangle might equally well symbolize something else, such as the Nile delta, and so fertility—depending on the context. On a highway, however, a triangle means to yield the right of way, an act that bears no affinity to the triangle. So relieved of any requirement for affinity, the symbol becomes the sign, and the context becomes arbitrary, constructed, and relative. With signs, resemblance is unnecessary, and indeed any picture may stand for anything. These propositions underlie countless disciplines: aesthetics, structural linguistics, cognitive science, psychoanalysis, software engineering, signal processing, art.

Take text. Arguably the richest symbolic contexts occur in writing. According to the philologists, the meaning of even a single word depends on time, place, and usage. A complete text, then, is not only a construction of time and place and outlook of the author, but also those of other authors, and also (on each occasion) of a reader. No wonder that growing webs of intertextuality may merit a genuinely infinite number of studies—studies of the investigation of methodology, investigations of the methodology of study, methodologies of the study of investigation, and so on. And whatever is understood from such hermeneutics can then be taken as a metaphor to be applied to other symbolic contexts—the built environment for instance. Contexts are everywhere. So it would not be entirely facetious to speculate how among dogs there exists a metaphorical "text" composed of smells.

Perhaps the Enlightenment philosophers were anticipating just such difficulties when they sought to establish a universal language of discourse. The modern literary critic Hugh Kenner draws our attention to one Thomas Sprat, Bishop of Rochester, of the late seventeenth century, known today on the merits of just two sentences, his classic plea for scientific writing—an indictment of "Eloquence, Luxury, and Rhetorick," albeit amusingly phrased in those very manners.

> They have therefore been more rigorous in putting in Execution the only Remedy that can be found for this *Extravagance;* and that has been a constant Resolution to reject all Amplifications, Digressions and Swellings of Style; to return back to the primitive Purity and Shortness, when Men deliver'd so many *Things,* almost in an equal Number of *Words.* They have exacted from all their Members, a closed, naked, natural way of Speaking; positive Expressions, clear Senses; a native Easiness; bringing all Things as near the mathematicall Plainness as they can; and preferring the language of Artizans, Countrymen, and Merchants, before that of Wits, or Scholars.[6]

It was in a similar spirit that Gottfried Leibniz proposed the *Lingua Philosophica* (1666). The great mathematician was convinced that a universal logic would help solve political misunderstandings resulting from the inadequacies and multiplicities of language. His logic would be applied to basic elements of reason, and it would be operable by formal manipulations of characters—a *calculus ratiocinator.* Such reasoning processes could be executed automatically, and indeed Leibniz was the first to propose a reasoning machine.[7]

Of course it was impossible to foresee the difficulties of achieving a universal formal language. From what we now know about linguistics, it was utterly naive. But it was also impossible to foresee the power of some particular formal systems. It turns out that the route to a more generally useful *Lingua Philosophica* was to get more explicit about semantics and notation. When in the twentieth century Alan Turing specified a symbol-processing scheme that could be implemented in an electronic machine, there finally existed the means to do just this. Some time would have to pass before these schemes would develop sufficient vocabulary and structure to pass for languages, but Turing understood his formalism to be for much more than just numerical calculation. Today we might say that programming language differs from natural language mainly in its basis for semantics, that is, in the unambiguously declared meanings of words. Even when contemporary computer languages extend this idea to high-level abstractions such as class libraries, code is pure convention.

Convention is a form of abstraction, or a means to abstraction. A mathematician might tell you that choosing the right symbols is half the battle in proving a theorem. Although the symbols are merely conventions, and the theorem itself is the main focus of abstraction, the choice of notation does affect the relative ease or difficulty or achieving the results.

Formal Notation

Mathematical symbols are an explicitly formal notation, and formal notation is a special case of symbol usage. Although any representation might loosely be understood as a notation, certain formal systems deserve particular attention. This is not an easy subject for conversation, nor one that summarizes well, but it is one worth getting a sense about as a foundation for studying the computer as a medium.

For a rigorous theory of formal notation and its relation to creative work, we may turn to Nelson Goodman's groundbreaking book, *Languages of Art* (1976). Notation, as formulated by Goodman, is essentially defined as a "symbol system" consisting of a symbol scheme unambiguously correlated with a field of reference. For example, letters unambiguously represent quantities in algebra. A symbol scheme is generally a set of distinct characters plus a syntax for combining them. The essential features of such a scheme are that the characters are finitely differentiable (ultimately you can tell which is which) and that the syntax is character-indifferent (or substitutable—one instance of a character is as good as another). These properties are common to many familiar schemes, including alphabetical, numerical, binary, telegraphic, and basic musical characters. They are not universal, however: they are absent from informal representations such as sketches. A sketch with its dense field of overlapping, ambiguous, uniquely executed marks is not a symbol scheme.

According to Goodman, a symbol *system* is the correspondence by which meanings comply with characters in a symbol scheme. This has similar properties of articulation. For example, all inscriptions of a given character must have the same semantic reference, or compliant. No one compliant can be referred to by multiple characters. And for the system to be a useful notation, these semantic distinctions themselves must be finitely differentiable. For example, in a musical notation, a C sharp quarter note represents a particular pitch and relative duration; all instances of this note in a given register have the same meaning; those are intelligible from other sounds; it is clear when you have an instance of the one; and no other note means the same sound.[8]

The most elegant instances of formal notation occur in music. Standard musical notation has endured for centuries, is common to many different cultures and languages, and has successfully incorporated many

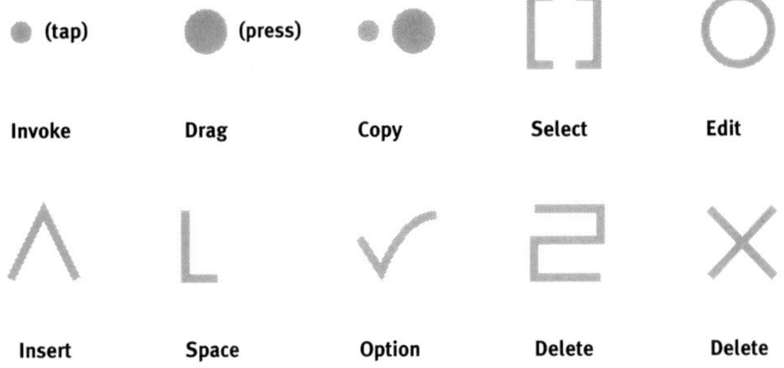

4.2 A very small system of differentiable symbols: gestures for a pen-based computer

modern practices. It has also extended well into digital media such as time-coded sequencers. A work of music exists in the abstract, and it may be performed, transcribed, arranged, etc., according to its notation. Two different performances are clearly instances of the same work. Note the preeminence of the score. Goodman observed, "The composer's work is done when he has written the score, even though the performances are the end-products, while the painter has to finish the picture."[9]

Painting is different. Here, authorship and execution are united. Even the most accurately duplicated copy would not be the same as an original. Painting defies notation, which Goodman claimed is because we lack any real definition of what constitutes a work of painting. We can develop a nominal notation that is essentially a new coinage for each piece of work; we can develop a procedural notation based on history of production (e.g., an advanced color-by-number for producing copies); but not both.[10]

Architecture is a mixed case. It does use intermediate representations—drawings—yet we do not think of these as the work. Construction plans, in which relative position, script dimensions, and established tolerances govern the reading, and in which appearance to scale is just for convenience, are true notations, whereas sketches are not. Yet plans are not like scores. "We are not as comfortable about identifying an architectural work with a design rather than a building as we are about identifying a musical work with a composition rather than a performance."[11]

Goodman introduced terminology to distinguish fine arts on the basis of notation. Arts such as painting for which the artifact is the work and there exists only one original he calls "autographic." Arts such as music where the notation carries the work and multiple instances are possible he calls "allographic."[12] We may note that the latter is more abstract. One route to abstraction is to incorporate formal notation.

At first consideration, traditional crafts are purely autographic. They lack notation, are made by hand, and produce no two pieces exactly alike. Yet if we discount the exception of the masterworks, and concentrate on routine artisanry, we find a different situation. Here among the countless indifferent pieces made according to any one trade, one piece is as good as the next.[13] Although the pieces are not identical, or modular, like machine-made wares, nevertheless they are effectively interchangeable. No one stands out as the original, and certainly there are no forgeries. Here one might argue that the intellectual property is not so much the artifact as the tradition by which it is made—such was the stuff of apprenticeships. As we have noted, this tradition is tacit. Even in the unusual case where there exists a written specification or a drawing, that notation is not considered the work. The work of craft is neither the design nor the individual artifact: it is the tradition of the very production. It is the presence of many objects identical in their conception, and interchangeable in their use, but unique in their execution.

Notation confers several advantages besides the obvious capacity to obtain multiple instances of the end product. For one thing, it is reproducible also in the sense that the score itself may be copied. Ownership is not of an object but a copyright. But more important, notation allows composition in the abstract. This means that modifications proceed quickly without the encumbrance of executing or performing every stage of the evolving composition. Multiple instances of the notation might represent different stages or versions of that work. The intrinsic syntax of the notation might suggest compositional approaches. At the simplest level, these might include elementary shifts and substitutions. One could think in terms of variables and transformations. There would be nothing to prevent the use of logical variables. Thus at an advanced level, the nature of notation might invite us to employ iterations and conditionals, which together with variables and their relations would turn scripts and scores into true programs. In sum, symbolic processing may assist compositional explorations. We can make rules, and we can identify structure.

Structure

Formal notation invites the study of structure, which in natural language consists of grammar. It is a cornerstone of twentieth-century intellectual history that comparative grammars reveal common underlying structures. Words themselves may vary between languages, and indeed may be arbitrary, but certain correspondences exist between languages at the level of phonetic systems. Ferdinand de Saussure's *Course in General Linguistics* (1916) established these principles and in so doing opened the floodgates for the development of disciplines such as semiology, structural linguisitics, developmental psychology, and structural anthropology. These many endeavors have adapted the notion of structural equivalence from descriptive grammars of language to interpretation of culture at large. In the process, there emerged much thought that linguistic structure somehow reflected the structure of the mind itself. Structure was inherent, and could be latent. The psychologist Jean Piaget wrote: "The discovery of structure may, either immediately or at a much later stage, give rise to formalization. Such formalization is however always the creature of the theoretician, whereas structure itself exists apart from him."[14]

By midcentury, there reemerged an interest in *building* symbolic expressions, rather than merely analyzing them, and this redefined grammars once again. Noam Chomsky's *Syntactic Structures* (1957) introduced the idea of generative grammars, as Chomsky emphasized the creative use of language for constantly developing new expressions. Unlike his predecessors,

Chomsky felt that a more general grasp had to underlie the process of inventing or understanding legitimate sentences that had not been uttered before. He thus renewed the interest in universal language with his distinction between the syntax of any particular language, which he called "surface" structure, and this more general cognitive process, or "deep" structure. Furthermore, he focused new attention on formalism by developing a notational system of rules for generating syntactic structures.[15]

Abstraction in Data Structure

Not surprisingly, many computational theorists share an interest in generative notations and grammars. After all, computing is essentially the use of symbolic notation on a huge range of scales, from microscopic arrangements of charges that yield logical interpretations (e.g., memory) right on up to planetary webs of computer networks.

Computing is structure manipulation. It is an abstract medium based on generative symbolic notation, particularly data structure, which can represent increasingly high-level concepts. To begin to see how, it is worth reciting two fundamental tenets of computer science: data structure, and data abstraction.

Data structure characterizes software: what you can do, and how a program looks and feels, depends on its underlying abstractions and assumptions. In essence a data structure organizes symbols for specific purposes. It formulates vocabulary and operators useful to some specific end, whether its record of symbols is to be treated as a document or an artifact, as real or as virtual. For example, one kind of structure might define a repertoire of shapes and area fills for use in an illustration program. This structure is itself a notation in a programming language, and it also establishes a format for creating and recording specific notations in the language of data elements it defines. What to the computer is a record of specific instances of elements within a defined repertoire is to you a drawing—a record of a session or body of work in a particular symbolic context.

Much as in Vieta's simple algebra, declaring a variable is the most fundamental act of building a data structure. A particular selection of variables opens up a particular set of possibilities, or casts the solution to a given problem in a very particular way. Of course, individual variables are grouped into compound elements—specifically structured types—such as shapes in an illustration program. Thus despite being based on the simplest, atomistic, data types of numbers, letters, and true/false values, a limitless variety of formal elements can be described: from words to sounds to forms to motions. Once established, these data objects may be given names, associated with positions in menus or maps, identified with pictographs, manipulated with sliders and knobs, and so on—there is no limit to the operations. As use of abstract data structures, computing is not so much calculation as generalized symbol manipulation. What makes data structure such an essential characteristic of a digital medium, then, is *which* kinds of elements and operations it establishes in any given context. A robust illustration program such as *Freehand* has a very rich data structure that shapes a useful symbolic context for fine linework. You can draw beautiful splines with control over second derivative of curvature, for example, but you cannot sweep those curves into surfaces, or animate them in time. To do so would require some other data structure.

This should already suggest something about this second and related fundamental idea, namely data abstraction. The history of programming may be understood as largely a matter of increasing abstraction. The earliest, most primitive software stored data solely in terms of indexed addresses in physical memory registers, and to use it required physical knowledge of the computer memory. Since that time, there have been three major advances in the independence of data structure from data storage technology. First came the capacity for named variables, which allowed memory allocation to be accomplished in software, and for this the new languages were heralded as "high-level languages." Second, languages introduced pointers, such as the identifier keys used in relational databases, which allowed for much more efficient programs by processing simple addresses rather than manipulating the more cumbersome data itself that is stored at those locations. (This is analogous to using weightless words rather than holding up bulky objects like the sages of Lagado). Third, and more recently, came the means to represent the identity of an instance independently of how it is found, where it is stored, or what it contains. This is known as object orientation.

The basic idea behind object orientation is to provide a single identity for any arbitrary set of properties and capacities. By uniting the two main acts of earlier programming methods, namely declaring structure and defining procedure, it enables a level higher of abstraction that insulates the outward behavior of a system of elements from its underlying implementation. This fundamental building block is known as an abstract data type, or class, instances of which are objects.

Programmers may find this trivial and nonprogrammers may find it opaque, but object orientation has several consequences for the growing perception of computing as a medium. Much of this simply reflects increasingly flexible software engineering. Three particular conceptual constructions obtain: first, one class may inherit properties (structure) from another; second, one same operation may be "overloaded" to be applicable to many different object classes; third, different operations now have a way of finding out whether they are referring to the same object. All this allows higher-level software design with greater independence of specific technological implementation. It makes for a more robust and modular structure capable of underpinning a much greater variety of software artifacts and operations. It is more than engineering performance, then: better abstraction lets programmers manipulate concepts at a higher level. Abstract data types have been a big advance, because like Vieta's alphabetic symbols, they allow semantic ideas to be manipulated independently of their actual compliants. From a software designer's standpoint, then, a class library is a powerful generative structure.[16]

The non-technician should note: here in what is fittingly known as object orientation is the very root of one of the biggest advantages of digital media, namely the ability to operate on abstractions as if they were things.

Generative Structure

Much as mathematics is largely a matter of choosing the right symbols, software design is a matter of defining an appropriate structure for serving a task or problem. Likewise software usage is a matter of grasping the uses and limitations of such structure. Often the best way to do this is through manipulation. Generative structure is the beginnings of a medium largely because it invites manipulation. Piaget wrote:

> As a first approximation, we may say that a structure is a system of transformations. Inasmuch as it is a system and not a collection of elements and their properties, these transformations involve laws: their structure is preserved or enriched by the interplay of transformation laws, which never yield results external to the system nor employ elements that are external to it. In short, the notion of structure is comprised of three key ideas: the idea of wholeness, the idea of transformation, and the idea of self-regulation.[17]

A structure has a feel based on internal laws and self-regulation, which we experience by working on it—through transformation. This is a fundamental idea behind any understanding of the computer as a medium. The structures we manipulate are more than collections of elements: they are dense notational *contexts for action.* The experience of structure is difficult to describe in words, but obvious to anyone using software. Available operations, accumulated work, and the organization of sessions all contribute to a strong sense of the rules of the game.

Creative computing gives special emphasis to generative structure. Developing new artifacts and expressions depends on sound aesthetic theory informed by syntax and grammar. Computing is not a radical departure but a natural extension of intellectual development that can be expressed in terms of our knowledge of notations.

As a point of departure for a digital aesthetic, Steven Holtzman has summarized the history, function and significance of generative structures in his recent book, *Digital Mantras* (1994). Holtzman places Chomsky's deep structures and generative grammars squarely in the path of an intellectual history dating back to ancient India and Panini's formulation of the *Astadhyayi* grammar of classical Sanskrit (which literally meant "perfected"). According to this interpretation, the *Astadhyayi* was the first generative grammar, and its preeminence at such an early point in intellectual history may suggest some fundamental human dispositions. Thus it comes as no surprise that there are counterparts today: using examples from modern music and painting, Holtzman explores the use of structured symbolic processing as the basis for creative expression.

For example, he studies examples of tonality in Western music. In particular, the interval of seven semitones, called the fifth, which since the ancient Pythagoreans has been thought to be especially harmonious, allows us to cycle though the twelve semitones of an octave in such a manner that each of the notes will be heard once before any is reached a second time: (C, G, D, A, E, B, F#, C#, G#, D#, A#, E#).[18] Holtzman describes classical Western music essentially as "an exploration of the circle of fifths, an exploration of the expressive possibilities of a system of music based on the special characteristics of the interval of the fifth, [and] also an exploration of the musical structures that can be built exploiting these expressive possibilities."[19]

This approach generalizes effectively to other notations. Formal structure provides a basis for understanding—and generating—expression within a variety of media. Computation introduces formal notation and structure where formerly there were none. We might say that it makes some autographic media allographic.

For example, sculpture now has a notation. Surface and solid modeling systems construct formal representations of complex forms. Constructive solid geometry hierarchies based on the union, intersection, and subtraction of elemental forms such as boxes and cylinders introduce a sense of cutting or filling volume, like with clay. Spline surface lofting systems based on sweeping arbitrary curves along arbitrary paths introduce a sense of bending and morphing surfaces, like with sheets of plastic or metal. Forms so described may then be fabricated in physical material—even carved in stone—or else they can be animated like Spielberg dinosaurs. Faster technology continually improves the capacity to work these notations not only by the measures and constructions of design, but by the free-form gestures of sculpture. You may believe that sculpture requires

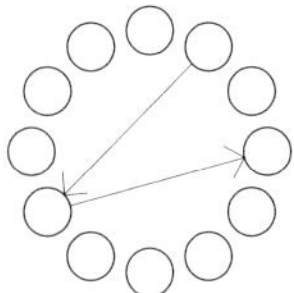

Starting points precess through set of twelve without omission or repetition

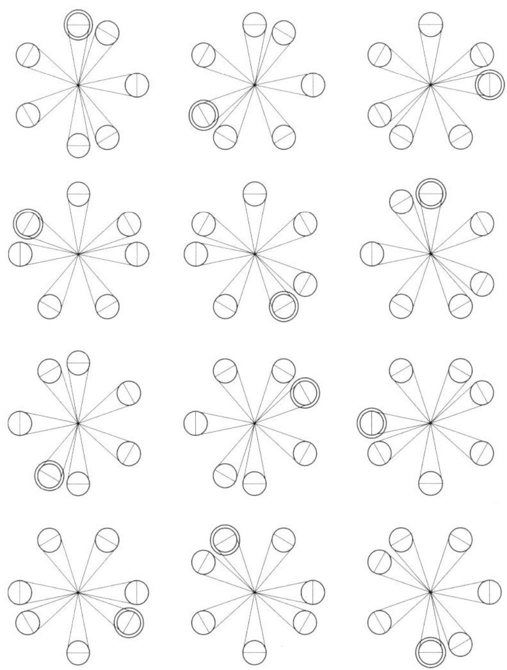

Each version differs from the original by one more (or fewer) element than its predecessor

4.3 A graphical rendition of the circle of fifths

palpable mass—and certainly we will have to examine the perception of medium in immaterial form—but many artists are happily exploring the possibilities of these highly structured three-dimensional notations.

In a generative system, symbolic processing of data structures establishes an underlying structure, which under the proper conditions can take on aspects of a medium. This structuralist argument is therefore an important contribution to the question of digital craft. As Holtzman puts it, "The essence of the structuralist view is that the key to studying language is the distinctions and relationships that emanate from the underlying system—and that this view is applicable to all systems of meaning." This condition is general: "All languages (in the broader sense) can be studied in terms of formal structure. Even the most expressive and subtlest languages can be studied in terms of formal structure, including the languages of poetry, painting, sculpture, and music."[20]

This Platonic and universalist position stands in obvious contrast to the relativistic, poststructuralist and (perhaps not coincidentally) anti-computational stance of much current academic theory. Yet its renewed structuralist emphasis may reflect a widespread interest at least among the digerati. And as a polemical approach toward a digital aesthetic (which Holtzman does call just a stake in the ground) its focus on generative structure seems appropriate and welcome.

So here is another stake in the ground. Although it is important to respect generative structures, we must also acknowledge that their power will be realized through the complementary role of personal sensibility, and that this may occur through the perception and practice of medium. *Theories of design computing demand attention to the skillful nature of accomplished symbolic manipulation.* Explorations of generative structure obtain power from hand, eye, and tools. They arise from personal knowledge, practice, and commitment of the sort found in traditional handicrafts, now applied to symbolic systems. Skillful operations of physical devices are given leverage through effective symbolic structures such as human-computer interfaces and cumulative software constructions. Through the abstraction of symbolic representation, practiced, playful talent finds new outlets and develops new kinds of appreciation.

The Limits of Structured Symbolic Thinking

One might argue that the ultimate symbolic systems—great software—could eventually just do all the work. But this is not the case, for there will always be intentions that we cannot or choose not to express in symbols. Specifically, there are limits to the domain of formalized code. In all likelihood, a human-computer partnership will continue to surpass either the unaided human or the autonomous algorithm for some (important) aspects of work. Neither decidable formal manipulations alone, nor traditional craft unleveraged by symbolic systems, should be able to keep pace with a partnership between inarticulable insight, or impetus, and rigorous symbolic reasoning. So long as this is the case, personal practice will prosper primarily in its coupling to digital notational systems, and digital notational systems will be useful just as much as they encourage human imagination.

According to a great many contemporary theorists, the mind has a structure of its own. It is generally agreed that particular knowledge does not reside in any explicit place, but that the mind is an epiphenomenon of brain structure, perhaps like the glow on burning coals. Nevertheless it is believed that language, vision, and perhaps even creativity may have corresponding physio-neurological structures. And though much of such thinking has centered on the formality of language, more general propositions have appeared on the formality of mind. Jung's archetypes, Saussure's linguistics, Lévi-Strauss's mythologies, Piaget's developmental stages, and a host of related theories all have emphasized structure.

It has been very easy, then, for some people to impute a symbolic processing model of mind. Because computers are the product of our minds, the mind must be somehow like a computer. The artificial intelligence research community of the 1980s was especially prone to take this view. Techniques such as inference chains, connectionist learning (neural nets), case-based and frame-based reasoning, etc., were at the vanguard of design research, and the rapidly emerging discipline of cognitive science informed and built a foundation for these investigations. The educational psychologist Howard Gardner became a most articulate advocate of symbolic-processing models of mind, and he has taken a special interest in the role of symbol systems in creativity.

> To my mind, there is a crucial leap that a structuralist study of the mind must take. The leap involves a recognition that the basic unit of human thought is the symbol, and that the basic entities with which humans operate in a meaningful context are symbol systems. Attention to symbol systems is possible (indeed natural) within a structuralist framework, but such a focus opens up the possibility of the endless devising of meaningful worlds—in the arts, in the sciences, indeed in every realm of human activity . . . The key to an understanding of artistic creation lies, I believe, in a judicious wedding of structuralist approaches to philosophical and psychological investigation of human symbolic activity.[21]

There is something of a jump from believing that symbolic processing reflects the mind to believing that symbolic processing *is* the mind. This is an especially appealing prospect to academicians, who presumably wish to build more complete, possibly definitive theories of mind, as opposed to "endless devising of meaningful worlds."

As a result, many recent studies of creative computation have confined themselves to decidable methods in symbolic processing. Despite the loss of certainty having been demonstrated even in mathematics, orthodox academics in countless disciplines hold fast to deterministic knowledge. It is as if scientism is the only way to legitimate creativity, as though otherwise we are spiraling back, hermeneutically, to square one—which you may recall as some courtly "Eloquence, Luxury, and Rhetorick."

Of course this very obsession with externalized knowledge has stigmatized this research in the eyes of traditionally creative people. Professional designers, for instance, have mostly spurned computation for anything other than task automation by direct manipulation. This has not just been out of necessity, but of choice. We have yet to escape the state where a sensible person can quickly dismiss computer usage for creative work on very simple grounds: one, it's too arbitrary; two, it cannot record feelings; three, you cannot get a hold of it; four, it is difficult and time-consuming; and five, it's not much fun.

On the other hand, we have arrived at the time where there exist people who would challenge every one of those grounds. This is largely a generational issue: younger people who have grown up with computing do not seem to experience as much frustration. Furthermore, each next generation of technology (far more frequent than generations of human beings) becomes more usable on the basis of faster components, increasing practicality of more intuitive designs, and general accumulation of technological wisdom.

Maybe you can't touch it now, but there are signs that haptic interaction will arise. Maybe it can't record feelings, but no medium captures anything but a partial and implicit record of the state of an author. In any case, the growing perception of computer as medium demonstrates a slowly increasing capacity for implicit emotional content.

However, there is no denying the arbitrariness of symbol systems. Like any other medium or notation before them, digital media have no special claims on reflecting any creative processes more directly. Consider that notations are improvised ad hoc. For instance, you could keep time by hand. Start tapping your foot to a regular rhythm, and then count twelve beats. Count them on one hand, as the ancient Babylonians did, by moving the thumb from fingertip to fingertip, then from midsection to midsection, then across the bottom segments of each of four fingers on the same hand. This lets you count to twelve. Using your other hand, raise one finger for each round of twelve on the first. This way you could count to sixty. The Babylonians built a whole mathematics on this practice—base sixty—but it didn't last because it made arithmetic unusually difficult. But one aspect of it is still with us on the face of a clock. Since the Babylonians gave us timekeeping, to this day there are sixty seconds in a minute, and sixty minutes in an hour.[22]

We must remember that the most basic symbolic systems were created out of convenient objects, long before there existed any theories of mind. Such ad hoc arrangements act in partnership with the human brain, but even in the most modern, sophisticated cases, such as computer programs, they don't necessarily work in the same way.[23]

Advocates of symbolic reasoning therefore need to recognize ways in which the mind is unlike a computer. For example, although rigorous symbolic contexts may help articulate qualities of imagination, they are no substitute for insight. We have explored this relationship as it pertains to visual thinking: human learning is by example, by context, and by intent—but not necessarily by rules. All of this makes it especially difficult for any notation, even with the power of computers, to extract useful information from pictures. It also suggests that we are mistaken to assume that even if the mind has intrinsic structure, it has *only* structure. It has structure *sometimes,* or it *changes* structures in the process of exerting multiple intelligences. We humans are very agile.

Besides, there seems to be a problem with symbolic systems that are completely context free. Consider the fact that being context free is both the main strength and the main weakness of numerical models. It is a strength in intelligibility: whereas extracting much content from pictures or texts remains beyond today's computing methods, extracting *all* the content from well-formed numerical expressions is the very basis of the technology. As demonstrated by Vieta, formal symbolic manipulations arrive at indicated solutions that suggest new concepts. But it is a weakness in contextual interpretation: numerical models have the unfortunate disadvantage of containing no information about when their contents are appropriate.

Inappropriateness might be an issue at a micro scale; for example, using a particular inventory and distribution model might be very profitable for one business and disastrous for another. Or, as the critics of computing point out, it could become global, and indeed become our biggest problem: abstractions such as bottom lines, admirably optimized in context-free numerical models, seem to have negative effects on social and environmental milieus. Pure abstraction and solely formal reasoning obviously need to be governed by human practice and context-based understanding. Perhaps this is why medievalists played it safe by sticking to the natural numbers. But where else, without rejecting modern mathematics, logic, and computer programming as a whole, might we begin to draw the line? How can we represent skill and judgment?

Inspiration and Intent

To uphold reflectivity, imagination, and contextual appropriateness as practicable but unknowable does not require one to become a hippie mystic—it is an increasingly legitimate intellectual position, whose heritage includes philosopher-biologists such as Henri Bergson, Pierre Teilhard de Chardin, and Gregory Bateson. Its current label is "biological naturalism."[24] It is an intellectual direction being taken by a lot of other fields besides visual studies.

In *The Rediscovery of the Mind* (1992), John Searle has provided a good recent summary of this position. Searle, a perennial opponent of the dualist crowd who regard the body as a mere "meat machine," argues that cognitive scientists have been working on false assumptions. Here are his opening assertions:

1. Consciousness does matter.
2. Not all of reality is objective; some of it is subjective.
3. Because it is a mistake to suppose that the ontology of the mental is objective, it is a mistake to suppose that the methodology of a science of the mind must concern itself with only objectively observable behavior.
4. It is a mistake to suppose that we know of the existence of mental phenomena in others only by observing their behavior.
5. Behavior or causal relations to behavior are not essential to the existence of mental phenomena.
6. It is inconsistent with what we in fact know about the universe and our place in it to suppose that everything is knowable by us.
7. The Cartesian conception of the physical, and the conception of physical reality as *res extensa,* is simply not adequate to describe the facts that correspond to statements about physical reality.[25]

Searle has effectively challenged the lack of affect in cognitive science, the overreliance on behavioralism in the study of software usage, and the wisdom of confining our discourse only to what shows up on our instruments. He has argued how consciousness is a natural feature of certain biological structures, much like being wet is a feature of the structure of water molecules. He asserts that intent is an undeniable component of behavior, but that you cannot detect intent in a detached experimental setting—you have to ask.

This argument is as pertinent to the humble digital craftsperson as to any lofty theorists of mind. If in essence consciousness is natural, and neither we nor our technology should ignore it, then more advanced conditions of design computing should differ from algorithmic, industrial machine operation precisely by reflectivity and intent. Yet generally, our routine computer usage has involved not the fullest and best forms of consciousness, and because computers are powerful means of production, which amplify and transmit our states, the results have often been unsatisfactory. This situation ought to be changed at the source—both the technology and its practitioners. Here again are some central themes. Digital craft is to will some sort of reflective consciousness in the practice of habitual computer-based work. It is to use the phenomena of tools, media, artifacts, and settings as means for focusing that consciousness. It is to cultivate contextual awareness.

Searle emphasizes how active intent occurs against a background context of capacities and presuppositions.[26] Here we might strike a crude analogy in the relation between a tool and a medium: a tool conducts intent, a medium forms a background of possibilities, and the two are inseparable. Note too how Searle's discussion of background ability bears similarity to Polanyi's concept of personal knowledge. An example used by Searle: a beginner may require a simple functional intent, for example to put his or her weight on the downhill ski; an intermediate skier can intend to "turn left"; and an expert can just "ski the slope."[27] Similarly in interpretive intent: one person might see colored patches in a painting, another might see a picture of a woman standing next to a window, and another might see Vermeer's respect for a newfound rigor in spatial illumination principles.

It is as if vision, thought, work all occur on a spectrum. David Gelertner has recently presented just this idea in his book, *The Muse in the Machine* (1994). Not only must there be a relation between focused reasoning and free association, he argues, but this relation is spectral, and not just not polarized as in the tired right-brain/left-brain metaphor. Gelertner's spectrum ranges from a "high" of detached formalism all the way down "low" to pure reverie. This spectrum essentially measures focus, as opposed to alertness. High focus suppresses associative reasoning. This focused, analytic state is best for manipulating abstractions, because it adheres best to syntactic and symbolic rigor. It suppresses associations like "Sheep—are we counting sheep—you can't have negative two sheep!" By contrast, other states benefit from association. Practical, intermediate levels of focus such as concrete problem solving maintain a deliberative thread but allow for recollection out of the blue, as in, "Didn't we do it this way that time?" Lower, still partially focused states may lack any thread, but nevertheless maintain a sensibility for when two recollections engender the same feeling. This latter condition is the best for creative insight.[28] Gelertner emphasizes that moving up and down this spectrum is more effective than maintaining a uniformly analytic focus. Those who confine themselves to just one part of the spectrum, even if at a higher focus, are missing some opportunities. This is of course the big problem with computation. Although complete thought includes what Gelertner calls "affect linking," nevertheless cognitive scientists have been ignoring affect (feeling) for years. This Gelertner likens to sailors who, knowing how to measure latitude but not yet longitude, were just as good as lost.[29] Searle, incidentally, draws a similar comparison between exclusively functional-analytic mind theorists and the drunk who, having lost his keys in the dark bushes, looks for them out under the streetlight, because the light is better there.[30]

Achieving a Balance

In the balance, symbolic processing is too powerful to ignore, but not powerful enough to rely upon exclusively. We must balance the use of powerful notations with the use of tacit knowledge: visual thinking, kinetic skill,

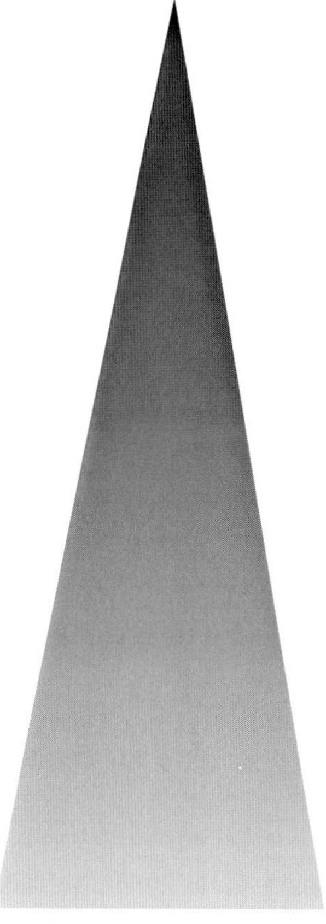

4.4 Spectrum of focal attention

and symbolic reasoning can complement one another, whether in business planning, scientific analysis, or artistic improvisation. They not only can; they must.

How can we approach these theoretical propositions from the standpoint of practical artisanry? If rapidly improving dynamics of structured symbolic processing lead to wider use of computers in the creative process, does that mandate that we understand the role of talent, skill, and insight? Does it suggest that creative computation overcome the traditional separation between tool users and symbol users? Will the balance shift as physical images, forms, and fabrication processes become abstractly coded?

Or conversely, will the balance shift as abstract schemas are given sensory manifestation? Can the power of visual and kinetic understanding allow us to pursue new realms of abstraction, different from the ones opened up by nonvisual, nonmanual computing?

So we must ask—as increasingly it all comes down to bits—can there be a reunion of manual and mental work? May the coordinated hand, eye, and tool at last benefit from what has traditionally been the most powerful means of abstraction—processed symbols? And conversely, may the work of symbolic processing be made more human by the ways of the eye and the hand?

In our pursuit of answers to these many questions, there is wisdom in coupling symbolic processing to all the human insight and skill we can muster. Here amid rapid advances in formal symbolic knowledge, this is no time to forget tacit, personal knowledge. After all, only human beings will make computing humane. Human beings like to make things; they like to use their hands at least as much as their brains; they like to play; they tend to do better with practice. If we are to tap the increasing visuality and dynamics of computing in order to open new realms of abstraction, we should depend very much on these humane traits to do so. So if there is a digital aesthetic to be had, getting there may well be a matter of abstracting craft.

5 Interfaces

How to Operate a Computer?

Most people would just as soon know no more about computers than whatever it takes to get some work done. But what is important to know? You could quickly lose your sense of proportion amid so much technical detail.

The only way to make sense of endless techniques is to address them with some higher conceptual framework, but this is just what the circumstances of training so often fail to do. Some huge majority of computer operation occurs without much notion of abstractions, but only as trained sequences of actions. This condition is understandable given the pressures of getting business done, but it is hardly the best approach even for that. Circumstantial knowledge tends to automate rather than eliminate unnecessary tasks, to miss opportunities for new processes and practices, and to deny the importance of psychology.

There is no better example of circumstantial knowledge than the way some people perceive the computer as its input and output devices

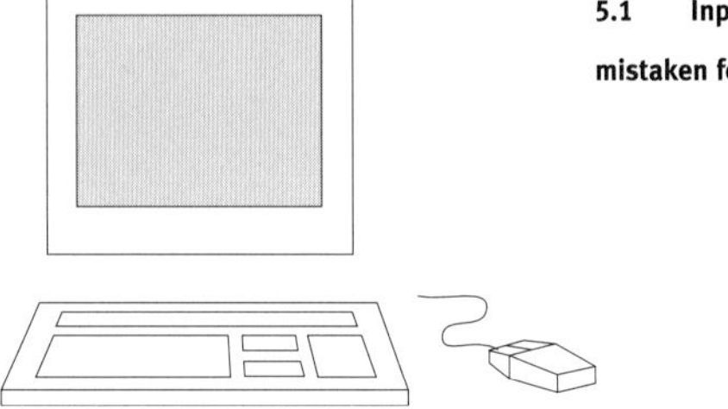

5.1 Input and output devices, frequently mistaken for the computer

alone—as if the screen is the computer. This too is excusable given that physical devices are the only tangible elements of the technology. But so long as this mentality persists, computing remains little more than things to type and places to point, and learning tends to consist solely of immediate instruction in rote operations—often command by command.

To make matters worse, there persists a perception that anyone properly instructed can operate a computer more or less equally well. This outlook is perpetuated by the instruction books and training courses that flood the marketplace. It is also sustained by veteran programmers who refer to everyone from beginners to experts as "users," and it is particularly acute among computer salesmen and middlemen, who tend to refer to their consumer/customers as "end users." Much of this owes to the remarkable uniformity of software over the last decade—and to the fact that computing is still relatively primitive.

You should have no trouble imagining how computer usage could be better. For example, instead of working *with* a computer, you might want a chance to feel that you work *through* it—with other people, with your work, *in* your work. As a part of this feeling, you might expect to find your senses more fully engaged. You might be able to handle a lot more actions subconsciously, and so not have to fill up your head with arcane details. This in turn would free you to build more stimulating mental models. Your actions might not be alone, but take part in a shared world rich with powerful constructions. Given enough of these various conditions, your way of working would become much more your own.

Often the key to working more satisfactorily is to understand the computer as a medium. Note that working on abstract structure requires *mediation* between action and notation. Work not only takes shape with an abstract medium, but (at least in comparison with traditional practices) it can actively reshape the medium itself. That is, software designers tend to engineer mediation, which they generally do in terms of a "human-computer interface." Mediation between physical devices and symbolic contexts defines the experience of a digital medium. A human-computer interface constructs enough representations to let us work intelligibly: spatial layouts, toolkits, object behaviors, process rates, multisensory feedback, messages, and conversations all contribute to a world where we participate. A well-designed interface reflects a variety of psychological factors, such as workspace context, orchestration in time, and the development of clear mental models. Like traditional tools and media, human-computer interfaces can help focus our tasks and methods.

Remember that the human-computer interface is a relatively recent phenomenon. Back when computer hardware was frightfully expensive, all programming efforts went toward optimizing the use of limited computation, and the few specialists who used the stuff were sufficiently motivated to learn tedious but machine-efficient operations. As hardware became more powerful and less expensive (which it continues to do at an astonishing rate) designs could evolve away from convenience for computers toward convenience for people. When the technology became practical for casual work by versatile people who demanded and could suggest still more intuitive methods, interaction design emerged as a substantive discipline. This field is still young and just getting going. Already it has demonstrated a great diversity of methods, beyond what prevails in the market, that allow for tremendous differences in working style and skill.[1]

Many forthcoming technologies should increase such opportunities. Large flat-panel displays, gestural tracking, social computing, smart rooms, multisensory perception, and haptic feedback are all in the works. Moreover, the psychology of how to forge all of this together into an inobtrusive, coherent, augmented reality has gained equal stature with so much device engineering. Increasing sensory-psychological sophistication might ultimately transform computers into some of the most pleasant technologies ever to have existed. Along the way, what may now seem contrived questions about digital craft may well become moot.

But there is no need to speculate. Today's rudimentary technology is more than enough of a beginning in digital craft. Its very lack of diversity gives us a common base of study. This may not be easy to explain in a manner that strikes evenly between the obvious and the esoteric, but human-computer interaction is an essential grounding for more easily appreciable matters of medium and practice. Reconsider what it means to work with a computer, then. Survey the technical elements and psychological factors that shape human-computer interaction. Beginning with the mundane graphical user interface, reconsider more fundamental issues such as space, time, language, psychology, grasp, and imagination.

Elements of the Technology

Graphical User Interface

Today, despite major differences in the internal workings and external interconnections, most computers' interfaces have become surprisingly similar. This uniformity results from the tremendous success of the point-and-click, desktop-and-windows "graphical user interface" (GUI). If you use a computer, you probably understand the nature of this interface, but you might not have stopped to consider it explicitly, especially if you have never encountered any alternatives. Its success is based on a breakthrough made a little over a decade ago, which has only recently been absorbed into the mainstream business marketplace. This breakthrough was quite simply the beginnings of hand-eye coordination in computer usage: for the first time, the computer placed all procedures and data in plain view and in reach of the hand. This advance proved to be exactly what was necessary to make computing acceptable to most people, and it has done more than anything else to support the proliferation of computing. But because it has opened up the technology to so many people, it has quickly become the only approach to computer operation that most people have ever known.

Due to the power of the market that it has created, this graphical approach has overshadowed other developments. Its properties serve as benchmarks against which alternatives and advances must be measured. Its applications extend even to processes that do not necessarily benefit from its graphical operations. Despite quite a bit of research about alternatives, much development gets confined to studying and measuring what makes a better GUI. In a world where technological change is supposedly revolutionary, we have lived with this basically unchanged idea for quite a long time.

The best single explanation of the graphical user interface is as a symbolic context for pointing. The ideas behind it are quite simple. First, pointing combines well with language—general conversation rarely operates without both of them. Second, pointing reduces tedious typing by offering commands and data-entry fields on screen. Third, recognition works better than recall, so graphical displays present options and suggest operations. Finally, pointing is better than question-and-answer dialogues for freely deciding the course of action. This latter freedom should be familiar as the basis for today's systems in which windows represent tasks, between which one may jump at will. The big change that transformed the experience and acceptability of computing was that now one could decide what the computer would do next without waiting for the computer to ask. The technical term for a system having this freedom is "event driven." By "event" this approach implies that the computer immediately handles whatever you do, regardless of the device and logical context of its source. Thus such a system is "modeless," meaning that you do not have to back

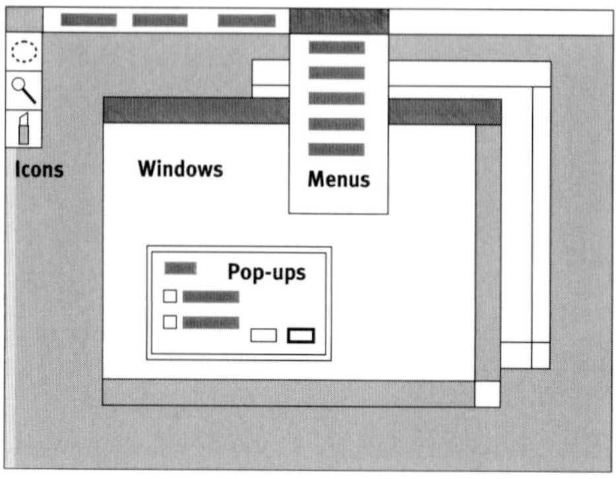

5.2 Characteristic (but arbitrary) features of the graphical user interface

out of the current activity to go on to the next one. One typical modeless event, incidentally, is to pick up a different tool.

Pointing alone was only half the breakthrough; the remainder was continuous graphical display. Hand-eye coordination was impossible without the latter as a source of feedback. Without graphical feedback, pointing could do no more than transform text-based question-and-answer into text-based form filling—based on pointing at menu options and keying names or numbers into fields in tables. With continuous graphical feedback, the way was opened for direct manipulation. As you may recall from chapter 1, direct manipulation consists of an object-action coupling with continuously visible results—what you see is what you get. This was responsible for the first beginnings of craft in computer operations.

The theory behind this creed was quite elegant. Alan Kay, a chief pioneer of this strategy, emphasized three kinds of knowledge commonly discussed by educational psychologists. *Symbolic* knowledge uses long abstract sequences of reasoning, such as those found in text, logic, or mathematics. It is the most powerful form of knowledge, but it is the least vivid. It is the most easily translated into the sequential symbolic processing that computers do, but the most difficult to learn. The second form, *iconic* knowledge is visual. Images are especially easy to recognize and compare (often preconsciously), and they seem to concretize other ways of knowing. Furthermore, if images are the basis of postmodern culture, we might believe that innate knowledge is increasingly iconic. The third type of knowledge is *enactive.* It is inherently tied to actions, and it is the craftsperson's way of knowing. It is the most intuitive and so the easiest to learn. What Kay recognized in these three forms was that even if symbolic knowledge of command languages was to remain the most powerful form of human-computer interaction, these nonsymbolic forms could contribute to learning and discovery processes that would make computing more acceptable to nonspecialists. "Doing with images makes symbols," he said. Actions and images help people develop mental maps of abstract possibilities.[2]

Symbolic Contexts and Physical Devices

Why is the idea of a symbolic context so important? After all, as one classic textbook put it, computer operation comes down to just a few essential tasks: entering text, numbers, or positions; setting modes or controls; selecting objects; initiating processes; obtaining feedback; establishing sequences; conducting communications; and validating results.[3] But to say that computing is limited because it consists of no more than these few tasks is like saying painting is no good because about all you can do is apply color to canvas. The value of the activity comes in skillfully executing, combining, and accumulating the effects of these basic moves. Few moves, even in physical media, have much meaning without a context. Symbolic processing media add the extra requirement of coupling physical devices to abstract actions. The effect, meaning, and accumulation of such moves need a very well structured setting, that is, a symbolic context. Symbolic context determines the nature of our moves: it relates physical tools to the abstractions of tools and media in software.

You might understand this matter in terms of three basic needs. First, we expect software to establish an appropriate instructional framework—a repertoire of operations—whether command language, toolkit, workable objects, or all the above. Next, we must have the means to construct sufficient mental models: there has to be a way to understand operations conceptually if work is to seem anything but rote tool usage. Finally, we want to orchestrate activities both in time and in relation to the work of others. Altogether, by meeting these three needs, we want to establish a world of actions—a medium. This may sound easy enough, but not enough people make the leap from physical device operations to abstract mental models.

Not only does symbolic context shape computational experience, but the manner in which it does so can change substantially. Consider where we are and how we got here. In his essay "Through the Looking Glass" (1989), *AutoCAD* author John Walker summarized:

> Today's fascination with user interfaces is an artifact of how we currently operate computers—with screens, keyboards, and pointing devices. Earliest manipulations were direct: twiddling bit switches, dedicated use. Next came batch jobs: stacks of cards. Next conversational, interactive, time-sharing. Next, text menu-driven. Next, graphical, object oriented, event-driven.
>
> Barriers were: first, front panel; second, countertop; third, terminal; fourth, menu hierarchy; fifth, screen. What comes next is a cyberspace system that provides a three-dimensional interaction experience that includes the illusion that one is inside a world rather than observing an image.[4]

Walker was suggesting that symbolic contexts have steadily evolved toward greater continuity of engagement. Note that a most thorough engagement would eliminate any awareness of an interface—and this is the appeal of "cyberspace."

From an engineering standpoint, faster processing allows richer symbolic contexts. Much as the graphical interface became practical when there was at last enough capacity to deliver mouse pointing and the two-dimensional desktop image, today many new possibilities have become practical—thanks to the capacity to deliver sounds, spatial images, bodily gestures, and remote communications in realtime. As computers continue to get faster, cheaper, and better, symbolic contexts will develop that will make today's pointing and clicking at menus appear nearly as crude as using stacks of punched cards. Eventually our three main input and output devices—keyboard, mouse, and screen—will seem quite arbitrary. For example, although nothing is likely to replace the keyboard immediately, many substitutes have emerged, including voice recognizers and optical character scanners for text entry, valuators such as dials and sliders for numerical entry, and pen-based notepads for combining sketches with written instructions. Similarly, screen alternatives exist (and some of these are more glamorous) including holograms, immersive stereoscopic goggles, and projected video overlays.

Virtual Reality?

The expression "virtual reality" has been used to describe any and all of these developments. It is not great terminology, but it has stuck. Part of the problem is that it is used in reference to many simple technologies having any degree of verisimilitude. More specifically, it should refer to gestural navigation in spatial images. The particular arrangement that fueled all the hype was three-dimensional pointing input with head-mounted stereo output: an interesting combination, admittedly, but hardly the incontestable future of human-computer interaction. Consider one alternative: in "augmented reality" physical devices that we already know how to use become embedded with audio/visual sensors and microprocessors for use in symbolic constructions. This might include your own real desktop now made digital, as well as the likes of smart rooms, and maybe the occasional use of your own bare hands.[5]

The appeal of these realities, whether augmented or virtual, is their better match of new technologies to existing human skills. One especially appealing existing capacity (that presumably everyone knows something about) is to work in three dimensions. Much as support for two-dimensional gesture and image recognition opened up initial possibilities, there is good

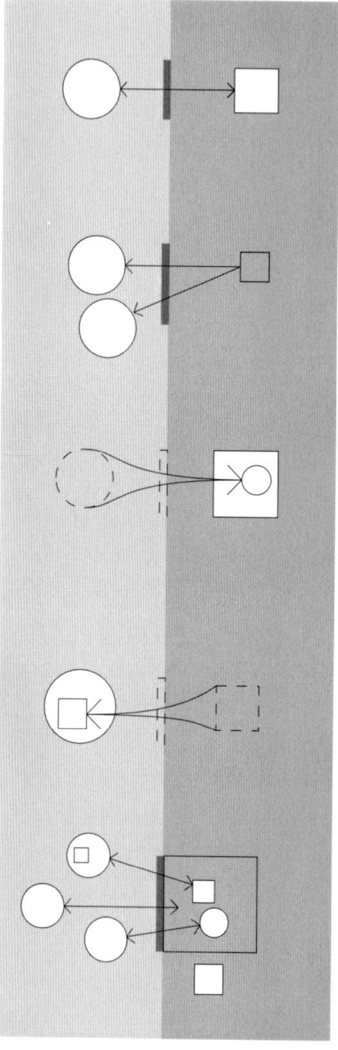

5.3 The two-worlds problem: linking the physical and the virtual

reason to expect that three-dimensional action and spatial thinking will expand the potential for digital craft. Therefore we might frame a more detailed exploration of computer operations in terms of increasing dimensions.

Language

One-dimensional, word-based interaction is far from obsolete. The endurance of command language makes sense if you remember that computation essentially manipulates structures of textual notations. Note that textual command languages are an intrinsic product of the programming process. As names of objects and processes, command languages mediate between computer language and natural language.

We might expect that computer languages would ultimately tend toward natural language, but this is not necessarily the case.[6] The concise specificity of nonspoken verbal instructions has many advantages. Although there is nothing to stop us from having a command language composed of bodily gestures coupled to three-dimensional sounds (so long as its underlying basis is a formal symbol system), purely text-based command language remains invaluable. Command language endures because of its abstraction.

Language in general can deal in arbitrary propositions, simply by representing them in words. As has been noted, words are often easier to manipulate than the things they represent. When a word exists, using it is usually quicker and more accurate than gesturing. Words can refer to things not visibly present (whereas a mouse can only point at what is on the screen). New words can always be added. Words can be modified by sequence and relations. A textual trail is also particularly conducive to scripting and programming. And because words do not take up space or otherwise interfere with one another, the language can accommodate any number of them.

Of course not everyone achieves or aspires to command language mastery. A keyboard alone forms a sufficient barrier, for most people cannot type very quickly. Memorizing an arcane vocabulary and syntax is uncomfortable too, and seeing options onscreen is an easier way to recall operations. Arbitrary command language is less easily learned and retained than natural words (or visual icons), because its elements are not conducive to preconscious cognition and therefore demand more attention.[7] For example, the Unix operating system has about a thousand commands, but hardly anyone seems to master more than a quarter of them. When some of the basics are "mv" (but not "move") for "rename," "grep" for "search," and "lpr" for "print," there is little wonder why. To most people, such a command stream, albeit scriptable and precisely modifiable, feels less like a language than a tedious and unnatural code. No wonder pointing changed everything.

Pointing

As noted, the prevailing form of two-dimensional interaction depends on pointing plus continuously refreshed image display. Of these elements, pointing offers the greater variety of devices and possibilities. This is good, because the hands, not the eyes, need more to do. If better hand-held tools are to become a main key to richer computing, we might begin by making pointing better.

We can certainly challenge several properties of the mouse. For example, the chief advantage of the mouse is that it is a relative pointing device, which means that you can pick it up anywhere, you can give it arbitrarily large displacements, and you may use several small, short strokes in place of a single long gesture. Yet absolute devices such as touchscreens and digitizing tablets have their advantages too, and these will become more prevalent as computing becomes embedded in more pieces of our environment. Another regular property of the mouse is its use of buttons, both on itself and in combination with keyboard reflexes on the second hand. Probably the most familiar example of this is the Macintosh's shift-drag, which means "move orthogonally only." You may have trouble retaining any but a small repertoire of such motions, partly depending on your level of comfort in working with two hands in different modes. Other modes are possible, of course: how about a device in each hand—one selector and one effector? Or more practically, combine voice with pointing. Or how about hand signals instead of any devices at all?

Modified Pointing

Pointing can control other variables besides location in a plane, and software filters can endlessly modify pointer actions. Software routinely translates mouse motions into indirect (but nevertheless continuous) manipulations. For example, the common one-dimensional scroll bar or slider applies the mouse to all variety of nongeometric variables, such as sound levels, color selections, and task allocations. A two-dimensional curve on a graph can indirectly control complex properties of digital constructions, such as tone distribution graphs for images, differential cross-sectional scaling graphs for lofted forms, or motion derivative graphs for use in animation. Some people refer to such graphical devices for indirect manipulation as "widgets."

Software modifications can also modify direct manipulations by tracking motion derivatives. Currently there is no better return on investment in digital craft than that obtained from a simple $30 accelerator mouse. This allows large displacements to be based on quicker rather than longer wrist motions, and this added subtlety is very helpful. Alternatively motion derivatives can be applied after sampling mouse position, that is, to the cursor. This results in an uncanny, elegant dexterity that is particulary useful in tracking, the first popular example of which may have been the game *CrystalQuest* (1988).

By combining widgets with direct-motion derivatives, two-dimensional pointing can support three-dimensional navigation. For example, an operation called tumbling alters the altitude and azimuth of viewing position simultaneously according to horizontal and vertical

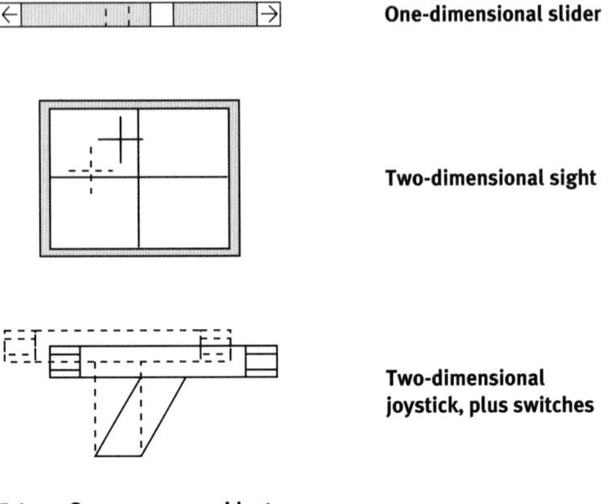

5.4 Some common widgets

pointer motions. This is useful in axonometric projections, but for navigating in perspective, systems must add a control for shifting between choosing a viewing direction and moving in and out along that direction.

Some systems map motion variables of a wireless stylus, such as pressure, speed, and orientation, onto time- and surface-dependent operations to increase the fluidity of mark making. Many programs such as Fractal Design's *Painter* take great advantage of this added fluidity. Other systems expand the lexicons of meaningful marks. This is how pen-based computing elaborates pointing into alphabetic writing. Given these many avenues of development, there is little question that pointing will soon escape the confines of mouse and desktop.

Pointing, in Three Dimensions

Pointing gets much more interesting in three dimensions. Understanding three-dimensional pointing begins with degrees of freedom. A two-dimensional mouse uses just two degrees of freedom: left-right (x-axis) and up-down (y-axis) translations. (It also can turn, but this is rarely useful.) A three-dimensional mouse has six degrees of freedom: x-, y-, and z- axis motions and rotations, the latter known as pitch, roll, and yaw. Tracking these

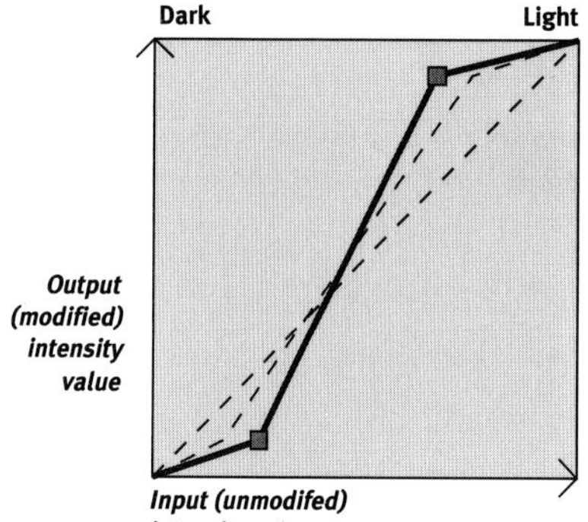

Contrast adjustment in image processing: curve slope controls contrast, or cutoff points control tonal range.

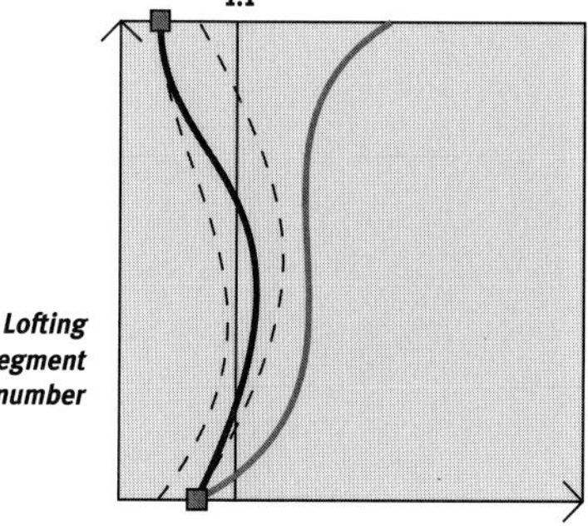

Profile scale in lofting: curve controls deformations over length of object. Maybe separate curves for horizontal and vertical scaling.

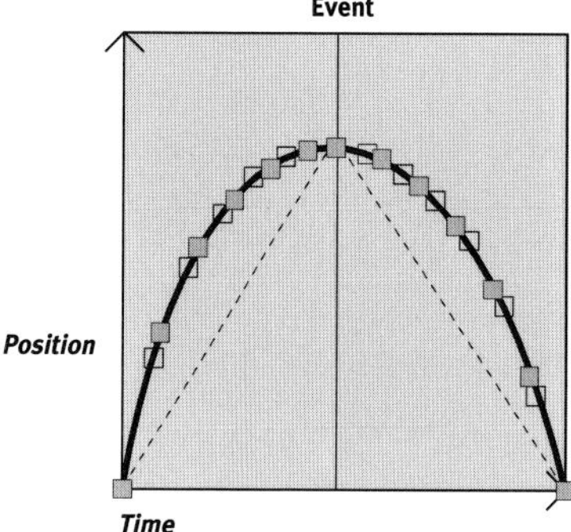

Motion transition in keyframe animation: curve continuity corresponds to event continuity, and segment spacing controls slow-in.

5.5 Three common examples of indirect manipulation by means of function curves

degrees must address the inherent problem of leaving the work surface. One response is to use rigid spaceballs that sense forces and torques in any direction. The more usual approach is to introduce electromagnetic trackers known as Polhemus digitizers. These devices employ the basic principle of physics that a current moving in a coil creates an axial magnetic field, and vice versa. By using two sets of three perpendicular coils and moving one of them relative to the other, it is possible to process signal changes to construct three-dimensional position and orientation.

Three-dimensional tracking devices have opened up a whole new class of interactive tools.[8] For example, with a "2–6 mouse," you can switch between using the usual two degrees of freedom and the full six: you can pick it up off the table and wave it around in the air when necessary. With a three-dimensional pointing pen, you can digitize an arbitrary sculptural form by systematically touching points on its surface. And for navigating you can use a dataglove, which has been by far the most celebrated new pointer of them all.

Spatial Action

If we may judge by the popularity of its image, the dataglove has many more significances beyond pointing and tracking. For one thing, it enables a sign language of sorts, based on using finger motions as choice and selection devices. It also suggests the possibility of pointing devices for other parts of the body. Some of these, such as the foot-mouse, or "mole," already do exist. Beyond these extensions, the main significance of the dataglove is that you do not hold it so much as you *wear* it. Not only does this free up the hand, but it represents a basic idea that can be extended straightforwardly into a full-body "datasuit." Beyond three-dimensional pointing, then, researchers are exploring interaction based on gesture, pose, and dance.

This suggests that the real appeal of "virtual reality" lies in better use of the hands, and not necessarily in the saturation of the eyes. Much has been made of visual saturation and stereoscopic immersion as a means for hopping-up passive entertainment. Certainly there is appeal to the idea that where current screen displays let you look *at* your work, stereoscopy lets you look *in* it. But not enough has been said (at least in proportion to the hype over goggles) about the manual, *active* possibilities. Too little has been said about sophisticated computer input, as opposed to stimulating output. Vision is largely passive, but constructed realities need not be passively received—indeed they should become more richly participatory. What if Kay's aphorism generalizes well—into, say, "doing with tactile forms makes mental topologies." What of spatial thinking? Consider that our definition of tools is kinetic, that the mastery of craft involves spatial dexterity, and that form giving is inherently a three-dimensional process. On the grounds that computer designs need to do more with what people already know and expect about handling their physical environment, there is no reason to downplay the physical, as some virtual reality prototypes have done. If we are to bridge the physical and the virtual worlds, then dematerialization is not the answer.

Ergonomics, or Fit

The study of physical human factors begins from good fit. Like physical tools, such as a good set of wrenches, digital devices should emphasize physical properties geared to human dimensions. Good fit generally permits greater facility. For example, fit helps the craftsperson choose the right tool and use it more effectively. We choose our conventional tools by the right size and weight for the job. In the case of hand tools, the fit of the grip is very important. For example, note how luggage with better handles seems lighter, because better handles distribute the load more evenly. The same is true subliminally for pens, for knives, and also for mouses. Better fit contributes to transparency and maneuverability. It also reduces fatigue.

The human factors of size, shape, and reach have always been important to traditional tool design, and it makes sense that they will remain so with computers. As limitations such as processing speed and memory requirements give way, technology designers may more directly address the ergonomic criteria for physical input devices. The accelerator mouse mentioned earlier is a good example of this. A computer that is worn, not held, might ideally fit very well—like a glove. This might make more complex forms of human-computer interaction more acceptable.

Taken to its fullest extremes, a catalogue of physical interaction tools might range all the way from the crudest bit switches on the earliest computers to the fantastical neural implants used in William Gibson's seminal cyberpunk novel, *Neuromancer.* This range could be measured on scales of precision, speed, or degrees of freedom, but none of these would be more apt than fit. What Gibson was implying, and what even the mouse represents as an advance over arrow keys, is the ability to fit the machine to the will of the human in a way that is direct, continuous, and without interference by intellectual constructs. Physical fit may be achieved soon enough, but logical fit is going to be more difficult. To almost anyone but a beginner unfamiliar with basic motor reflexes, it is logical frameworks, such as desktop graphical user interfaces, and not physical input tools that form the main obstacle to transparent computing. Meanwhile, physical fit is just one aspect of a much larger issue. Half the excitement about datagloves owes to the focus on the hand itself, for the hand is a symbol of touch.

Touch

No other sense is so important psychologically, but touch has yet to be a part of everyday computing. Touch technology is underdeveloped, and few interaction devices provide force or tactile feedback. Without touch, currently the most common complaint about computers is not about overload, but deprivation. It is about the inability to touch one's work. Being *out of touch* is considered an occupational hazard: regular sensory deprivation turns you into a nerd.

In *A Natural History of the Senses,* Diane Ackerman explains: "In many ways, touch is difficult to research. Every other sense has a key organ

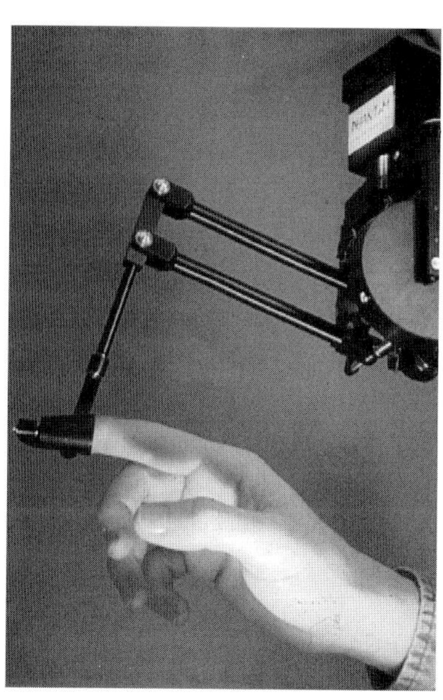

5.6 One of the first commercially available devices for force-feedback at the fingertip

to study; for touch, that organ is the skin, and it stretches over the entire body. Every sense has at least one key research center, except touch. Touch is a sensory system, the influence of which is hard to isolate or eliminate."[9] Nevertheless touch has identifiable components. Skin feels contact, temperature, pressure, vibration, and texture. Coordinated joints and muscles provide a feel for bodily kinematics, by which we can perceive phenomena such as weight, solidity, and inertia.[10] These perceptions combine with those registered by the other specific senses, such as hearing, and with general conditions, such as focus or fatigue, to create complex challenges for the designers of software. Multimodal interaction seems at least as interesting as multimedia documents as an immediate future for computing.

Remember that the hand works two ways: effecting and probing. The former is easier than the latter to engineer. Although pointing is extremely useful, it will remain unsatisfactory until balanced by sensation. And for anything more than pointing or button pushing to be effective, some degree of tactile feedback will be necessary.

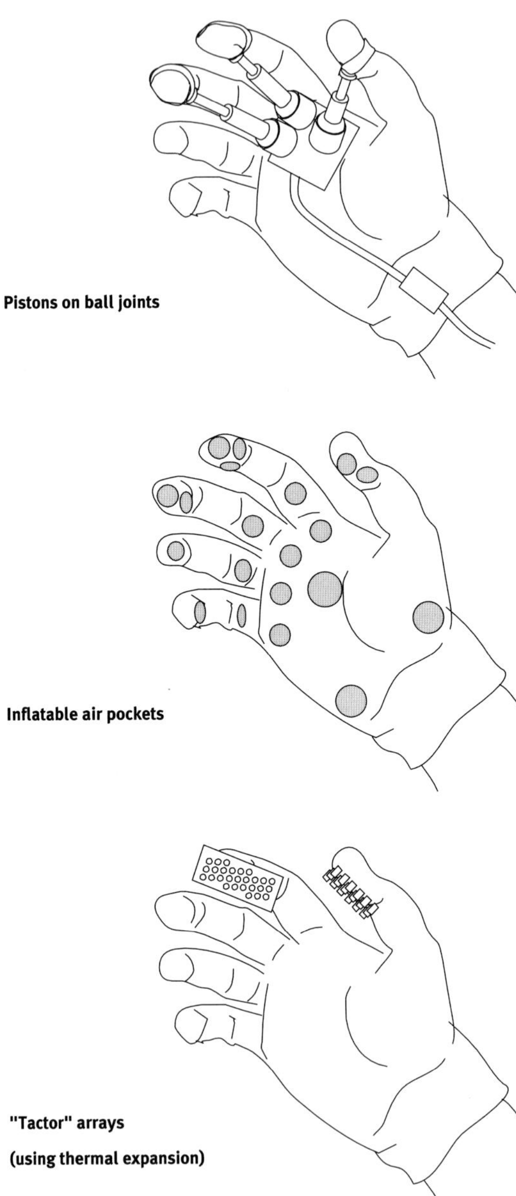

5.7 Some ways of adding haptic sense to a dataglove device

Tactile devices have various ways to convert electronic signals into something tangible. For example, datagloves can be equipped with air pockets or thermal grids for tactile feedback. The term *taxel* has been introduced to describe small units of tactile differentiation that make up these grids.[11] Taxels are fit more finely to the fingertips, which can resolve stimuli much better than, say, a forearm.

Force feedback is of course very well developed in the servomechanisms used in mechanical engineering, and researchers have applied it to the hand for a variety of applications.[12] For example, for work in hazardous surroundings, hand-worn remote controllers use joints and pistons to provide the hand force feedback from pressure sensors on robots. In immersive virtual environments, force feedback on pointing devices adds a sense of bumping into impenetrable objects, rather than passing, disorientingly, right through them. Even in routine two-dimensional desktop pointing, force feedback can help reinforce or acknowledge certain actions. A fairly simple device called a "feelmouse" has been developed to modulate the pressure needed to click on a mouse key depending on the context and location of the pointer.[13] As noted in chapter 1, a variety of tactile controls have advanced fairly well in specialized settings such as medicine, music, and gaming simulations. But most of these are hardly practical: at this writing, one haptic feedback pointing device advertised in a popular magazine costs about the same as an ordinary personal computer.

Response Time

More than anything else, including touch, the growing possibility of craft depends on continuous operations. Craft flows, and the technology must reflect this. If self-pacing is essential to traditional craft, it is also fundamental to the object-action coupling that underlies direct manipulation software tools. Work must occur at its own intrinsic pace, without interruptions, delays, or rush. Performance becomes an important measure of software, and response time is an important quality of performance. Only with adequate response may skill be served, concentration maintained, innovation accommodated, production furthered.

Response time depends mostly on the capacity for transmitting data streams between continuous processes. Better bandwidth, more frequent samples, more modes of representation, and more information about context all contribute to the perception of better response time. You can feel it just by running a familiar program on a faster computer. As technology evolves, an increasing range of activities becomes deliverable with acceptable response times. Continuous photographic image processing was inconceivable two decades ago, but today it has become normal. Continuous stereo image delivery is now possible, but not yet practical.[14] Full body motion can be captured for use in animation, but it is not yet pratical for driving arbitrary, everyday processes.

Note that computational events occur along a huge spectrum of time measures, ranging from nanoseconds to days, but the human pace of work demands that computers report all this without perceptible interruptions or delays. The condition in which data are delivered quickly enough to prevent any perception of discontinuity or lag is normally referred to as *realtime.* This condition is especially important for continuous operations, where the response to a *stream* of input must be dynamically calculated and displayed at least as quickly as it is anticipated.

Realtime thresholds vary. The hand is quicker than the eye, for instance. Perceptible lag may be as low as a hundredth of a second, whereas for moving images, we know it to be about a thirtieth of a second. Tolerable lag on a manual mechanical device like a mouse is about a tenth of a second, whereas the acceptable rate on a visual operation like placing an image in a document layout may be as high as two whole seconds.[15]

Masters will often increase their tolerance for delay in order to expand the range of processes that they can conduct in a quasi-continuous manner. In other words, they compensate for time impedance. We might refer to this state as near realtime. For example, moving a viewpoint in a three-dimensional display involves trade-offs between how much you can view and how much the display lags the mouse motion. Too much lag increases the likelihood of error, for you cannot see what you are getting. Near realtime responses of this sort cause stress, for expectations are raised, and full attention is required, but unnatural slow-motion gestures are employed, and subliminal interruptions occur.[16]

It is important to remember that many operations are asynchronous; that is, they need not be conducted continuously. For example, batch operations that require no intervention between start and finish can be managed indirectly. All we require of these is the ability to run independently. More specifically, processes must give an estimate of when we should check in on them, or, if that is indeterminate, they must report back to us whenever further input becomes necessary. Batch operations are desirable for computationally intensive processes that would be very tedious to perform directly, for example, frame-by-frame renderings. They are also very useful for processes that need to be delivered at a rate *slower* than their calculation. One special form of batch process called a daemon awaits a particular condition before activating, like an alarm clock, but with many other kinds of possible actions. As computers keep getting faster, there will be no point in having them wait for us, any more than we should wait for them, and periodic reporting strategies such as agents will assume a greater role.

Dialogue

Most operations are neither completely batch nor truly continuous, but involve some amount of dialogue. We conduct interactive computing primarily through dialogue. Question-and-answer dialogue was the only mode of operation for some time before pointing, and even with pointing, the dialogue box still surpasses the tool metaphor as the most characteristic element of the graphical user interface.

Response times for dialogues are rather more difficult to measure, because here tolerable delay is a matter of patience. Psychology researchers have generalized rules of thumb: two seconds is a suitable average delay; anything over twelve seconds results in distractions and errors. But patience depends on many factors: one's desire for the result, the convenience of going on to some other task, the need to maintain concentration, overall fatigue, a sense of self-pacing. Some short discontinuities just cause irritation, but others provide welcome time to rest or think. It makes a big difference whether delays are of predictable length. Like near realtime response, near interactive response is a source of stress: too much waiting destroys one's concentration. But predictably managable response times seem to be acceptable once learned. Thus progress reporting devices are a hallmark of this state.

Software dialogues are improving in many other ways besides faster response. For one thing, increasingly we have them with other people, and not just with our software. Sometimes we have them between ongoing processes without having to stop and take turns. Increasingly we may conduct dialogues with less rigid protocols and with less suspension of other activities. We have more modes, including pictures and sounds. We are learning how to butt in, or change the subject. These various capacities depend as much on the robustness and adaptability of the software as on the bandwidth of the hardware. Increasingly, they suggest the importance of timing.

Orchestration

If graphical desktop and virtual reality approaches treat symbolic context as a space, another alternative is to organize it in time. The next (third) dimension could be time, not space; or there could be space and time—four-dimensional interfaces. In any case, as the technology continues to improve, there will remain little reason for people and computers to take turns, little need to confine interaction to one device at a time, and little barrier to collaborative working environments.[18] Operating a computer may then seem less like sitting alone with a machine and more like entering a world of action in which you are the narrator.

All this suggests emphasis on the narrative trail. A trail is a documented series of actions and states. Command by command, event by event, everything that occurs on a computer happens in a coded sequence that can be recorded. Many applications do this already, for a trail is also easy to keep in one-dimensional text-based operation. For example, *AutoCAD* was one of the first programs to provide a complete trail of a session, including all steps and settings as well as changes to the artifact.

Nevertheless, more sophisticated time-structured working contexts are clearly possible. For example, it should become easier to move back and forth in the history of a session. More interestingly, it should become possible to introduce forks and junctions in the trail. The representation known as multithreading allows multiple processes, whether interactive or autonomous, to be at work in a shared software environment without upsetting one another's contexts. Such capacity is especially important in networks, and this accounts for the rise of multithreaded scripting languages such as Java.

As in a physical workplace, we can schedule time for synchronous actions. For example, collaborative workspaces are environments specifically engineered for scheduled, multimodal, multiparticipant dialogue—commonly known as meetings. In an online meeting, people can transmit and demonstrate much more interesting documents. They can marvel at artifacts. They can still sketch on boards, and pass the chalk. They can yell and gesticulate. They can dress for success.

Meanwhile we can improve our management of asynchronous autonomous processes. For example, a reliable independent process can be represented with a character identity and encapsulated as an "agent." Giving instructions will involve managing these agents. An agent may serve you like an apprentice, and its software may reside only on your computer. Or it may move about over networks: an agent may carry information between you and others, like a messenger, or it may come and go on its own, like a traveling salesman.[19]

We are likely to find all these actions easier to manage in time than in space. Thus the tired old desktop becomes even less useful when adapted to less similar environments such as process management. Moreover, its event-driven framework that places all the responsibility for scheduling on us becomes a liability. Therefore, much of the current research in human-computer interaction invites us to consider all these actions as narratives involving characters, including but not limited to ourselves.

	Before	"Graphical user interface"	After
Hardware basis	Terminal, printer	Keyboard, mouse, screen	"Augmented reality": embedded, ubiquitous computing
Dimension	1-dimensional, text-based	2-dimensional, laid out in desktop plane	3-and 4-dimensional: navigable space, and/ or orchestrated time
Sequence of activity	Computer-controlled question-and-answer	Pointer-controlled; taking turns acting and waiting	Agenda-controlled; persistent activity and computation
Interaction stream	None; all batch	Single device and channel	Multi-channel
Scope of reference	Reference by name; visibility unimportant	Reference by position; everything visible	Reference by action; perceptible objects, environment, and agents
Sensory range	Specialized vision (text)	Mostly vision	Multisensory: vision, hearing, touch
Input/output balance	Crude input and output	Crude input, sophisticated output	Sophisticated input and output
Spectrum of awareness	Language only	Variety of foreground cognition	Foreground cognition and background sense
Scope of control	Batch session on central computer	Whole personal computer	Distributed work domain
Protocols and conventions	Designated by local computer center	Established by bestselling applications	Practiced by professional workgroups

5.8 Before and after the graphical user interface

Psychological Factors

Participation

By now it should be clear that how to use computers is a much more complex and diversifying question than most popular instruction manuals imply. How to operate technology is not enough; it might be better to ask *how to be* when using technology. If it were possible to summarize this psychology in a single word, that word would be "participation." As is increasingly acknowledged by managers and technologists alike, effective, satisfactory work depends on conscious involvement.[20] This very sense is perhaps all that is meant by the new usage of the word "craft." Participation normally benefits from some degree of physical involvement, but it also relates to pyschological identification, which in turn benefits from habit and mastery. The control of process, engagement with material, and identification with work that we admire in the traditional craftsman are clearly qualities of participation.

Psychologists and software designers use a wide variety of terminology to discuss participation: intentionality, focus, assimilation, cognitive guides, enactive knowledge, engagement, transparency, attention.[21] "Everyone knows what attention is," wrote William James. "It is the taking possession of mind, in clear and vivid form, of one out of what seem several simultaneously possible objects or trains of thought . . . It requires withdrawal from some things in order to deal effectively with others."[22] We have seen examples related to skill: attention withdraws from lower-level execution in order to participate at a higher level of intent. The pianist plays the music; the skier skis the slope.

Better human-computer interfaces improve our sense of participation. Good software designs engage us with a credible representation of a world in which we work. They let us know we are in charge, and they let us focus on our work. Like good traditional tools, they go unnoticed. We may say that they become transparent.

You may find it hard to feel this way about contemporary software. Computers are notoriously distracting. Interfaces are clumsy. "Users" do not always feel that they are party to programmers' goals. Anxiety and detachment seem to be more common than participation as descriptions of the computational experience. Software psychologists' term for these various frustrations is "perceptual load."[23]

An excess of perceptual load prevents us from finding tools to be transparent or actions to be continuous. Distraction interferes with the participatory practice of talent. This is reflected in the fact that beginners get frustrated where experts somehow manage to overcome any sources of stress. If you use a computer, you can probably name some sources of perceptual load, including time delays, visual strain, repetition, unretainable physical skills, bad fit, and other considerations generally in the domain of comfort. Ben Shneiderman has enumerated the following factors for mitigating perceptual load: consistency; availability of shortcuts; continual feedback; closure; error handling; reversibility; sense of causation; limited use of short-term memory.[24] You probably know the last factor as a common rule of thumb that says we can successfully pay attention to no more than seven things at a time.

Assimilation

Consider another popular criterion: "the principle of least astonishment." This is an expression of conceptual load. Software should not surprise us with inconsistent symbolic contexts or unfamiliar abstractions. To avoid producing astonishment, interface designers pursue various means of assimilation. One obvious technique is to avoid discontinuities, since quick jumps disorient us, and long delays break our concentration. Better software performance assists assimilation by use of continuous transitions. For instance, if you close a window on the Macintosh, it appears to zoom back into the icon that then represents it on the desktop. That way you know where it "went." Another common means of assimilation is reminders: like a small yellow tag stuck on a printed report, software uses alerts, handles, and highlights to tell you how to orient yourself to a given symbolic context.

Assimilation also benefits from sensory engagement. If software needs to get our attention, one of the best ways for it to do so is through a variety of perceptualizations. Note that immersion is not the same as assimilation. Too much of the former without enough of the latter quickly produces "simulation sickness"—something familiar to anyone who has spent even a few minutes under a virtual reality headset. But a proper balance of sensory stimulation with cues for conceptual assimilation usually improves engagement.

Our most natural way to assimilate is to combine senses. Multisensory interaction, or at least multiple media, assist our understanding and synthesis. Psychologists generally agree that when more than one sense confirms a perception, the perception becomes deeper, or more credible. Cognitive correspondences between gestures, images, sounds, or symbols help us build an intuition about logical states for which there are no easy words or phrases. This may be as simple as reinforcing a logical distinction with a physical action and a visual image, such as deleting a file by physically dragging and dropping an icon. It may be a composite construction such as a spatial-audio field mapping the same space as a visual surface model. It may aspire to match the natural multimodal interaction we know as conversation, or to the powerful coupling of vision and touch we expect when using a tool Pointing-plus-seeing was one of the first such couplings to be demonstrated, as in Richard Bolt's famous system, "Put-That-There" (1980).[25] Audio-plus-gesture is another combination now becoming popular. As noted, the psychological criterion of response time influences these developments. Advances in multimodal interaction have the potential to become the main source of assimilation and participation in the richer symbolic contexts of the future. And in the end, we get the most engagement from touch.

Conscious attention and skilled action are closely interrelated, and this is one reason why traditional craft has meditative qualities. Participation depends on both lowest, automatic-level, perceptor-motor actions, as well as the highest understandings of focus and intent. If your mood did not affect your work, computers would be very dreary indeed. Psychological factors such as excitement, tedium, anticipation, and fatigue are known to affect work and performance.[26]

All this is notoriously difficult to measure, however. Software designers like to test and evaluate interface prototypes by surveying and monitoring test "users." This process has an uncanny resemblance to time-and-motion studies used by modernist industrialists earlier in the twentieth century. Of course cognitive psychology has developed considerably since then, but nevertheless interface metrics must occasionally fall back on some mechanistic assumptions and cannot often manage to measure quiescent states such as satisfaction, reflectivity, or intent. Furthermore, testing is usually applied only to new software and in support of design for usability by beginners. Much less has been done to test experts, and indeed expertise is much more difficult to test.

Foreground, Background, and Compensation

If psychological principles permeate the study of human-computer interaction, then skillful computational practice should have its psychological challenge and rewards. Moreover, the philosophy implicit in the proposition of craft should depend to some degree on an appropriate approach to human-computer interfaces.

Better technology shifts psychological load from foreground cognition to background awareness. In other words, it establishes contexts that free us from having to keep too many considerations actively in mind. For example, some research has focused on developing symbolic contexts that subjugate any awareness of linguistic formalism. Other research has focused on getting the entire computer out of the way, by embedding it in the physical context.[27] These are admirable goals, but the process of reaching them remains inadequately understood. Contextual awareness is clearly a dimension of expertise, but establishing this awareness requires more than just the right tools, languages, and settings. Developing a fuller back-

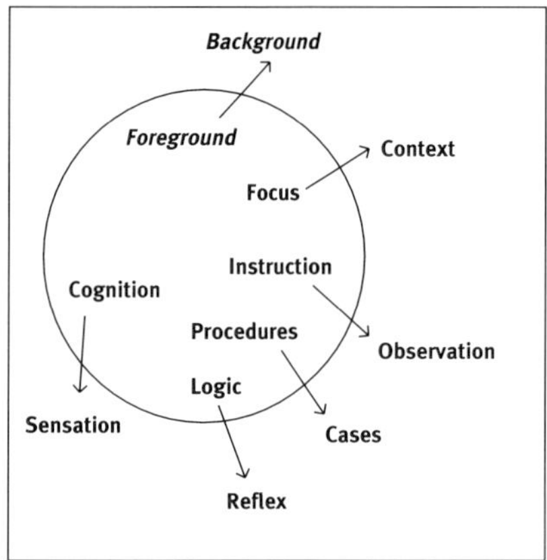

5.9 The foreground/background issue: reducing cognitive load by building up contextual awareness

ground awareness may not be easy, for the design of software remains largely based on questionable assumptions of a cognitive science that give insufficient credence to intent, feeling, vision, personal knowledge, critical praxis, or any of the other cultural contexts of creative computing raised in the first half of this book. It may be easy to say that background awareness is the main thing missing from primitive computational strategies, but it is not so easy to say what exactly that is.

For the moment, then, the role of the humane worker is to withstand the psychological demands of fledgling software that places too many considerations in foreground awareness. *There is an art of computer usage based on handling the psychological dimensions of an imperfect medium.* Of course there has never been an ultimate medium, and craftsmen of all past ages have exhibited patience, sympathy, and innovation with their imperfect traditional media. The same will be true for the digital realm. The digital craftsperson will not only practice knowing the properties of the general digital medium, but also will seek opportunities for transparency of software tools, work around psychological-technical barriers, manage sensory imbalance, and handle perceptual and cognitive loads.

To anyone without this ability to balance, the crude technology may seem overwhelming. Like Polanyi's pianist, who after noticing his fingers, fell out of the music, a software beginner will often notice the computer and so lose focus on his work. A newcomer watching an accomplished master at work will see a fine manual coordination that lets fingers dart around keyboards and glide back and forth with a mouse. But behind these operations the master psychologically balances between cognition, action, and intent, and behind this balance lies a refined mental model of an abstract world that is being operated on through the computer. This abstract model is the object of action, and the computer is only the framework.

Mental Models

Mental modeling is the key to effective computing. Working on abstract structure requires mediation between action and notation, not only by the technology, but also within our imagination. To put it within the terms used to structure this survey, mental models are the meeting of symbolic contexts with operational psychology. They are the beginning of understanding software as a tool and computer as a medium. They are exactly what is missing in the rote procedural knowledge conveyed by so many popular training guides. They are the difference between struggling beginners and seasoned experts.

Effective mental models of computer system states are able to predict outcomes of untried procedures, whereas rote knowledge of procedures does not necessarily include an understanding of underlying system states. Such models are essential for learning how to combine elements of the digital repertoire. You must know the elements and be able to visualize their combinations. Masters teaching such conceptual frameworks to beginners may feel like they are taking a bunch of Martians to the neighborhood hardware store.[28]

Can you count the number of windows in your house? This is an example commonly used by psychologists to demonstrate the use of mental models. To answer the question, you do not walk around counting windows, but simply construct a model in your mind. This capacity is not limited to memories and experiences, but can be propositional. One common experiment uses mental rotation to see if two objects are equivalent.

The ability to envision structure varies among people, and is one of the main reasons that we may say that computing takes talent. Even within a clearly defined hierarchy, envisioning a structure makes it easier to grasp longer paths and relations. We know from the work of file management that some people are capable of imagining only one or two levels away from their current directory, while others can "see" whole directory trees. In more free-form organizational structures, the ability to navigate varies much more, and it seems to relate to an ability for spatial orientation.

There is a substantial tradition of using analogous spatial access structures for nonspatial data. As Frances Yates described in *The Art of Memory* (1964), classical orators were able to recall segments of long speeches or stories by correspondence with architectural elements of an auditorium.[29] This architecture could be real or imaginary—all that mattered to the orator was to memorize the mappings. Researchers and cyberspace enthusiasts have seized on this phenomenon of the memory palace as a promise of forthcoming developments in the architecture of information.

Spatial abstraction reduces psychological loads by using our latent abilities in recognition, orientation, and positional memory, thus shifting the challenges of navigation and assimilation from reasoning to simple perception.[30] This is useful not only for analyzing but also for generating new formal structures. Text-based narrative adventure games have routinely played on this phenomenon. They provide descriptions (e.g., "you are in a long, dark hallway with doors on the left and behind you") and challenge you to mentally map a spatial world. More recent multimedia games such as *Myst* (1993) do this with pictures and sounds, and with a hundredfold increase in the vividness of the results.

These gamers' dungeons and the orators' memory palaces are examples of knowledge in distributed relations. They demonstrate implicit structural equivalencies between different symbolic contexts. Like the

5.10 Use of images for mentally mapping a fictional world: one of over 2,600 views from the hit game *Myst*

symbolic reasoning demonstrated in the example from Vieta in chapter 4, however, these equivalencies invite us to endow them with an emergent reality. We cannot say, "these names are a house," or even "these names are like a house." But we can put names in rooms, and rooms in relations, and soon enough have a mental picture of a house.

It follows that we can use arrangements of other familiar phenomena as means of access to unfamiliar, abstract system states. An access structure is simply a means of finding things, like street addresses or mug shots. It may be a formal classification, like a library index, or a less hierarchical organization, like the placement of tools around a workshop floor.

A particularly interesting case arises when there is similarity—isomorphism—between a data structure and its access structure. For example, access from one item to another in a collection of views of rooms could be accomplished by pointing at doorways in those views. Clicking on a doorway would bring up a view of the adjacent rooms that one would

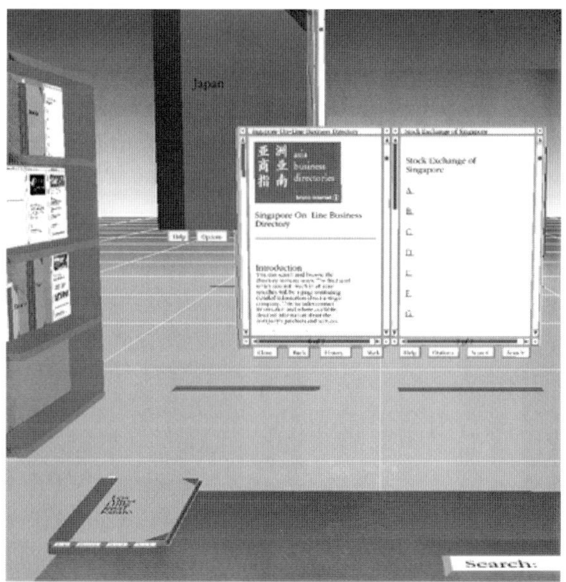

5.11 Escaping the bounded, flat, virtual desktop: a virtual book of web pages (taken from shelf at left in this view) in a navigable set of rooms, using Xerox *Web Forager*

enter by passing through that doorway. In this way a better perception is constructed of being in the data. This is what happens in *Myst.*

The idea of pictorial perspective used in virtual buildings (or islands) may be generalized: we can move about any abstract space, such as a semantic network of words arranged in space, according to the principle that our point of interest occupies most of our vision and reveals the most detail, and related points in the web recede logarithmically in size and detail.[31]

Besides having different arrangements, then, access structures may employ different visual representations. Items might be represented as one-dimensional text names, two-dimensional icons, or at least text names presented in two-dimensional menus, two-dimensional views of three-dimensional space, three-dimensional objects themselves, three-dimensional projections of four-dimensional data structures, and so on. Selections might be made by typing, pointing, or "occupying." The last method might mean spatial navigation in an immersive interface, or some other combination of actions in some other multimodal format, such as simultaneously speaking and making a hand sign.

A visual access structure populated by objects, some of which are tools, creates a new logical framework for human-computer interaction. In this world, where you are in the same space as your tools and your artifacts, the need for other interaction frameworks such as command names or graphical menus diminishes. Children's software such as *Silly Noisy House* (1993) has explored this possibility and created what we may call "randomly interactive" worlds. Working in such a world is well suited to that basic form of learning in which we poke at things to see what happens. It also lets menus go the way of punch cards.

Rich information spaces resemble well-directed theatrical productions in their appeal to our imagination. As such we may recognize them as elements of social framing—something that is practical even without visual representation. Collaborative systems such as public-access bulletin boards do this with their chat rooms. Of course denser representations can yield much more verisimilitude. The more intervening states, the more continuity used to assist assimilation when moving between neighboring states, the more cross-modal reinforcement (e.g., with audio) and the more detail that comes forth only when we focus on something, the easier it will become to develop not only rich mental models, but also skillful navigation and manipulation of increasingly abstract conceptions. *Myst* demonstrated this very well, too, with its tectonic representation of logical puzzles. Mental models are not just static; they function. That is, they represent not only configurations but also dynamics. Through motions, they reveal structure and mechanism. Thus a mental model can represent how it actually works, or is set up.

Imagine searching for an identity or structure by which to give a concept form. Designers and craftspeople tend to do this well, and we call this vision. One might argue that craft involves using a medium to convey vision. In design, vision includes looking for a class of design solutions that is the best reflection of the class of design problem.

In language this art of analogy is known as metaphor. In the verbal realm, metaphor's implicit comparisons between the new and the familiar permeate our thinking. So too in design. So too in computing. Already, in everyday software, metaphors map logical structure with visual images, such as desktop, finger, spool, subscriber. Spreadsheets use the metaphor of a ledger; hypertext uses notecards; training software uses guided tours; games use rooms. But throughout a more general range of software, no metaphor has been more common than that of the tool.

Tool as Metaphor, Medium as Structure

The tool metaphor provides visible form and physical action to a logical operation. As discussed in chapter 3, a tool helps us to identify and take hold of a process. Any tool's purpose is immediately apparent. When using it, nothing occurs out of our reach or sight. Sets of related tools provide incremental differences in function. Workspaces or toolkits lay out many tools within easy reach.[32]

We are now in a position to examine more carefully the relation between the software tool metaphor and the hand-held pointing device. To begin, recall that the tool metaphor dictates a temporary role for the general hand-held pointing device. In current implementations, the computer represents this role visually by substituting the generic cursor with a specific icon. Like a physical tool, this icon may include some measuring or controlling devices. Besides these, the tool defines its role with pointer motion, which is not necessarily analogous to tool actions. For example, double click means pick, and holding down and dragging means move. Using more sophisticated devices, such as a multibutton mouse (or a lexicon of dataglove signals), increases the number of definable motions.

As a part of giving scope to pointing, a tool metaphor must construct a process identity. To do this it needs a symbolic representation (normally a visual icon) plus a means of application that affects data entities in a manner somehow visibly related to the presence of the tool. Warren Wake has noted that for the metaphor to hold, the tool must be a coherent entity; it must be applied to the objects of one's work (and not to some supporting framework such as a menu or a window); it must not have any side effects outside its visual proximity. "Merely performing a task does not imply we have a tool."[33]

A well-constructed tool metaphor relieves cognitive load. A currently selected tool helps define what tasks are possible. It expresses an unambiguous context for action, both relative to the purposes of tools and toward a particular kind of artifact. It frames an operation (which the software may support with many unseen settings), and picking up another tool becomes a quick and intuitive way to change frames of reference.

But it is only a metaphor. A tool should have some affinity to a conventional process, but not become unnecessarily bound by limitations of its physical analog. (No need, for example, to be able to spill coffee on the desktop.) It should not prevent us from improvising alternative metaphors. Lakoff observed that "If metaphors are a means of learning, then people will build their own when necessary."[34] Composite metaphors are a commonplace outside software, Wake suggests. Adjusting, customizing, and linking tools need to become routine in software, much like improvising jigs and setups in mechanical shops. Of course there is no need for sharpening, and no washing up. What then does being tool-like suggest? Sometimes there is no clear distinction between tool and medium. Sometimes found objects serve as tools. We might then say there are clusters of meanings. We have defined tools by the continuity of guided action. When does such usage emerge?

Despite widespread reliance on direct manipulation, genuine tool metaphors are underdeveloped. We need to infer the usage of a tool from prior experience with other tools. We discover new uses for old tools. We often combine tools. We understand our tools within the contexts of our workplaces. For example, many people keep a mental model of their work space. A particular office or shop that appears a total mess to visitors might be the perfect access structure to its various contents for its resident. But move a tool to a different (albeit equally visible) location, and it might as well have disappeared.

Structural mental models of context also underlie the experience of a medium. If you want to understand a process as something more than a sequence of steps to follow, you have to know something about the context. This context might include your intent, as well as your grasp of some tool-programmer's assumptions. It must include extrinsic factors such as a system configuration and network environment. Intrinsically, it depends on the use of a specific data structure. You need to know that a particular symbolic record is being created within a particular logical environment, and this should help you build it.

Creating a sense of medium especially depends on developing a dense structure of contexts for the operation of tools. As we shall explore later on, a medium conveys a sense of possibilities through the continuous probing and action of a tool. This, too, becomes a mental model—a design world—and part of the challenge of effective software design is to impart a convincing representation of such worlds of action, in such a manner that we become willing participants.

This suggests that medium is ultimately more important than tools, and that participatory mental models are the way forward from the current overreliance on tool-based graphical user interfaces. Interactivity authority Brenda Laurel advanced this position in *Computers as Theater* (1991). Laurel asserted that "knowing what is going on in this representation is ultimately more important than knowing what is going on in the computer itself." Within the representation, participation may involve defining presentation of oneself as well as choosing one's prosthetic tools. This is especially pertinent in distributed, shared environments. Moving about from medium to medium amounts to exchanging one set of roles and constraints for another. The computer, then, is a "web of representational contexts for action."[35]

This suggests the need for a mental model of a digital repertoire. In form-giving media, we must imagine design worlds; in social media (including many manifestations of the internet), we must imagine participatory worlds; and in presentation media, we must imagine narrative worlds. But these are interrelated. Understanding the digital repertoire requires us to construct mental models of design, participation, and presentation, together. To move elements of a project, representations of yourself, or pieces of communication from one medium and representational context to another, and then another, is an inherent advantage of digital media.

We will explore how the constraints of a particular medium define its usefulness, especially relative to similar media. We will see how the increasing density of notation enabled by computing gives more symbolic activities the feel of a medium. We must remember that improved capacity for the hand and gesture are on the horizon. We might see a proliferation of possibilities, just in ways of working and interaction. Between the virtual environments described above and capacities for speech, gesture, three-dimensional sound, not to mention other forthcoming possibilities such as ubiquitous computing, it is difficult to imagine that a single, unified approach to human-computer interaction will hold sway much longer.[36]

When computing comes to mean something different for each of us, there can no longer be any doubt about the role of personal practices in the configuration and use of computing environments. We will have our own sets of representational contexts, just as much as we have our own offices, libraries, and workshops. The digital craftsperson is therefore likely to master a repertoire of media just as much as a repertoire of tools—indeed the two will be closely interrelated. Michael Polanyi predicted this extension: "We are faced here with the general principle by which our beliefs are anchored in ourselves. Hammers and probes can be replaced by intellectual tools; think of any interpretive framework and particularly of the formalism of the hard sciences. I am not speaking of the specific assertions which fill the textbooks, but of the suppositions which underlie the method by which these assertions are arrived at."[37]

No two personal practices built on computing tools need be alike. More than the technologies themselves, accumulations of personal knowledge will influence what we do with the new digital tools, and how well we do it.

6 Constructions

Think of a digital artifact, shaped by software operations, made up of data assemblies. Although lacking in physical substance, it is a thing with an appearance, spatiality, structure, workable properties, and a history. Although it does not bear the mark of someone's hands, as a clay pot does, neither is it the product of a standardized industrial process, like an aluminum skillet. It is individual, and reveals authorship at the level of its internal organization. It is unique, for although flawless copies can be made, nobody is going to make another just like it unless by copying. It is abstract: a symbolic structure, a workable construction, in a digital medium, showing the effects of manipulation by software tools.

This artifact is not a unitary piece like a carving, but a cumulative composition more like a work of architecture. Like a traditionally made form, it represents the results of many simple repetitive actions, where one move enables the next. We build up digital artifacts one step a time, one piece on top of another, with what is already there affecting what is to come. If there is an art to visual computing, then, it is at least partly in making cumulative moves within the medium of abstract constructions.

6.1 A complex digital artifact: a city model built by indirect constructions plus direct manipulation

Like knowledge representation or interaction design, the theory and practice of formal constructions constitutes a substantial discipline, or more accurately, multiple disciplines, including architecture, animation, music, manufacturing, multimedia publication, web design—a growing list. If computers let us operate on abstractions as though they were things, or take part in representations as though they were spaces, it follows that formal constructions should have widespread application. Presumably the most developed and representative case will remain computer-aided design, in which form is an end in itself. To complement the preceding chapter's broad sweep over interaction design, here let us probe deeper into the case of computer-aided design.

Software as Mechanism

Software is designed for particular purposes. You might think of a data structure as a framework for building up statements about a design. A particular set of data types establishes a set of elements and operations intended for a specific application. Like the grain of a material, this repertoire of data constructions shapes our work on digital artifacts. It

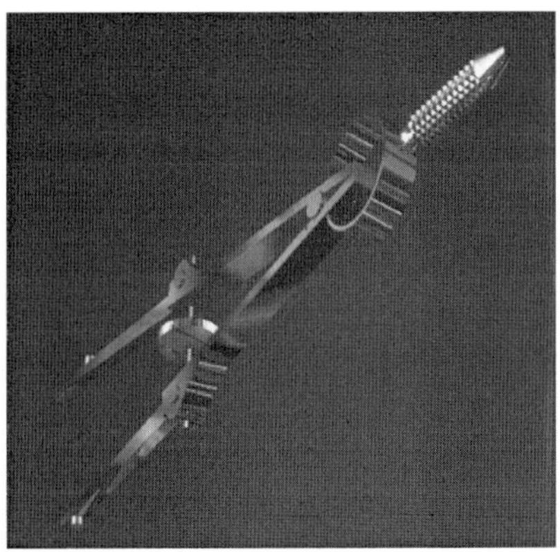

6.2 A mechanism for translating and constraining motions

determines what kinds of entities are available for placement, how to combine them, and how to interrelate them.[1] More significantly, it is constructed of composite operations, which add leverage to our simple moves. Like the gears and levers of a physical apparatus, a chain of geometric constructions may translate our simple gestures into motions at different shapes or scales. In this manner, indirect constructions can modify the effect of the hand-held pointing device: they might somehow translate, amplify, or repeat our driving action; they might trigger related actions. You may recognize these various properties as those of a *mechanism.* In this sense it is quite reasonable to refer to a computer as a machine. More generally, if any abstract construction can be shown to be independent of its technical implementation, we might refer to it as a virtual machine.[2]

Some constructions operate on collections. In software we define general types of objects and then obtain particular instances of them. This requires some logic of similarity and selection on our part, plus some representation of families and sets in the technology. Working in this manner overcomes a common failing of direct manipulation at too low a level: far too many people work by making one object at a time, without a thought to how this next object might be an instance or transformation of another existing object. To paraphrase Aristotle, one of the most basic acts of human intelligence is to discover that *this* is one of *those.* For example, in drawing software there is no need to work line by line—the idea is to identify patterns and classifications. There is no need to specify every element of a composition when higher-level descriptions can generate them automatically. This can be as simple as a copy-paste transform operation, or as complex as resolving a series of interrelated formal prototypes.

Constructive processes can appear as objects themselves. For example, an animated tree can visualize a file structure. The tree represents a hierarchy as an explicit, editable graph, and such representation helps build new tool metaphors by providing opportunities for direct manipulation of schematic diagrams. More complex trees are possible: for example, animators use articulation trees to perform "inverse kinematics," which is the process of calculating how a constrained motion hierarchy such as an arm can reach a desired position such as pointing a finger.

The potential for software-as-mechanism invites us to think about the geometry of translated and leveraged motions. CAD offers the most developed case of using mechanical constructions to generate higher-level descriptions of artifacts, but this is only one example. Hypertext compilation, audio composition, illustration—even personal information management—all rely on specialized constructions that lend practicality and leverage to the manipulation of notational structures. When you drag an event around on your calendar, that is one thing, but if you propagate it across all Tuesdays for the next three months, or add a new meeting by copying and transforming a similar, earlier meeting (rather then having to enter all details again), that is another. Call it indirect manipulation.

Indirect Manipulation

Although "indirect" implies a loss of direct analogy between manual motion and tool action, "manipulation" still indicates the controllable action of skillfully handling objects set before us. That is, we are not simply referring to all computer operations that are not direct manipulation—for example,

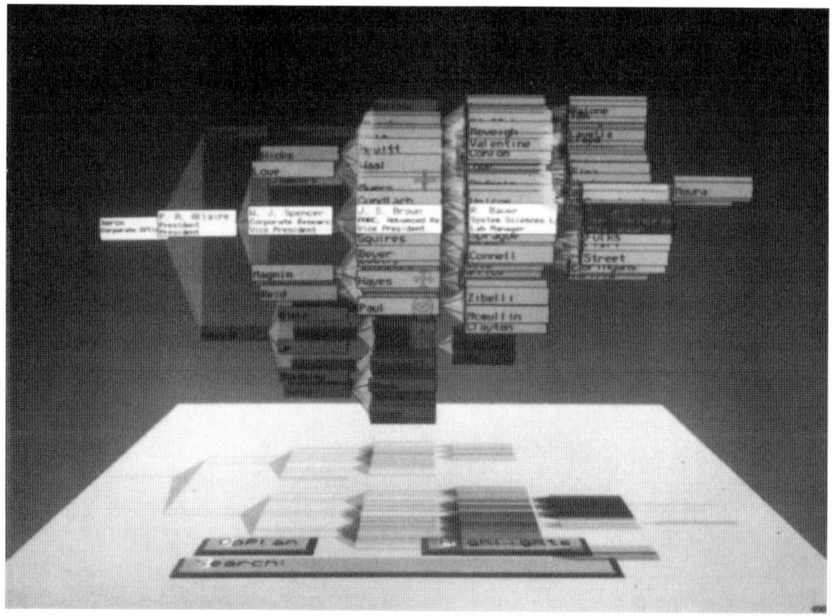

6.3 Abstraction as thing: animated cone tree for manipulating file hierarchy in realtime, using Xerox *Information Visualizer*

scientific calculations performed offscreen. Indirect manipulation does not so much eliminate the role of the hand as give it leverage. As with the use of sophisticated machine tools, the results remain visible, and the impetus remains our own.

Indirect manipulation demonstrates unprecedented applications of software more inherently than direct manipulation, for it is not so prone to mimic the usage of corresponding traditional media. It engages the hand, but modifies its action into an abstract, not necessarily geometrical operation. You may use software for layout and publication, or for time-coded multimedia arrangement, rather than CAD, but the principles to be inferred from our representative case should be essentially the same. Using constructions, you can establish specialized realms of possibilities, in which you can define whole classes of designs rather than isolated artifacts. Thus by means of indirect manipulations, you can improve your power to explore particular design worlds.

We have seen that direct manipulation is the great advantage of traditional craft. Direct contact of the hand with the material allows playful, humane expression. The quality of handicrafts obviously demands practiced skill, but it also depends quite a bit on the appropriateness and condition of the individual hand-held tool. This criterion is unlikely to be surpassed in electronic media—so unlikely that propositions about electronic craft remain easy to dismiss. However, new genres of work may emerge not only by emulating the strengths of tradition, but also by mitigating weaknesses.

The perennial limitation on craft has been the strength of the human body. No human being can summon the strength to work some materials, such as ingots of steel. None can sustain the power to mass produce an everyday artifact, like a glass bottle, at a practical rate. Moreover, for tasks within human capacity, the exertion of strength normally preempts the application of finer skills. "Brute force" implies a lack of elegance, even in abstract work such as programming.

The twin responses to this weakness are of course the machine and the engine. Recall that the two are distinguished by their roles with power: the machine amplifies and directs power; the engine simply generates power at beyond-human magnitudes from latent sources (i.e., fuel). The former is our focus here, for it is the very embodiment of construction; the latter is not of interest except as a remote supply of electricity. The former can accomplish much without the latter, and indeed did so for centuries in the guise of what we now call the simple machine. Consider the block and tackle. The very form of this machine reveals its purpose of amplifying a comfortable tug on a rope to the point where it can lift a very heavy object: the mechanical advantage is basically equal to the number of strands supporting the load.

This mechanism is at the same time a response to another inherent manual weakness: limited inability to combine tools. The hand can only hold one thing at a time, and the craftsperson has only two hands. Artisans constructed simple constraints like vices, clamps, or fences to mitigate this limitation, but electronic designers and fabricators have already surpassed these in many ways. The many constraints, locks, and links available in several software genres, particularly CAD systems, represent a fundamental advance on an age-old weakness of craft.

Making Moves

Recall Diderot's definition of craft: simple, intelligent, repetitive motions—mechanical operations. If you look at somebody using a geometric modeling system, where a skilled person might accumulate as many as a hundred steps in a single minute, many aspects of this definition fit. The work is habitual. The hands are always active, and their moves give a cadence to the work. The motions work the material incrementally: no one master stroke affects the work so much as the accumulation and combination of many routine moves. Adding elements, moving things around, configuring guides, assigning properties, embedding or combining, and sometimes backing up or starting over all again, occur in a quick series of steps. This repetition involves some tedium, but perhaps also some contemplation. Knowledge of these actions is internalized, and attention is directed higher, to intent.

We all know an example of carefully synchronized simple actions, and that is driving. There are not too many options: step on the gas, turn the wheel, etc. Using just these few moves is enough to get you where you are going, if you repeat enough of them, and provided you synchronize them properly. Otherwise you end up in the ditch. The car itself makes moves (such as piston cycles) that amplify simple human operations such as pressing on pedals. It rules out all but a few operations: pushing forward on the rim of the steering wheel does nothing, for example—only pulling it left or right has any effect. Many moves are guided: a stick shift has only five or six possible positions, for instance, and it cannot be moved at all until the clutch is applied. All of these controls are widgets of sorts: rigid mechanical devices that translate geometric motion into direct control of some useful variation on the system.

Software abounds with virtual widgets, with necessary sequences of control, and therefore with analogies to driving. But if even such a simple system as a car must be learned, then a more complex mechanism such as a CAD system might take much time and effort to master. Synchronizing its countless moves is a highly specialized skill, as any frustrated beginner will tell you. Subjugating so many synchronized moves to a creative intent is a yet greater skill. Constructions affect how one might develop tactics of work. Attaining such a condition makes working the software somewhat like playing an instrument—and indeed, skillful players develop distinctive working styles.

Moreover, with computers you must not only learn so many moves, but also come to understand the state of the system in terms of a higher-level abstract context that it gives to those moves. As has been emphasized in the previous chapter, effective mental modeling distinguishes more masterful activity from semiskilled rote operations. Mental modeling gives the ability to choose moves, rather than following instructions. In the previous chapter we examined time frames, tool metaphors, and pointing strategies; here let us explore the symbolic contexts and underlying constructions of the entities being manipulated.

For example, a familiar drawing program such as *AutoCAD* works with traditional Euclidean construction. The software introduces algebraic calculations for what were traditionally graphical constructions performed by means of instruments such as compasses and triangles. Not only does this improve the accuracy of these constructions, but also it makes them very practical to perform in three dimensions.

Consider the textbook example of constructing the midpoint of a straight line.[3] Euclid's elegant solution is first to construct two arcs of equal radius, one about each endpoint, and then to construct a line passing though the intersections of those arcs to locate the midpoint of the line. The computational solution, which can be executed in a fraction of a second, is to calculate the midpoint by taking the average of the x-coordinates and the y-coordinates of the two endpoints of the line. This solution is not only faster, but also more easily generalized to multiple subdivisions of the line—in fifths, for example—and to subdivisions of curves. Furthermore it may be applied to a line at any orientation in space. Thus, for example, it makes it very easy to draw a triangle between the quarterpoints of three perpendicular edges of a cube. If you were to work this example in software such as *AutoCAD,* you would perceive such a midpoint construction as a modifier on the motion of your hand. You would simply instruct the system to look for a midpoint, point anywhere at the line, and your pointer would automatically snap to the appropriate location on the object. Such constraint simultaneously improves the precision and the speed of the system (whereas in traditional drafting those two qualities may have been opposed). This alone makes a drafting system a very powerful tool.

Imagine a digital drawing as a mechanism. Its parts are generated from a basic repertoire of shapes, constructions, and transformations. For example, constructions might include subdivisions like above, parallels, perpendiculars, concentric curves, fit curves, breaks, trims, extensions, angular constructions, and alignments. An expert could easily elaborate this set by combining elementary constructions into more specialized composite constructions, much as a mathematician might concatenate complex functions from simpler ones. Basic transformations would include the ability to translate, rotate, scale, or reflect shapes or groups of shapes, and again an expert could combine these operations quite elegantly. Additional transformations such as stretching and shearing would change the shapes themselves, and not just their size or placement. Like initial inputs for shape constructions, any of these geometric transformations can be fixed by existing geometry. For example, you could rotate a rectangle until it matched the orientation of a line. You could scale a circle until it passed through a particular vertex of a nearby triangle. As you executed these transformations in realtime, you would experience them as geometrically constrained motion, that is, as mechanism.

The result is a qualitative change: much as word processing is more than automated typing, line processing is more than automated drafting. The latter difference is greater because the activity is more complex. Analogously we could refer to three-dimensional geometric modeling as *form processing.* Digital form processing differs from both traditional drawing and traditional model making, neither of which it automates or replaces so much as complements and transforms. For example, spline surface constructions introduce new capacity to sculpt complex curvatures of form by means of a transferable, reusable notation. Solid constructions introduce the union, intersection, and subtraction of forms. Coordinate hierarchies enable articulated rigid motions. Cumulative geometric constructions are the essence of the generative medium of geometric modeling.

Structures that relate objects and moves add still more power. The simplest of these is classification. Layers can organize sets of objects, and blocks or groups can create new composite objects, making it possible to manipulate them as single entities. Positional constraints increase accuracy by means a simple as snapping a new object onto an existing one, or as complex as resolving the combined effect of alignments, displacements, size limits, and other dimensional relations. Generative constructions can amplify any move made on a single object to affect many other related objects. For example, refine one window on a facade and all others of its kind automatically reflect the change. Or change the minimum thickness of a thin-shelled cast form and have all the dimensions adjusted automatically.

As mentioned in the discussion of interaction design, software widgets (the most common example of which is the slider bar) transpose linear gestures into manipulations of nongeometric variables or simultaneous geometric variables. Examples haven been taken from geometry, but the same would be true for sounds, animated text titles, or any other established vocabulary. By now it should be clear that indirect but continuously controlled actions offer great leverage on sophisticated formal structures.

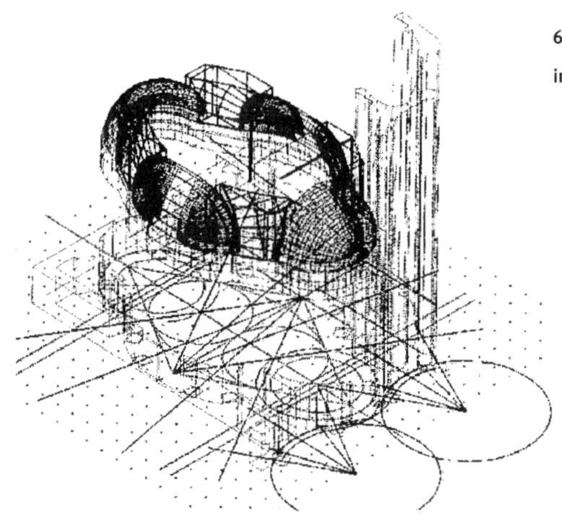

6.4 Extending Euclidean constructions into three dimensions

Virtual Artifacts

Some possibility of craft should be obvious enough within the accumulation of constructions, but how this applies to intangible symbolic structures requires more explanation. We have seen how a notational scheme comprises finite, articulable elements, and therefore how a digital artifact is composed of discrete data records. These records might be characters in a text, sounds in a musical sequence, tones in an image, forms in a model, frames in a movie, or any such fundamental building blocks. Their content gets defined by the symbolic structures of the software with which they are made, and their accumulation gives rise to virtual artifacts.

Computer files have normally been treated as documents, but now the increasing richness of digital representations invites us to understand some of them as artifacts. A document is a symbolic record of intellectual action. Documents are held as proof of things. They are business communications. Many notations are documents, and most documents are notations.

An artifact has history. Its form has some fixity, and intrinsically shows something about where it came from and how it was made. Where a document is to be read, an artifact is to be handled. If a document depends more on a context for its meaning, an artifact may have obvious or intrinsic function or significance. An artifact has, to use Benjamin's term, aura. It is a unique accumulation of responses to material imperfections. It is a material record of tool usage. Something about its authorship or origins is inescapably bound up in it.

Some pieces of digital production are both objects and notations. They can be both handled and read. They have both intrinsic sensory significance and coded intellectual meaning. They are both implements and records. The concept of a virtual artifact needs more development and defense than we have known how to give it so far, but it is not absurd.

The question of durability remains unsolved. Electronic productions vanish—they are ephemeral. Digital media also proliferate versions because software makes it so easy to save each stage while we endlessly rework, revise, and reuse pieces. Playback and storage media change quite often, as do the design programs and operating systems, and so even the best archival techniques fall far short of carving something in stone. Yet for all these problems, digital productions have their own kind of permanence. Copies proliferate, for one thing. Reconstructions are easier—in fact every instance is reconstructed from a bit code every time.

Although digital objects are coded and reproducible, they are not trivial, obvious, or conveniently reproducible other than by direct copying. Anyone who has tried to radically change a detailed geometric model knows this quite well. The structuring effort that goes into a digital production is not easily modified or replaced. This is not just a matter of time and money: talented execution of continuous processes produces unique artifacts. Objects have a grain, as if they might as well have cracks and wrinkles. This grain consists of internal hierarchies and classifications, external formats and displays, and accumulations of specifically modified generic formal vocabulary elements. Understanding these constructive frameworks is at the heart of digital form-giving expertise. As in conventional practices it helps to have a good mental model of the underlying structure of the medium.

Constructive Vocabularies of Form

Entities

Two chapters ago, we noted the basis of treating notations as things. Abstract data types encapsulate their own public interfaces, and the resulting objects become quite direct to handle. For example, an abstract transition such as a diagonal screen wipe in a two-dimensional animation program becomes an object. You can drag it around, copy it, assign conditions to it, substitute another transition into the circumstances of this one, and so on—and that is how you orchestrate transitions.

In computer-aided design, naturally the objects are geometric entities, such as cones, cylinders, or cubes. Technically, any form that is visible, spatially continuous, finite, and used as a unit of construction may be defined as an entity, but a parsimonious system will provide just a few fundamental elements at an appropriate level of abstraction. For example it is more convenient to represent a surface in terms of faces rather than edges, and it is sometimes possible to describe those faces in terms of a swept profile. It is more elegant to define a rectangle than to draw four separate lines every time, and to the software this is a difference between one entity and four.

If represented at the right level, almost any element of a composition can be specified as a variation on one of just a few a essential constructions. For example, a complex but radially symmetric object such as a bottle may be described as a simple surface of revolution. Different bottles may be obtained simply by manipulating the profile.

The fundamental process for generating a particular type of entity normally has a corresponding representation in an interface, which constitutes a low-level construction normally involving direct manipulation, for example, placing and sizing a cylinder. Like tools, such graphic primitives come with moves by which they are applied. (Indeed, tools and primitives sometimes get conflated, as in "rectangle tool.") Highlights, grips or handles placed on provisional states of an instance indicate available moves. A "rubber band" vector, stretching from an established starting point to the continuously varying position of the mouse in search of a suitable ending point, becomes the best way to draw a line. More sophisticated constructions, such as spline curves and surfaces, generalize this principle by interpolated forms according to independent control points, like puppets on strings. This often makes it easier to manipulate the control points instead of the form. That in turn makes it easier to place the construction in explicit relationship to other objects.

Also like tools, formal constructors come in sets, members of which differ incrementally in their functions. For example, a set of surface mesh constructions might offer differing degrees of curvature and continuity derivatives, the choice between which would depend on intended purpose of the model. Similarly in terrain surface modeling, triangulating from spot elevations would serve one purpose, and lofting from a regularized succession of evolving cross sections would serve another.

From Entity to Type

With the idea of formal types, we begin to make the jump from mechanical mastery to a more thoughtful kind of work. To begin, note that all entities made by a given primitive share a single data structure. The underlying representation of the primitive encodes an essential relation between particular dimensional variables. The entities share some essential qualities, but differ by some accidental qualities. The essential properties are inferred in the encoded relation of design variables, and the accidental properties are indicated by the arbitrary values given to those variables. This allows particular constructions to be adaptable to a wider variety of situations, which is especially useful for repeatable prototypes. For example, a spotlight prototype in a geometric rendering system defines an essential configuration of a directional cone of light to be added to the system's summation calculation of surface brightness and shadowing. Each light created from this prototype may have unique position, aim, intensity, color, beam width, etc.

This principle of type and transformation may be generalized by application to groups of entities. We can define a composite entity as an entity made out of other entities, all of which surrender their respective identities to the whole. For example, a truncated cone plus a cylinder with appropriate radius might make a useful, repeatable form—and one could designate this funnel as an entity type. Note that a composite entity encodes an inherent formal relation between its elements. All instances of this composite will share this essential relation.

If the entity dimensions and relations are fixed, the composite is treated as a block or a group. This enables a powerful indirect manipulation: revising the definition automatically updates all the instances.

If the entity relations are somehow variable, however, the composite is treated as a prototype. In this more sophisticated case, the definition includes variables according to which particular instances may differ. The selection of variables establishes a family of forms. This is accomplished by treating some of the entries in the composite construction's data structure as variables, and then specifying relations through which some of these variables are made dependent on others. The few independent parameters are made interactive, and inputs to them are resolved to calculate the values of the dependent variables in order to create an instance of the composite entity. Once a suitable set of relations is established, one can create any number of formally similar but geometrically distinct entities, without need to draw or model them directly, but simply by giving different inputs to a few parameters. Here then is a fundamental mechanism of indirect manipulation. We can define geometric parameterization as the imposition of constrained relationships on the elements of constructed form, and parametric variation as the exploration of the formal types implicit in those relationships.

In geometric modeling, parameters may be positions, orientations, or counts (such as how many subdivisions), but most often they are dimensions. Dimensional parametric variation is a powerful addition to the repertoire of operations, for unlike simple geometric transformations it can revise the internal compositions of composite forms. For example, one

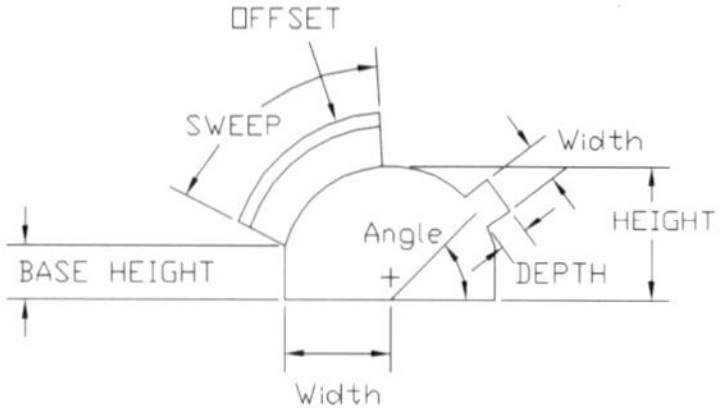

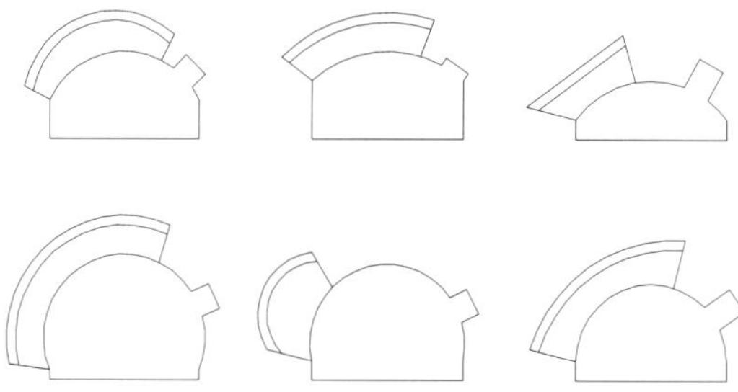

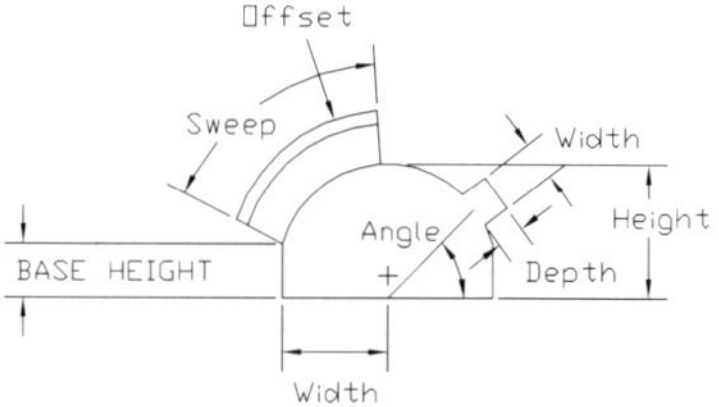

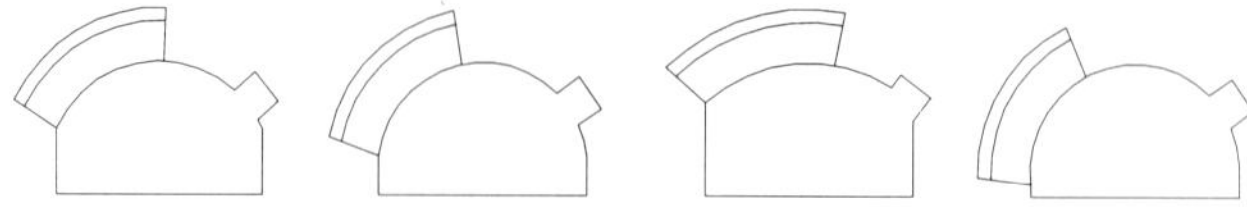

6.5 Type and transformation: a parametric object. Two sets of variations, one with many independent variables, and one with a single independent variable

might describe a teapot in terms of just a few dimensions such as bottom radius, overall height, shell curvature, handle size, handle orientation, and spout length. Other dependent geometric measures would be calculated from these given values for these independent variables, and from the results a specific teapot would be determined. Other teapots could be obtained by altering any or all of the design variables. Each of these would be an instance of the prototype. Some instances might be more appropriate than others, but all would share an implicit essence resulting from the fixed relation of dimensional dependencies. As the parameterization yields a family of objects, in one sense it is not so many designs, but one.

Realtime Transformations

The great advantage of parametric objects and relations is that you can supply values to the independent design variables systematically. For example, arguments given as input to parameters may be taken from the output of other processes, such as orders or analyses. This in turn may depend on essential variables in production processes, such as allowable size range and rotational degrees of freedom in machining. Within established ranges, design arguments may be varied incrementally to generate large numbers of parametric variations from which to identify suitable versions. Given enough processing power, you can accomplish such variation quasi-continuously in realtime.

Consider how this happens. Manual action on one axis (such as a slider widget) can be mapped to changing the state of a particular design dimension. Actions in two or three dimensions might be measured on principal axes in order to vary multiple parameters simultaneously. Different widgets might construct different meanings of an input gesture. We could develop a mental model of a design space: if the cross product of all possible variations produces an abstract n-dimensional space of designs, where n is the total number of parameters, then manipulation of any single parameter value constitutes a vector through that space. Because these realtime design excursions in mental models occur along single dimensions in design space, we could call them "design vectors." Nicholas Negroponte once amusingly referred to them as "design space Harleys."[4]

By whatever name, realtime transformations have a distinct advantage over the discontinuous iterations of trial and error more typical of traditional processes such as drawing on tracing paper. You will get to explore more states, and instead of having to imagine each state before you model it, you might *discover* a state while you continuously manipulate a particular design variable. Furthermore, some manipulations to a single variable can gain quite a bit of formal leverage through geometric constructions. The richer these dependencies—the better the parameterization—the more powerful the design variations. Imagine a case where a whole design is reduced to a single variable, like the size of a jacket, but where other dependent qualities come forth depending on size as you manipulate that single variable. Realtime transformations increase the importance of having a good eye. You must be on the lookout for things to try, and configurations to retain. To accomplish this you must have some inner vision, perhaps not yet sufficiently literal that you could simply draw it up, but adequately formed that you might be able to *recognize* formal configurations that embody its essence. Thus the mind's eye couples with realtime structural manipulations. This happens especially well on the computer, but it is essentially the same process by which a traditional craftsman continuously, incrementally, coaxes a physical material into visual or structural equivalence with an inarticulable vision.

The ability to explore a continuum of design states represents a fundamental advance toward using the computer as a medium. In some cases this malleability may be sufficient to compensate for the lack of physicality. At least this has been the initial justification of virtual artifacts. In most cases, more highly iterative design exploration will lend insight into the way the a design problem has been conceived. Therefore computer-aided design is largely about expressing design problems computationally—about strategies for manipulating symbolic structures. Thus there is a twofold approach to design. First, one may frame the problem, then one may explore the domain of possibilities that one has established. Geometric

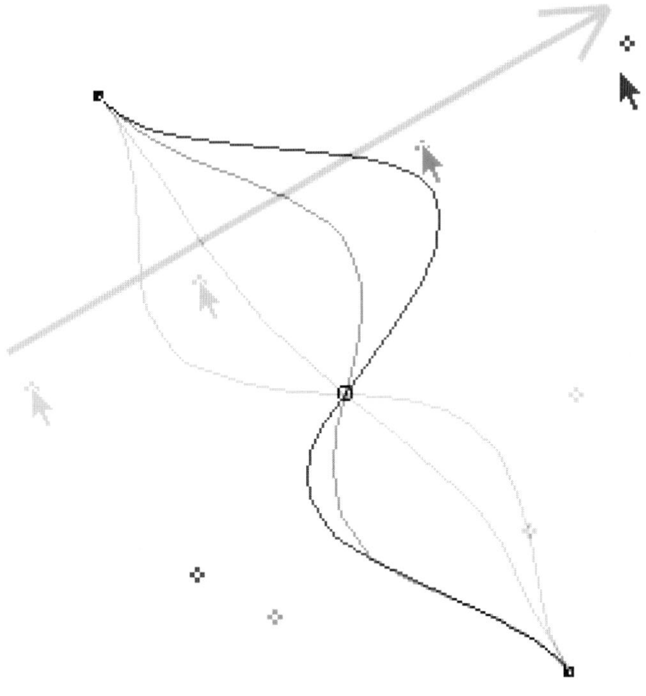

6.6 Realtime parametric variation of a spline curve

constructions are just one example. Other possibilities for parametric variation might be as simple as choosing a color or as complex as optimizing an engineering solution.

Because explorations themselves depend on how much information the computer can deliver in realtime, faster computers will allow us richer explorations. Not only does this let us develop and explore more sophisticated parameterizations, but also it allows for better interfaces to those explorations. Because discovery is so important to the process of exploring variations, and discovery benefits from rich sensory and conceptual contexts (serving our design vision), we are in a position to develop methods

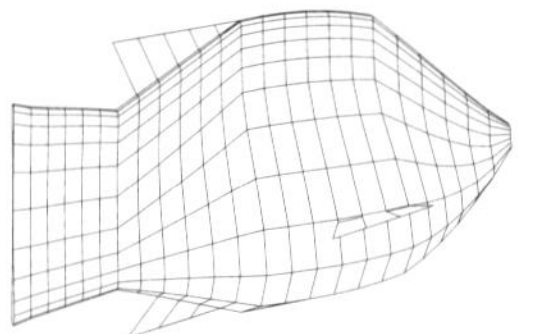

6.7 Near-realtime variables in the the lofting process: different scaling, profile displacement, profile substitution, profile tilt, profile spacing

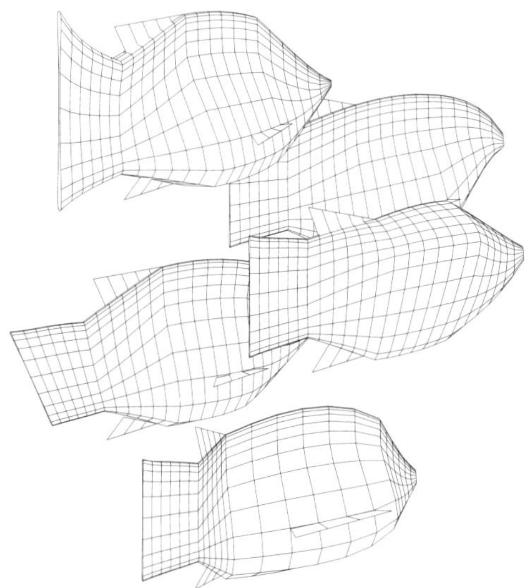

whose fluidity more closely resembles that of a workable material than that which we expect of static traditional notations.

Relational Modeling

Although processing speed alone will continue to increase the fluidity of the geometric modeling medium, additional responsiveness can result from richer data structures built to take advantage of increasingly powerful computers. More sophisticated CAD software has the capacity to store and reinterpret parameterizations.[5] Simpler systems that only store lists of discrete geometric objects cannot do this: even if they can create objects by parametric procedures, they cannot vary them afterward, but require that instances be remade, which process includes reentry of values for all the parameters. Storing the parameterizations can alleviate this problem. Stored parameterization also provides the ability to look up the state of one entity's parameters while creating an instance of another, which permits the exploration of relations between the shape or position of several compositional elements. In some cases where the value of a variable is independent, its range may be dependent, for example. Thus the range of one parameter may be subject to the values of other parameters. This is known as constraint.

Relational modeling, built on the use of parametric modeling and constraints, is the most powerful manner of indirectly manipulating form today. It has appeared only in the 1990s because it is computationally intensive and, in some cases, procedurally problematic. One wicked problem is that relations can be transitive, that is, one relation depends on another, which depends on another, and so on. Computational requirements for checking long chains of constraint at each cycle of a realtime variation are often prohibitive. Delays of several minutes for a single move are not unusual. Moreover, procedural problems may arise from inconsistent relations. Implicit inconsistencies embedded in chains of relations are notoriously difficult to anticipate. Most inconsistency is a case of overconstraint. However, both underconstrained and overconstrained situations are commonly quite difficult to resolve without complicated interventions.

Software engineers often mitigate these consistency problems by concentrating on particular, frequently used classes of practical formal relations. Specific parametric forms having specific constraints are implemented as specialized constructions known as features.[6] These are common in manufacturing (e.g., blends between fillets meeting at a corner, countersinks centered on bores, and so on). As recurrent conditions demanding designers' attention and characterizing classes of production problems, some such feature constructions bear an interesting similarity to the contents of traditional artisans' pattern books.

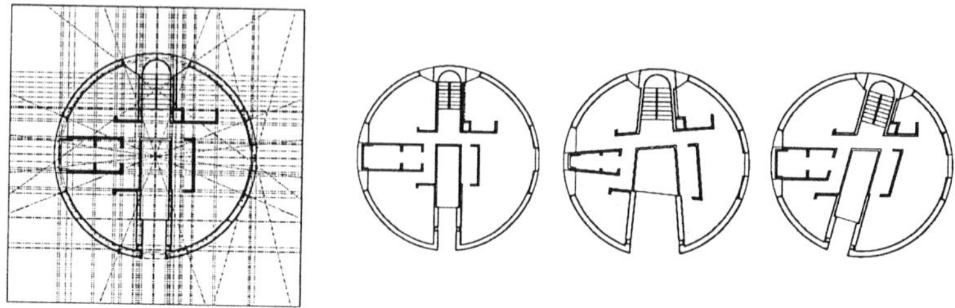

6.8 Relational modeling: single-step variations on a composition produced by solving constraint relations

Although standard features can anticipate only a few classes of relations, a generalized capacity for constraints can accommodate many more. So long as relations do not accumulate into long or interconnecting chains of relations, software can manage arbitrary constructions based on specific relations such as alignment, proportion, spacing, or concentricity. This condition means that relations must be exclusive if conflicting relations are not to arise. A single object may not be placed in relation to more than one other object, or when multiple relations are necessary, they must be given explicit prioritization. For example, consider three parallel lines that are also constrained to fall within a given rectangular boundary. Rotating one line will rotate the other two to preserve the alignment relation, but this may cause the outermost line to fall outside the rectangle. Depending on prioritization, this operation could cause the outermost line to be eliminated, or it could prohibit the rotation from reaching such magnitude.

Constraint of position, orientation, and alignment is of course a defining property of mechanisms. The components of a mechanism have degrees of freedom. For example, the two plates of a hinge have freedom to rotate about one axis only, and not to slide at all. Mechanisms construct motion transfers in hierarchical series, like the drive train in your car. The study of constrained motion in serial mechanisms is known as kinematics. In essence, this discipline studies motion hierarchies of rigid bodies.

Motion hierarchies resolve compound local coordinate systems, like the moon revolving around the earth revolving around the sun. Motion analysis employs an abstraction known as kinematic chains, which are graph representations based on degrees of freedom at the joints of serial linkages. Some contemporary animation software represents kinematic chains as articulation trees, which may themselves become visible, transformable, and edited by direct manipulation. Alternatively, articulation trees may be modified indirectly, by establishing the position of an outer node of the chain, and this is known as inverse kinematics. Either case is a good example of how software is capable of converting abstractions into workable things.

Motion hierarchies present a clear case of mechanism, but many other abstract structures may be mapped as chains. For example, spatial audio presents clear possibilities of hierarchical linkage that are currently under research. Some audio designers use graphic software to manipulate diagrams that control structurally equivalent sound compositions.[7] Some multimedia designs produce form and audio together: isomorphic doubles. Some allow the equivalency relation to change at human impetus—they let us drive the multimedia mapping. Such multimodal structures revive the nineteenth-century poetic notion of sensory synthesis known as *synaesthesia.* Huysmans' famous olifactory organ anticipated the control of structural equivalencies from a keyboard. This fantasy may yet come true, but first smells will have to be expressed as symbolic constructions.

Fabrication Process Models

Consider an especially well developed case of equivalent symbolic constructions. Because better design has always been grounded in the realities of fabrication, obviously the most meaningful approach to parametric modeling is to take manufacturing criteria as the basis for variation and constraint. When this is accomplished properly in computer-aided design and manufacturing, the result is a close-coupled loop in which both design variations and fabrication process criteria can drive one another. The essence of this coupling is that the input to physical fabrication operations is symbolic, and the output from geometric derivations is tangible. Tightening this loop between conception and execution has the potential to reconcile some of the separation of design and fabrication that industrialization had previously imposed on craft. Thus, after two centuries of separation, the conception and the execution of everyday objects are once again in the same hands. (So to speak—hands actually touch less than ever before.) But to the same extent that visual computing affords personal work habits of improvisation, invention, and imagination (in at least some of the ways described in this book), computer-integrated manufacturing supports organizational endeavors of factories, form processing, and fabrications. The question, then, is whether the feedback and flexibility provided by CAD/CAM methods is sufficient to give a new sense of a medium and to somehow make up for still further removal from direct manual work.

The background for CAD/CAM comes from the broader disciplinary context of industrial engineering. Fabrication is just one component of this discipline. For example, although it was less significant in traditional artisanry, assembly, too, is most essential to industry. Indeed, the archetypal image of industry is the assembly line. This in turn demands attention to materials handling. Because it requires more force than finesse, and is often quite costly, materials handling has always been a good candidate for mechanization. This then leads to a fourth component: process planning. Process planners study the likes of line balancing and stoppage handling. Because monitoring no longer occurs intrinsically, quality assurance then emerges as another distinct component of industrial engineering. Where once it is was implicit in the hand and the eye of the artisan, testing today involves specially designed sensors and employs statistical methods quite dependent on computation.[8]

All of these aspects of industrial engineering can be approached as abstract constructions in CAD/CAM process models. Moreover, they may apply numerical methods: the Laplacian mathematics of system control models the elements of process in terms of transfer functions. Thus process models are not so much representations of static form as of dynamic response. As computation supports experimentation with these models, the fixed assembly line gives way to a reconfigurable collection of particular process cells corresponding to classes of processes. As a result, manufacturing becomes much more adaptable than in conventional mass production.

This is not to discount the power of CAD/CAM at the level of individual fabrication operations. If traditional industrial engineering was about the flow of material, CAD/CAM is more about the flow of information: design prototypes become design specifications, then process models, then machine instructions.

Examples of coded instructions may be found well before the twentieth century, particularly for discrete processes such as weaving. Even in continuous processes, such as cutting or milling, many setup operations were discrete steps suitable for explicit codes. Since long before CAD/CAM, manufacturers have been recording setups by a variety of means ranging from keeping simple handwritten notes on paper, to implementing push-button mechanical control systems, to sophisticated programming-by-demonstration.[9]

A numerical code (NC) program written directly for a specially designed machine, and read in through a punched tape, can reliably reproduce objects from information. Computer numerical control (CNC) has many advantages, including the ability to build libraries of program modules, the capacity to manage multiple processes, and the ability to visually simulate results. Moreover, these advantages may be powerfully combined and automated themselves.

Manufacturing engineering software dramatically improves the work of preparing for numerically controlled fabrication. Besides providing a better framework for NC programming, and distributed NC control, manufacturing software opens up additional information sources by importing geometric models prepared in CAD programs. Manufacturing software automatically converts design geometry to machine instructions; but the NC programmer must usually assist with interpreting unusual or ambiguous constructions. NC programmers have substantial knowledge of the equipment, materials, and processes. Thus the formulation of the CAD model can influence—and ought to reflect—the practicalities of the manufacturing process.

One way to do this is by rigorous parameterization. Besides providing an excellent framework for building models directly, CAD software may generate forms indirectly by procedurally constructing from design specifications. Dimensionally driven models, based on parameters set by engineering or business considerations, are the latest source of manufacturing data. Design parameterizations represent knowledge about types of forms to be generated in geometric modeling. They are a way of expressing design classifications computationally; they are an approach to indirect manipulation of design prototypes.

With initial industrialization, the structure of designs once embedded in the inarticulate traditions of craft migrated to the explicit process model. Now the process model, once solely the province of large-scale manufacturing, has migrated to personal computing. If the means of fabrication follow a similar trajectory, masters and their small ateliers may reappear.

Generative Prototypes

The potential for a production method combining the power of industry with the flexibility of artisanry demands a deeper understanding of formal types. Formal type reflects the identity of design conception as well as the nature of artifact production. It is the shared essence of several incidentally dissimilar objects. Not surprisingly, then, type is an expression of structure.

In craft, type transmits particular traditions; in industry, particular process formulations; in software, particular conceptual abstractions. In any of these forms, type is the carrier of past solutions to frequently encountered problems. The essence of type lies in its repeatability.

In industry, the prototype is adapted to the particulars of the job at hand, the variables are shaped by business and production. Any habitual combination of constructions that amplifies or constrains creative moves in some singular way may be considered a prototype. A prototype implies a fixity of form. It is for replication but not necessarily adaptation. Such prototypes state explicit relationships based on formal similarity and do not provide for emergent solutions.

For one thing, industrial prototypes are not so useful for representing structural or functional equivalence without formal similarity. This is to say that the idea of type could be more mutable. It could do more to support mental agility, such as discovery that *this* is one of *those.* This is well expressed in the nineteenth-century architectural theorist Quatrèmere de Quincy's coinage of *typology:* "The word 'type' represents not so much the image of a thing to be copied or perfectly imitated as the idea of an element that must itself serve as a rule for the model . . . The model, understood in terms of the practical execution of art, is an object that must be repeated such as it is; type, on the contrary, is an object according to which one can conceive works which do not resemble one another at all. Everything is precise and given in the model; everything is more or less vague in the type."[10]

Note the similarity to the structuralism of a century later. Quatrèmere was one of the first to suggest a universal grammar in place of a lexicon or taxonomy of forms in architecture. His was a system of formulation: artifacts are related by an underlying essence, even if their outward appearance is quite different. This formulation became more important than depiction as a means of description. Formulas, as abstract constructions, could be modified according to their intrinsic syntax in order to produce new objects outside of previous experience.

Although typology may initially seem constricting, with practice it becomes liberating. Typology and invention complement one another in the creative process. Invention consists of overcoming past schematizations embedded in the type. It involves criticizing existing types as well as creating new types.

In practice there is not so much a problem with too few alternatives as with too many. Conventional design technologies were so cumbersome that very few possibilities could be explored, with the result that people tended toward previously successful arrangements: tradition. But now that

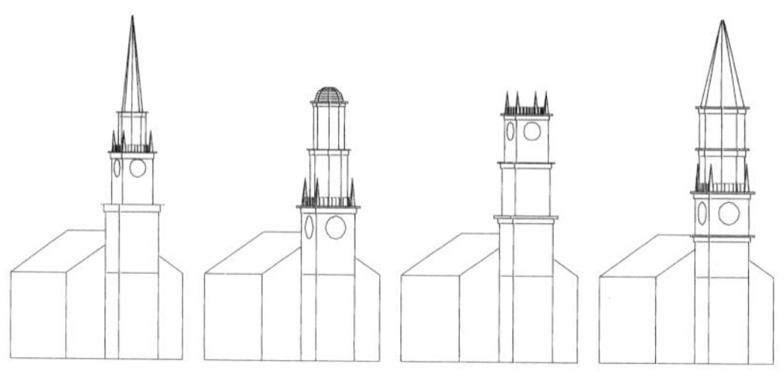

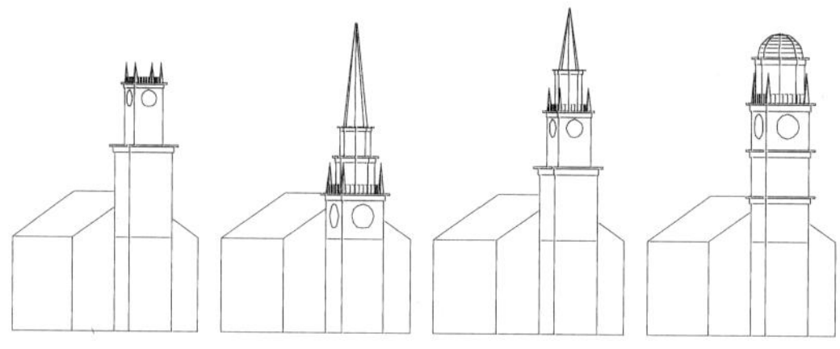

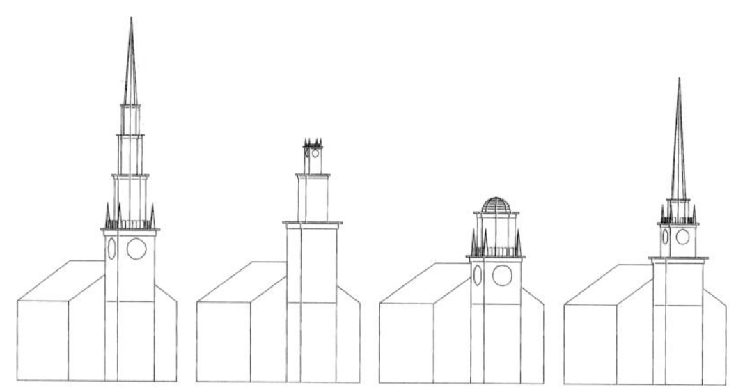

6.9 Variations on a theme of New England steeples, using parts substitution and dimensional variation

computing accelerates the production of alternatives, we need a better method of deciding which alternatives to explore. If one trouble with computer-assisted constructions is that they produce too many possibilities, one response is to incorporate sufficient typological knowledge in the system. Thus it has become something of a holy grail to design computing researchers to develop knowledge-based systems to assist designers in recognizing and transforming particular conditions. Many design theorists have followed the lead of structural linguists in this matter. In the recent history of creative computing, to restrain needless proliferation of types, many knowledge-based systems have taken the form of grammars.

A grammar essentially guides a process by establishing classes of recognizable situations within a symbol system. This is not limited to text or language. For example, the use of grammars for shape computations has been described quite effectively by William J. Mitchell in *The Logic of Architecture* (1990). A grammar basically defines initial states for which the designer should watch out, and resulting states that make particular responses worth considering. Its discourse is a sequence of well-formed depictions. A grammar can formally state combinations and accumulations of moves. It automatically constrains and amplifies various inputs. Its knowledge-based reduction of all possibilities in a set of vocabulary and operations places elements in fewer, more useful kinds of combinations. Its reduction can be bottom-up, as with classical prescriptive rules, or top-down, involving replacement rules, or both. The knowledge it encodes can be in a generation mechanism, or a test mechanism, or both.[11] The implication of a grammar is to automate design search by means of state-action trees not unlike those used in chess-playing programs. Approaches using rigorous control of when rules may be used or when state tree branches terminate may have shown some success for processes such as checking and diagnosis, but their application for synthesis tasks is only in its infancy. In particular, we must investigate the appropriateness of the degree to which grammars replace, rather than mediate, direct manipulation. Are grammars tools?

6.10 A grammatical construction: code-generated model of traditional Korean joinery

It may be more useful to think of grammars as constructive agents for giving substance to indirect manipulations through design mechanisms. They should be particularly applicable to assemblies, and because all digital artifacts are accumulations of one sort or another, in data structures that are frameworks for statements about designs, grammars could powerfully inform production. For example, much as a simple modifier such as snapping-to-vertices guides the elementary direct manipulation of a single geometric element, so a more complex syntactical constraint based on knowledge of particular design context might guide an accelerated design process. Paradoxically, by virtue of such generative structures, such processes would then become all the more improvisatory.

The implication of types and grammars for the proposition of craft is that structure and improvisation shape a richer process than improvisation alone. Indeed, improvisation must occur on a theme, type, or syntactic construction. Given that the initial advantage of the virtual artifact is its quick and structured malleability, the challenge to developing a constructive craft seems to lie in the framing of interesting potential families of artifacts. Perhaps this has less in common with traditional craft than with industrial design. Perhaps the reunion of intellectual and mechanical activities enabled by design computing, however, may create a condition that combines some of the individuality and responsiveness of craft with the process control of industry to create something new.

Design Worlds, Production Worlds

This section of the book has drawn several conclusions. Symbolic processing yields new possibilities not suggested by the operands themselves. Mental models are the key to human-computer interaction. Data constructions establish very particular realms in which improvisation gains leverage through structure. It follows that we should pay careful attention to mental models of constructive symbol-processing possibilities. For convenience, we can call them design worlds.

Much as the symbolic context presented through the software interface invites mental models, so a set of formal possibilities defined by a set of constructions can be understood as a design world. Much as different languages cast expressions of basic concepts in unique ways, so different design worlds can cast consideration of design problems in particular orientations. Much as the traditional craftsman takes care to select the appropriate tools and materials, so anyone engaged in creative computing alertly chooses a suitable design world in which to work. Mitchell put it very well: "The selection of axioms or primitives for a design world establishes a domain of formal possibilities for the designer to explore, and the designer must be concerned that the domain is appropriate to the task at hand."[12]

Design worlds are more than interfaces and constructions: they are invitations to construct particular mental models of generative strategy. They are different takes on creative computing. They are the working realities of different pieces in the software repertoire.

We have studied the example of geometric modeling here, but design worlds exist wherever sophisticated software is used in imaginative ways to generate classes of artifacts. We have seen that abstract notation is the best means to achieve generative structure: computers are symbol manipulators. We have seen that the devices and frameworks of human-computer interaction encourage the development of mental models, including tool as metaphor and medium as structure. For these, it should be evident that different design worlds correspond to different notations and interfaces, and that their constructions and mechanisms establish generative strategies with particular power. To the degree that these mechanisms can be coupled with denser notations and more engaging means of interaction, a technological context for skilled, reflective work may well develop.

What is more, many design worlds will gain credibility from coupling with the realities of production. Besides framing intangible worlds, we can apply symbol manipulations to physical manufacturing. In computer-integrated manufacturing, we can extend the idea of mechanism from a metaphor in software to a reality in hardware. And conversely, we can make the processes of production become workable in the abstract, and manipulate process abstractions together with the objects of design. This is not a new idea, but it has gained a lot of ground lately. Industry has of course had a couple hundred years to get organized, and process design has basically been inherent to mechanized industry. Computation clarifies, accelerates, and adapts this work to the point where both process models and their physical implementations become much more dynamic systems. Call them production worlds.

Industrial engineering has developed its philosophy about reconfigurable processes into a fundamental higher-level abstraction known as group technology, which in turn it couples to general strategy for business planning. The loop becomes product strategy plus process planning plus flexible manufacturing systems. What to make, and when to make it, are now at least as important as how many to make. Mass production is being displaced, as was artisanry before it.

Thus taken at the level of business planning, the practice of parametric constructions amounts to adaptive design. Fabrication process models therefore fit within what business administrators like to call enterprise workflow, and in this regard CAD/CAM may be understood as an information stream. This may sound like nails in the artisan's coffin, but upon closer inspection there appear to be some aspects of CAD/CAM that may well empower the small-scale worker and restore greater flexibility, particularly for industrial designers.

If attention to the material and organizational economy of machine processes is industrial engineering, then attention to the formal and expressive capacities of machine production is industrial design. In that it works solely with a palette of mechanically driven operations, without any human impetus behind the individual artifacts, industrial design is the ultimate art of indirect manipulation.

Industrial designers have other concerns, such as the economy and identity of visual perception, and effective presentation for usability, but at a fundamental level the discipline addresses the nature of mechanical processes and constructions.[13] For example, how can a piece of office equipment become easier to assemble in the factory? How light one can make an injection-molded part and still obtain sufficient strength? The fundamental premise is twofold: one, that everyday utilitarian constructions deserve consideration as design, and two, that material properties and fabrication processes play a significant role in that design. One can of course apply these assumptions to other disciplines such as architecture, and one can recognize them as inherent aspects of traditional craft, but industrial design is the discipline that depends most fully upon them today.

Not just coincidentally, these same principles are the most encouraging aspect of CAD/CAM. Computer-aided design improves the practicality of giving explicit design attention to ordinary objects—indeed it necessitates it. Computer-aided manufacturing improves specification and control of material properties and fabrication processes. Moreover, as we have seen, these activities work together as two-way conduits. CAD/CAM techniques let us both exert our will to control fabrication processes and obtain improved feedback about materials and operations. This makes it easier to probe what kinds of things want to be made. As this loop tightens, two interesting consequences emerge. First, the sense of working in a particular medium should become significantly better than in traditional manufacturing. Second, greater range and adaptability in practical fabrication processes should dramatically improve the expressive capacity of industrial production.

Consider the particular technology of rapid prototyping, for example. This process produces a complex, precisely specified form right at the scene of the design office, quickly, overnight or in just minutes—whereas a traditional mockup or tooling-up for actual production took weeks or months. Like the exploration of form in geometric modeling, rapid prototyping is accelerating the ability to explore related formal possibilities, except that it is doing it in physical form. Like the design worlds of parametric modeling, these production worlds of adaptive design are becoming a locus for talented improvisation and practice. As the cost of this method falls, as other technologies have done, rapid prototyping alone should achieve stature as an expressive medium. The act of making moves cumulatively on digital artifacts can occur in a variety of settings and scales, and in increasingly complementary relation to making physical form.

Experiencing Technology

What does this rich technological context suggest about the proposition of a digital craft? What is the newfound relation of individual talent and productive work? Is CAD/CAM—or even basic geometric modeling—a departure from past experiences with manufacturing automation, which has a consistent history of incompatibility with individual craft and artisanry? The common perception is that the introduction of still more mediating command-and-control technology will just further detach people from work. In the normal view, CAD/CAM is just another in a series of workplace mechanizations already including division of labor, application of machine power, substitution and deskilling of handwork, power distribution through electrification, organization in continuous line process, and so on.[14]

On the other hand, no other equally prevalent application of computers is so closely related to that traditional locus of artisanry: the making of three-dimensional things. Never before has form giving had such an effective notational system or means of connecting three-dimensional sensibilities to the power of computers. Perhaps theories of prototypes and grammars are not so alien to traditional production, but are more like contemporary counterparts to the pattern books used by traditional artisans. And if the tightening loop between design and fabrication does indeed give some people a renewed sense of workable material, responsive process, and mastery over the form-giving enterprise, then is that a renewed form of craft? How far can the extensions of man be taken?

With the benefit of computing, we have entered a golden age of industrial design. At the height of the first machine age, industrial designers protested that they needed to design in the actual materials of the factory and in the full stream of production, and not on paper drawings to be interpreted at the hands of unimaginative factory managers.[15] What was then an ideal—and quite hard to pull off—is now more of a reality. Industrial designers can work in the stream of the process, without disrupting it, by doing it virtually. Working with digital models of process and form, they may not only participate actively in production worlds but also connect with the managers and salesmen. In the business of producing an abundant variety of well-designed goods, things have never been better.

Yet this is not the end of the story. We have explored the power of constructive digital artifacts, but we need to know more about their applicability outside factory production. We also must ask what other mental models can be made into formal notations and process models, and what other kinds of creative processes might develop powerful and adaptive interfaces. What is more, we must turn to the personal context. What will it take for anyone to regain the sense of productive autonomy and personal impetus that we expect of a genuine craft? If and when such capacity develops, and whatever its technical balance of notation, interface, and construction, the test of abstract craft will depend mostly on personal experience. Therefore, as technology continues to provide us with increasingly compelling worlds of design and production, we need to think carefully about individual outlooks toward a medium, improvisation, and practice.

III Personal Context

7 Medium

To give work substance, we require a medium. The actions of our hands, eyes, and tools must be mediated. Our personal knowledge and skills must be given a habitual setting for practice.

The word "medium" has many meanings: a medium may be a material, such as plaster, or a means, an agency, or an instrumentality, such as the press. It may be an intervening person or thing, such as a messenger, or some other kind of carrier, like the liquid mixed with pigments to make paint flow. It may be a pervasive environment, in which bodies exist, like the air in which birds fly.

Quite often the word signifies a class of tools and raw materials. For example, metalworking is a medium, which includes welders, torches, hammers, and clamps, as well as aluminum, iron, and bronze. Because a type of material distinguishes a particular class of tools, the ensemble may be referred to on the whole as a medium. When the tools are complex, when the artifacts produced are abstract, or when tools provide the only means of access to the medium (all common conditions in high technology), it can be difficult to say where a tool ends and a medium begins. But we can say that under skilled practice even these tools become transparent, and that a sense of a medium eventually emerges.

Normally this is a more simple relation: a medium receives the work of tools. Where a tool is an effector or a probe, a medium is a substance that may be sensed or altered somehow by tools. If a tool is kinetic, and under active human guidance, a medium is static, and passively presents limits to human control. The meeting of tool and medium provides a locus for skills. As we push material around, we encounter structure. We find that we may work only in certain ways, and only at certain rates. We say that the medium has a feel, and we sense this quality only in action. Substance mediates action.

To mediate is not only to shape but also to communicate. Because a medium shapes the way a tool conducts an author's intent, it provides a locus for expression, and becomes subject to interpretation. In this way, a medium communicates between author and audience. The more tacit expression, subtle interpretation, or latent content a medium is capable of communicating, the richer it seems.

A richer medium invites interpretation. Its subtleties become subject to connoisseurship. The contexts and purposes under which it is used and interpreted create genres. In the case of craft, interpretations focus specifically on the way in which content takes form. With art, however, the relation of form and content varies constantly. Computing transforms this relation too: the same content (bits) may take many different forms quite easily, and it may do so after the fact. Of course there is considerable debate as to whether content must take material form, or whether the articulation of a more abstractly mediating substance, such as generative algorithms, may be subject to appreciation. But rather than entering a discussion on the merits of computer art, let us focus on the basis of an abstract medium.

Engagement, Affordance, Constraint

If it is to be anything at all, a medium must have sufficient effect on the senses in order to command our attention. It must stir our imagination.

7.1 A medium defines a practice

This quality of engagement is personal. If you are like most people, you probably work well only when your attention is focused on the task at hand. Something must draw your interest. This might be the pleasure of handling a material. It could be the concentration required not to ruin a piece of work. At a more abstract level, it could be the intricacies of solving a problem, whether technical or conceptual. It could be the anticipation of a finished product. It might be the ambition to succeed, or the fear of failure. Or it could simply be the calming effect of routine, based on soothing motions, habitual expertise, and a sustaining commitment to practice. If enough of these engaging qualities are sufficiently strong, nothing will distract you from your work—the hours will fly by, and you might not even hear the phone ringing. But if they are weak, the techniques of which they are a part may not make much of an impression on you, and your mind will drift.[1]

Many of these psychological factors depend directly on the properties of a medium. When we speak of richness, difficulty, or versatility, we are not only referring to the discipline of our practices, or the quality of our tools, but also to the very medium in which we work. In the sense of the word that means a pervasive context, these are the properties of a medium that surrounds us.

Thus the best way to begin understanding any medium is as a range of possibilities. Within traditional material craft, this is often articulated in terms of structure. Wood has a grain, paper has tooth, metal has temper. Understanding of structure is implicit; it is learned through experience. Although this becomes everyday knowledge, it does not become formalized. For example, although there are lumber grades based on the number of clear faces on a cut piece, we still have no formal scale or gradation for describing the texture and grain of wood. Moreover, the understanding is in terms of workability and practices, rather than according to any theoretical constitution. Thus people worked metals for centuries without any notion of lattices and free electrons. Acute knowledge of a medium's structure comes not by theory but through involvement.

For a medium to be engaging, it must be dense. This means that it must surround us in possibilities. Such immersion is more than sensory, for

Medium	*Continuous process*
Image processing	Tonal correction, layered composition
Paint	Finely controllable brushstrokes
Illustration	Drawing curves and shapes
Page layout	Placing elements
2d animation	Placing elements and transitions
Mapping	(rapidly iterative queries)
Geometric modeling	Position, scale, alignment
Sketch modeling	Geometric transformations
Parametric modeling	Parametric variation
Rapid prototyping	(iterative fabrications)
CNC machining	Programming by demonstration
3D object language	Navigating generative form
Rendering	Adjusting lights and cameras
3D animation	Path and transition control
Digital video	Cueing elements, editing orchestrations
Hypermedia	(following associative trail)

7.2 Continuous operations in digital media

it also serves the imagination with opportunities to coax the medium from one state to another. Ideally there should be enough states of the medium to create a sense of a *continuum* of possibilities. Continuity depends on the condition that between any two states there exists still another. It also means sensations of states cannot be disjoint: a neighboring state must appear, and feel, nearly like the present state. Only such density will produce continuous behavior that can be worked with continuous hand-guided processes, like coaxing a material. Although this is difficult to document, the importance of continuity to reflective, masterful processes cannot be underestimated. Work must flow.

Density supports engagement not only through continuity but also through variety. Only countless subtle differentiations of conditions will yield a heightened, satisfactory practice. A rich medium offers such an extent of possibilities that no one author or piece can incorporate them all, and only this is enough to sustain continued exploration.

Thus the attuned craftsman asks, "What can this medium do?" as much as "What do I wish to do with this medium?" It matters that one works in a medium whose properties suit one's purposes: sometimes a more forgiving medium; sometimes a more rewarding medium; occasionally rigor for rigor's sake; but always a medium whose intrinsic advantages are appropriate to the task at hand. An experienced craftsman knows how to choose the right medium and to push it as far as it will go—and no further.

Psychologists (and software experts) often employ the term "affordances" to describe the workable capacities of a medium.[2] This reflects the truism that opportunities shape outlook: "how we see the world depends on what we can do with it."[3] Or we sometimes speak of "what a medium can do." For example, every physical material has tolerances, within which it is workable and outside of which it breaks down. Wood can be cut across the grain more readily than along the grain, and it can be cut only so thin and still remain rigid. Each type of wood has distinct qualities. Harder woods afford more detailed forming processes, such as carving and sanding. Any wood can be carved more easily than stone. More resilient wood can be

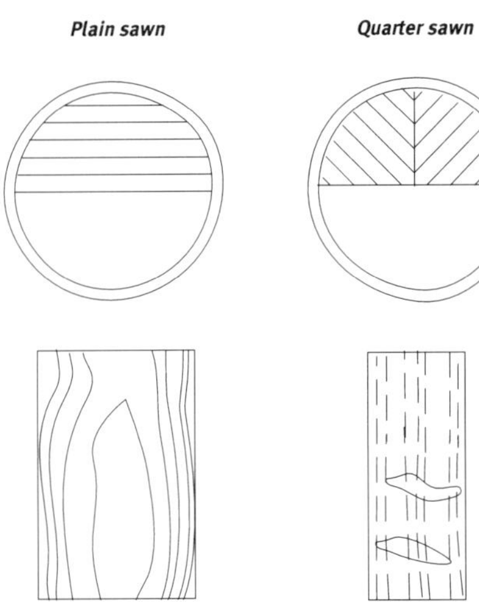

7.3 An example of material properties: quartersawn lumber looks better because of continuous ring lines, and is less likely to warp, but wastes more wood

worked further than less resilient wood of equal hardness. Of course, no two pieces of one wood are alike. Clear wood is stronger than knotty wood. Aged or dried wood is less likely to deform, but wood dried too rapidly will crack. Untreated wood is relatively cheap, and there tend to be left-over pieces of it lying around, which can be worked with relatively unspecialized tools, such as a penknife. Thus we might say that wood affords whittling.[4]

There is no guarantee that the affordances of a medium will be obvious. Unlike objects of industrial design, for which the term affordances is also used in describing the potential purpose and self-evident uses of things, a medium is not necessarily established for a particular intent. Rather, it is found. Its affordances are discovered. They may not be subject to identity or measure, but knowledge of their presence may be embodied implicitly in tradition.

Affordances seem to be meted out more or less equally among various desirable media. In this sense the word affordance implies a finite budget of opportunities, and so it is complemented with the idea of "constraint." For a medium must also have limits. It is not too difficult to imagine that an unconstrained medium would have little identity. Presumably it would be unpleasant. Being able to do whatever one wants does not induce creativity so much as paralysis. But in reality, there is no ultimate medium. Constraints define specific formal possibilities and guide creativity into specific channels, much like banks define a river.[5]

In other words, constraint is a source of strength. This is especially the case with respect to the nature of a material and the giving of form. Effective constraints are not explicit methods for the use of tools so much as implicit limitations learned from the behavior of a medium. Such limitations focus the scope of process without obstructing engagement the way explicit rules do. Thus, another way to think of constraint is as the rigor of substance. Note that this is not necessarily material so much as structural. As we continue to note, structure is a particularly constructive source of constraint. Only through the possibilities and limitations of structured substance does expression come into being—otherwise it remains only inspiration.

Together, affordances and constraints shape expression, and they do so in the process of giving form. Form establishes boundaries. A medium shapes the structure of expression. Its unique capabilities give rise to idioms. Some expressive forms, like a sonnet or sonata, may be more clearly constrained than others, like action painting. Gombrich wrote, "It is because art operates with a structured style governed by technique and the schemata of tradition that representation could become the instrument not only of information but also of expression."[6]

Understanding affordances and constraints is exactly what engineers, designers, artists, and craftspeople do well. Each of these expertises involves deep familiarity with possibilities and practicalities of particular media. Consider their respective approaches.

An engineer—most pertinently a manufacturing engineer—is concerned with measurable qualities that yield reproducible results. Armed with such certainties he or she can automate processes in a way that goes far beyond human strength, precision, patience, or endurance. Though experience and study—but also through predictive modeling—the engineer can become familiar with the practical possibilities of a technological configuration. Similarly, an industrial designer can master the aesthetic possibilities of a standardized production process, albeit without giving much personal charm to the individual products.

Almost any other kind of artist, by contrast, is released from practicality. This condition is especially pronounced in the freedom from having to put material to work economically. The artist, devoted to seeking pure expression, has little concern for optimal use of raw material. In this case, getting the most out of limited affordances matters less. Rather a coded intellectual context (aesthetic theory) serves as a guide, and individual vision assumes dominance over any practice of traditional skills.

But between these modes there remains some realm where scientific production cannot go, where mechanized industry finds too little demand to go, and where artistic discourse cares not to go. Where personal knowledge still combines with practical intent, where the expression is as much functional economy as aesthetic stance, where the products are individual and idiomatic, where the medium is the basis for mastery: there we find craft.

One better articulation of well-understood affordances dominates craft, and that is *workmanship.* Clearly this is a reflection of engagement: it is the quality with which a design vision takes form in a specific medium. It is also a matter of appropriate expression, in recognition that idioms seldom translate well from one medium to another, particularly from a finer to a cheaper material. For example you cannot replicate in Formica what you can accomplish in mahogany, and the results tend to be ugly if you try— although of course Formica has its own distinct possibilities. Good workmanship is sympathetic to such potentials of a medium and uses any idiosyncrasies to its advantage. In this regard, workmanship ultimately seems more a property of the process, or of the worker, than of the very medium.

Many people believe that workmanship is a fundamental human disposition. For example, in *The Instinct of Workmanship and the State of the*

Industrial Arts (1914), Thorstein Veblen affirmed how "The instinct of workmanship is effective in such consistent, ubiquitous, and resilient fashion that students of human culture will have to count it as one of the integral hereditary traits of mankind."[7] Veblen felt that this trait was being obstructed by mechanization, which distanced the worker from the medium, but he recognized that workmanship is largely a matter of functional economy. "Workmanship is not less the object of attention and sentiment in its own right. Efficient use of the means at hand, and adequate management of the resources available for the purposes of life, is itself an end of endeavor, and accomplishment of this kind is a source of gratification."[8] Moreover, Veblen took the view that "All instinctive action is intelligent and teleological." This supported his main thesis that if the craftsman could retain control of the process, even within an industrial setting, technological excellence would result. To put it simply, workmanship will find a way. In this sense, a new medium could be made, even within a more abstract and technologized context.[9]

Aesthetic historian David Pye has studied workmanship at length and asserted its primacy over material. "In speaking of good material we are paying an unconscious tribute to the enormous strength of the traditions of workmanship," he says. "We talk as though good material were found and not made."[10] Pye's central argument is very much along the lines of personal knowledge and commitment:

> Workmanship of the better sort is called, in an honorific way, craftsmanship. Nobody is prepared to say where craftsmanship ends and ordinary manufacture begins . . . [But] if I must ascribe a meaning to the word 'craftsmanship,' I shall say as a first approximation that it means simply workmanship using any kind of technique or apparatus, in which the quality of the result is not predetermined, but depends on the judgment, dexterity, and care which the maker exercises as he works. The essential idea is that the quality of the result is continually at risk during the process of making; and so I shall call this kind of workmanship "The Workmanship of Risk": an uncouth phrase, but at least descriptive.[11]

This kind of workmanship Pye contrasts with a "workmanship of certainty," which he presents as the basis of ordinary manufacturing. Certainty, particularly in the form of standardization, yields incontestable economies. But uncertainty, or diversity, can yield a wider range of practical endeavors and a more natural expression of material microstructure. By the latter is meant conditions where, like the wrinkles in finely tanned leather, diverse irregularities in the medium, which might be eliminated in standardizing processes, instead become a source of beauty.

Workmanship engages us with both functional and aesthetic qualities. It conveys a specific relation between form and content, such that the form realizes the content, in a manner that is enriched by the idiosyncrasies of the medium. In this sense it is an act of appreciation.

Appreciation

Usefulness and beauty are in the eye of the beholder: just as a medium must provide a context for skilled action, so it must provide a context for developed interpretation. Here the word "medium" is used in the sense of an intervening carrier. It allows authors to give form, whose users and audiences may interpret. It implies the necessity of intermediate objects, that is, artifacts. This was the essence of Focillon's phenomenological argument: "A work of art exists only in so far as it is form. In other words, a work of art is not the outline or the graph of art as an activity; it is art itself. It does not design art; it creates it. Art is made up, not of the artist's intentions, but of works of art."[12]

An artifact is a phenomenon in itself, and not just an exact representation of an abstract vision. Its expressiveness is shaped by the very properties of the medium. The manner in which an artifact employs known affordances and works within implicit constraints conveys vision indirectly, through the stuff of the medium. Repeated or related executions establish types and genres of form. Affordances for talented execution, and for a vivid record of an impassioned or contemplative state, improve the chances for a widely differentiated body of work, possibly including individual masterpieces. In other words, affordances give rise to expressive conventions, and they do so through the particularity of the artifacts. Gombrich summarized: "The forms of art, ancient and modern, are not duplications of what the artist has in mind any more than they are duplications of what he sees in the outer world. In both cases they are renderings within an acquired medium, a medium grown up through tradition and skill—that of the artist and that of the beholder."[13] Note the emphasis on the fact that a medium must be acquired, both in terms of skill and with respect to interpretation.

Obviously a piece must be received on a higher level than the purely sensory, like turning on the lights, or the purely literal, like retrieving a phone message. At minimum, its reception must somehow engage the subjective framework of its audience. For example, it might be decoded according to a shared body of meaning, such as engineering drawing conventions, or religious iconography. Or it might remain meaningful on an uncoded, sensory level, but appeal to some sort of shared experience—"digging it." However, normally, appreciation combines coded structure, shared sensation, and personal reflectivity into a higher level of reception. This was the essence of Gombrich's position in *Art and Illusion* (1960). "The true miracle of the language of art is not that it enables the artist to create an illusion of reality. It is that under the hands of a great master the image becomes translucent. In teaching us to see the visible world afresh, he gives us the illusion of looking into the invisible realms of the mind."[14]

The notion of artifact as translucent vessel brings forth the possibility of latent content, which can be defined as expression neither intended by the author nor read in by the recipient, but conveyed by the cultural context under which the artifact has been produced and received. Thus an author's intent is not the sole arbiter of meaning. Latent content dominates especially in craft artifacts that are not overtly artistic but simply the product of traditions.

Appreciation is a participatory practice, culturally positioned, and without explicit rules or grading. Here there are parallels to skill. Polanyi suggested connoisseurship as a dimension of active personal knowledge: "Connoisseurship, like skill, can be communicated only by example, not by precept. To become an expert wine taster, to acquire a knowledge of innumerable blends of tea or to be trained as a medical diagnostician, you must go through a long course of experience under the guidance of a master."[15] We don't just see: we study; we learn. Anything less would be mere apprehension, or mere projection. Appreciation requires exposure to a lot of pieces, for experience assists assimilation. Appreciation also benefits from repeated exposure to the same pieces, so that by reflecting our moods they may also reveal themselves.

Appreciation also incorporates intent. This may be unstudied disposition: as the critics say, "dogs see dogs." However, more usually intent is a matter of willful receptivity. For example, the difference between hearing and listening to a piece of music might be its relation to the last piece listened to, and this is why many people prefer media in which they get to choose the programming. Intent lets us decide the context in which we receive a piece: we might say that is lets us look at a medium or through it. For example, we might return to the theater to see a play a second or third time to study it at different levels, for example, the acting, the direction, or the lighting. Such intentional appreciation has a close relationship to craft. It doesn't hurt to have first-hand experience with the making.

More specifically, the interpretive process centers on familiar categories of forms within an acquired medium. We might say that appreciation can be *within* a genre or *of* a genre. The Parthenon is great primarily in relation to so many other Greek temples. Greek temples are great because they gave us so many related artifacts, including the Parthenon. We appreciate a genre in proportion to how many pleasing artifacts it has given us.

Octavio Paz evokes the simplicity of the craft artifact, the appreciation of which is based on the simplest relation of form and content:

> A glass jug, a wicker basket, a coarse muslin *huipul,* a wooden serving dish: beautiful objects, not despite their usefulness, but because of it. Their beauty is simply an inherent part of them, like the perfume and the color of flowers. It is inseparable from their function: they are beautiful things because they are useful things. Handcrafts belong to a world antedating the separation of the useful and the

> beautiful. Such a separation is more recent than is generally supposed.[16]

The separation of art and craft is a modern historical development. Increasing differentiation of skills, newly discovered respect for originals in an autographic medium, and growing freedom to explore personal visions combined to introduce a new kind of artifact: the work of art. If the history of art may be regarded a study of the ever-changing relation between form and content, then we may say that this kind of artifact established a new condition in which beauty was freed from necessity. This freedom has advanced in stages: first from necessity for utilitarian function, later from any necessity of literal representation, and finally from necessity of technique.

We cannot ask of the work of art what it is "for." Utility became the province of the industrial object, which especially in its early stages was crudely formed, banal in intent, its design unbalanced by infatuation with newly convenient processes, its ornament imitating traditional expression but in cheaper materials—in a word, ugly. Art appreciation generally ran away from the machine, at least until industrialism had a century to mature. The emergence of a "machine age" aesthetic in the 1920s was an exception to this divorce of function and beauty, and this had passing influence on earlier, therefore presumably higher arts. In architecture, for example, Le Corbusier celebrated grain elevators and ocean liners.

Herbert Read drew distinction between fine and applied arts, or cabinet arts and useful arts, as he called them. The problem of artistry in earlier industrial objects was that it was applied—literally. Ornament was derived from traditional materials, methods, and expressions, "distinct from the processes of machine production, and applied to the manufactured object."[17] Classical ("cabinet") taste had been the measure of nineteenth-century industrial art, with dreadful results, and forcing modernism to rise independently. "Meanwhile, by use of [modern streamlining] the man in the street is betraying his instinctive aesthetic judgements—aesthetic judgements which owe nothing to the standards of traditional taste and academic arts—judgements which are, in fact, evidence of a new aesthetic sensibility."[18] In other words, industrial design emerged because popular tastes became ready to recognize the possibility of an abstract art in the pervasive industrial vernacular—in products. The systematic modularity of production and product lines, and the disposable interchangeability of individual pieces, however beautiful, were a great departure from the previous understanding of art as individual works.

In opposition, the autonomy of academic Art deepened. Then, as today, any dominance by or widespread commercial use of a powerful new technique tended to taint its acceptance in the artistic academy. This happened with modern architecture, with photography, and above all with the early cinema. Industrial design, despite its initial achievements, eventually came to be seen as a form of marketing corporate identity—mere packaging. Altogether, industrial artifacts continued to be considered ugly. They had to lose their usefulness, like Pittsburgh blast furnaces, before they could be valued for their beauty. Utility was not only ignored in higher aesthetics; it was also denied. Oppenheim made fur-lined teacups (1936). "Ceci n'est pas un Pipe" (1950), painted Magritte, without need for adding: "only a referent."

But like the industrial object, the art object also broke away from codified representation. One might overgeneralize that if traditional appreciation was *within* a medium, then modern appreciation became more likely to be *of* a medium. Traditionally, functional objects created within aesthetic traditions had used the embellishments of necessary components as a means of expression. This was not limited to physical wares, which were displaced by the products of industry, but also included representative imagery. For example, interpreting religious iconography uses traditional conventions to reformulate content. Only certain elements and themes were expected to be subjected to artistry.

By contrast, more recent artistic expression defies such direct interpretation. Although traditional art was mimetic, the arrival of the camera, and more importantly the loss of shared mythology, undermined its representative function. Modern art, from Motherwell to Monk, is not *about;* it simply *is.* As is a matter of phenomenology it finds epiphanies in the simple. Under these conditions, conventional, codified interpretation was reduced to a means for bourgeois apologetics and academic pedantry, so the artists just got rid of it. In the case of painting, as Susan Sontag identified, modernism easily shook off the yoke of interpretation by using the twin tactics of abandoning representation, as in abstract expressionism, or resorting to literal representation of banal, nonsymbolic objects, as in pop.[19]

This same freedom enabled latent content to be engineered—or even eliminated—from intellectually richer artifacts. That is, works played more self-consciously with their cultural contexts. Because people who have acquired a sensibility naturally share an intellectual frame of reference, the possibility exists for an exclusive art that endeavors to confound all but a few insiders. As the shared frame goes beyond the sensory and improves communication independent of execution, there is a tendency toward works devoid of technique. Anyone who demands technique, or who otherwise fails to buy in to these subterfuges, can simply be dismissed as a philistine.

This is not to say that appreciation has stopped. On the contrary, art, however confounding, has been allowed to fill some of the void left by religion. Recall how with *In Praise of Hands,* Paz laid out this accusation of art in defense of the merits of craft.

> Art inherited from religion the power of consecrating things and imparting a sort of eternity to them. The museums are its temples; the critics, its theologians . . .
>
> [However] the modern religion of art continually circles back upon itself without ever finding the path to salvation: it keeps shifting back and forth from the negation of meaning for the sake of the object to the negation of the object for the sake of meaning.[20]

Perhaps this is one reason for a renewal of interest in craft: in Art, it would seem, the snake has long since swallowed its tail.

Meanwhile, any fissures between art, craft, and industry have by now been completely overshadowed by the popular culture of electronic communications. Not only does an electronic medium such as film, television, or recorded music allow an easier emphasis on form, with cheaply produced and reproduced content, but also it comes comparatively free from cultural baggage. In the 1960s, Sontag asserted that film had become the most important medium, because there "It is possible to elude the interpreters in another way, by making works of art whose surface is so unified and clean, whose momentum is so rapid, whose address is so direct that the work can be . . . just what it is."[21]

"The Medium is the Message" became Marshall McLuhan's famous slogan of this incipient electronic era. Factors such as instant total awareness, unity of form and function, and the lack of need to ask what a functional medium such as electric light was "about" all contributed to this emphasis on the medium in itself. Moreover, any direct effect of the content the media conveyed was felt to be secondary to the indirect social consequences of increasingly technological media. It did not matter what was on television, so much as that everyone was watching. McLuhan's creed was that "The message of any medium or technology is the change of scale or pace or pattern that it introduces into human affairs."[22]

The change of pattern that followed from the permeation of society by television has been the onset of postmodern consumerism. Postmodernity does restore a use value to aesthetic production, but the use is political and economic rather than simply functional. As noted in the earlier discussion of images and media culture, this condition is marked by dematerialization, simulation, and commodification of aesthetic artifacts, most of which are pure image. This state has been well charted by the academic left. To cite but one example, Fredric Jameson suggests that any formerly elite cultural appreciation has not so much vanished as exploded. "A prodigious expansion of culture throughout the social realm, to the point where everything in our social life—from economic value and state power to practices and to the very structure of the psyche itself—can be said to have become 'cultural' in some original and as yet untheorized sense."[23]

Twenty years into postmodernity, we have arrived at a condition where the ubiquitous fusion of economics and culture has transformed aesthetic production from the work of a fairly cloistered few into the play of the increasingly networked many. One of the consequences is that artifacts must be electronically transmissible if they are to be noticed. As was explored in the chapter on visuality, the necessities of information delivery both demand and invite new developments in abstract, electronic media.

The rise of digital media once again overturns the relation between form and content. We have begun to depart from the era of passive television, of information segregation by delivery media, rather than by content, and of primacy of form over content. Earlier media theories such as those of Sontag and McLuhan do not necessarily translate to this era, where both medium and message are streams of bits that demand (and often provide) interpretation. Negroponte observes that the two most important properties of bits are, one, that they commingle, intrinsically producing the condition known as multimedia, and two, that some bits exist specifically to tell you how to use other bits.[24] Notably, as an outgrowth of these conditions, particular content can be given many forms, according to the wishes of whomever receives it. "The medium is not the message in a digital world. It is an embodiment of it. A message might have several embodiments automatically deliverable from the same data."[25]

As evidence of a reemphasis on content, note that as the internet has begun to achieve critical mass, a new electronic profession, often a cottage industry, has emerged under the rubric of "content producers." Perhaps to the older media mogul this term is indicative of a subsidiary industry addressing the irritating but quickly dispatched need to have some stuff to push over the wires. But what if people pull instead? That is, what if people browse and download content of their own choosing, and "least common denominator" broadcast content simply fades from the scene? If the audience may choose between formats, the owner of the channel has less of a monopoly on their attention. When browsing among content headers (bits about bits) rather than tuning in at a specified broadcast time determines what will be received, then what will matter is content.

Interestingly, the content producers, working in digital media, are the ones talking about craft.

The Abstract Medium: Engaging Notational Density

It is in appreciation of abstract, notational media where we use the word craft most broadly. Consider the writer's craft, for example. Writing, is very much shaped by its artifacts, which are sentences and paragraphs. Formless thoughts must be executed in the quirky phenomenon of words. Ideas cannot be organized in just any manner, but must be joined from one to the next in such a manner that the sound of the language flows. Because of this need, small, idiosyncratic difficulties of putting one word after another can derail entire trains of thought. Like wood, language has a grain. Within the medium of words, the writer's craft incorporates countless devices to work this grain: specialized vocabulary, idioms of usage, tone, meter, voices, metaphors, allusions, similies, tropes, imagery, apostrophe. The experienced writer bridges ideas by means of these constructions—to varying degrees of success. A beginner who tries to use too many of these will suffer. Consistency without monotony is a very elusive goal to achieve, and elegance is more difficult still.

Note that even within intellectual pursuits, languages of expression may be influenced by production technology. For example, Hugh Kenner evokes the mechanical muses of the poet Ezra Pound:

> Pound uses the indents made easy by the typewriter as poetic device: to indicate change of voice. He uses the reference materials produced by the Victorian era to incorporate so much knowledge not necessarily his, e.g. elements of other languages. He abided by the spirit of accuracy, efficiency, and concentrated power. The aesthetic of a tool-and-die maker. Pound's ideal poem would consist solely in mobile parts and the parts required to keep 'em in their orbits or loci.[26]

Kenner appreciates how Pound used the medium of typewritten text to evoke the century of the machine. He infers: "Once we persuade ourselves that 'machine' need not connote iron nor hardware, that the word applies to any economic self-activating system for organizing resources, we can see mechanisms everywhere." For example, the reference materials used by Pound were a great machine: the *Oxford English Dictionary* was the crowning epic poem built by many thousands of toilers organizing and making accessible all that could be ascertained about the record of human speech.[27]

However, if the conditions within design computing were no different from this example in literature, the proposition of craft in digital media would be mostly semantic—and not very interesting. The word craft applied to a nonmaterial medium, such as poetry, has a distinctly different meaning—and not the one we are curious about—than the word craft applied to a physical medium, such as stone.

Must a craft medium have a material substance? Historically, physical materials have been the best source of mediating structure. The physical workability of a material is what defines its possibilities as a medium. Traditional arts and craft forms are identified as much by material as by any practices or modes of expression. Examples are everywhere in terms of material: woodblocks, lithographs, watercolors, oils, silver, ironwork, textiles. The working of these materials has been direct—without symbolic notation—and this directness has been the source of greater tacit affordances than can be obtained from notational media. In other words, historically there have been limits to mediation, and the ability to somehow execute work directly within the medium and work it in some unstated way has remained essential to expression.

For example, in Pye's conception of workmanship we have a fundamental challenge from tradition to the proposition of electronic craft: must a true medium entail sufficient risk and irreversibility to demand the rigor and devotion that have always been necessary for great works? Can a computer with its *undo* and *save as* functions ever demand sufficient concentration on our part to enable serious, expressive works to come forth? Can these functions enable us to take greater risks and therefore express ourselves all the better? Or do they render us noncommital and our work superficial?

Materiality is therefore pivotal to the question of craft in the electronic realm. Recall the opening discussion of touch technology. What good is the computer as medium if you can't even touch it? May we suspend the need for physical properties, or the subtlety of touch, or the durability of tangible artifacts, in exchange for a more dynamic manipulation of abstract structures of symbols? Is this question even reasonable? Or may we only ask the question to the degree that electronic media provide for manual dexterity through positional gesture, touch sense, and motion rates? Or is it that we are extending the sense of the word craft to apply to an different, more abstract situation, more like that of Pound, that only bears conceptual similarities to the working of physical materials?

Fortunately there is more to the issue. Today we are faced with conditions that transform age-old relations between material and notational artifacts. This intellectual understanding of craft based on the particularities of notation is merging with the more usual skillful kind of craft, based on the continuously workable medium. We might describe this unification in terms of four basic ideas.

To begin, the fundamental difference between digital and traditional media is rooted in microstructure: bits versus atoms. Processes that move physical atoms around are precisely the irreversible aspect of traditional work. According to very fundamental laws of physics, operations such as cutting, bonding, and mixing are irreversible. Mix black paint into white, and you've got grey for the duration. Crack a fine piece of laboriously refined jade work, and you have lost not only time but also expensive material—a rare configuration of atoms. By contrast, the microstructure of the computer medium is bits: a specified arrangement of symbols. The computer is made out of atoms, to be sure, but its logic employs symbols that quantize the physical charges they represent—it obtains stable bits. Because any physical deviations caused by atoms get rounded and corrected, these symbols built on bits do not degrade. In the microstructure of the digital medium, arrangements and values can always be reconstructed; their previous states can be stored and recalled; additional instances and versions can be replicated.

And this is the second principle: In electronic design media, format is often determined after content. Artifacts in many different formats may emerge from a single database. The structure of the abstract database is the content. Moreover, data structures are partially exchangeable. Once in digital format, the media become to some degree translatable into one another. Versions can proliferate as easily as invoking a *save as* operation. To use Goodman's terminology, these are obviously properties of an allographic medium, whereas craft, as it has been understood traditionally (and not in the manner of the recent example of the writer's craft), has depended on a continuous, autographic medium. But now the distinction is waning.

The third idea behind this merger is maybe the most important: *Increased notational density supports quasi-continuous operations formerly only available from physical materials.* The use of abstract data types based on high-precision numerical representations not only increases the density, but also expands the range of allographic media. Increased notational density distinguishes computing from earlier allographic media based on manual notations such as text or musical scores, which however rich were neither possible to manipulate in real time nor able to provide a continuum of potential states. By contrast, the data structures and variations described in the preceding chapter modify notations nearly continuously. Although there are not infinite possibilities, the mathematical resolution, of say, double-precision floating point calculations so exceeds the resolution of any devices by which they may be manipulated that in effect, there seem to be infinite possibilities. The fundamental condition of density is met: between any two practical possibilities, there exists a third. Similarly in images, both the number of pixels and the number of intensities available for them to take on are finite, and easily handled in notation, but are more than enough to provide the sense of continuity before the human eye.

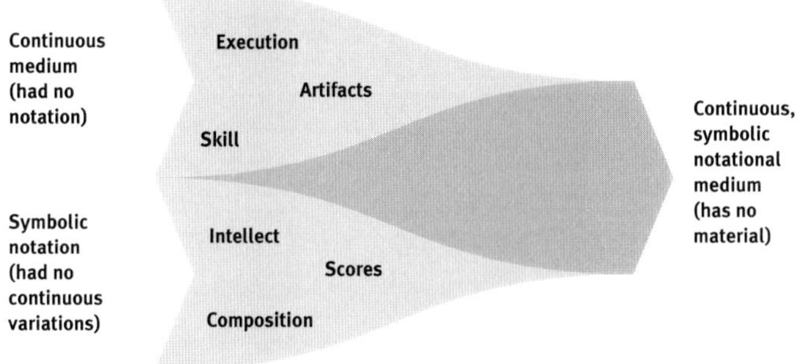

7.4 Dense, effectively continuous notation

Lastly, then, better human-computer interfaces, based on dense notations, provide increasing engagement in structural manipulations. In particular, they engage the hand in the modification of notation, and this begins to reunite skill and intellect.

Computer as Medium

In light of these various conditions, it is fair to assert that despite the lack of physicality there exists a growing possibility of constructing the experience of a medium in the world of the computer. Furthermore, there exists a growing collection of such rich symbolic contexts: a digital repertoire. Intentional differences in symbolic data structure, forms of interaction, and types of indirect constructions yield distinctions between a growing variety of digital media. One way to understand these is in terms of the dimensionality of the artifacts. One-dimensional media manipulate text or sounds; two-dimensional media are naturally for pixels, lines, and polygons; three-dimensional media place lines, surfaces, or solids in space; *n*-dimensional media introduce time, as in animation, and may also add links between a variety of items or formats, as in hypertext.[28] Each of these media is at least partly related to the others; translations between them are routine. Software is packaged and chosen not for specific tasks so much as for the kinds of vocabularies and operators provided. Working environments cobble together many such pieces of software into powerful design networks.

Notably, some media formerly lacking in notation now become describable, and therefore subject to generative constructions and compositions. Autographic media become allographic. For example, sculptural geometry now has a notation in solid modeling.

The data structures underlying dense notation become a source of affordance and constraint. We have explored how internal representations in software, such as graphic primitives, represent available actions and implicitly suggest suitable applications. For example, representations of surfaces in space suggest rendition in light and shadow, whereas the additional representation of occupied volume suggests sculpting by union, intersection, and subtraction, and is wasted on rendering. Such affordances are not binding. In theory you could draft with a paint system, if you set out to do so, but the raster data structure would hardly encourage the act; conversely, you could paint with a vector graphics system, but the experience would be clumsy at best. More subtly, you could render a three-dimensional interior scene by means of raytracing or an exterior by means of radiosity, but the respective advantages of the two methods would suggest doing thereverse, because raytracing does highlights and sharp shadows better, whereas radiosity does diffusion across surfaces better. Like understanding the affordances of physical materials, choosing the digital medium that best suits your purposes has emerged as an important component of software expertise.

At the same time the psychological dimensions of human-computer interaction determine the degree of engagement with these symbolic manipulation worlds. As we have seen two chapters ago, engagement depends partly on sensory-motor activity and partly on handling perceptual loads. These processes, too, may be understood in terms of affordance and constraint. Moreover, the experience of them depends very much on the dynamics of interaction, and is best when continuous. Thus the nature of the computer as a medium began with the introduction of direct manipulation, and continues to depend intensively upon the ever-improving quality and range of continuous interactions.

Establishing both design worlds and psychological engagement depends on building adequate mental models. This is the most essential requirement for the computer to be understood as a medium. The best way to approach these questions is to understand software as a representational context: software designed and used properly creates a world of possibilities within whose assumptions and parameters we operate. Desktops, studios, sequencers, and stages all are representational contexts for specific classes of actions. We base our actions and understandings on these contexts. Often to succeed, we must necessarily subjugate our awareness of outside contexts to participation in the representation. As Brenda Laurel has observed, this is similar to what we experience when attending a good play:

> Engagement, as I use the concept, is similar in many ways to the theatrical notion of the 'willing suspension of disbelief', a concept introduced by early nineteenth century critic and poet Samuel Coleridge. It is the state of mind that we must attain in order to enjoy a representation of an action. Coleridge believed that any idiot could see that the play on the stage was not real life. He noticed that, in order to enjoy a play, we must temporarily suspend (or attenuate) our knowledge that it is 'pretend'. We do this 'willingly' in order to experience other emotional responses as a result of viewing the action.[29]

Suspending disbelief is an act of *participation.* As participants we are involved with what is going on within the terms of the representation, and we are unconcerned about how the performance itself is working. Note the similarity to the subjugation of sensory-motor response described by Polanyi in the context of tool usage. Here in an intellectual framework it is a matter of appreciating the implicit assumptions that theatrically frame a medium. Thus we suspend our awareness that we are working with a computer, and we enter the mental model, as though our monitor were a proscenium, or better yet as if we were onstage ourselves. Incidentally, this explains much of the enthusiasm for interfaces that construct, at a lower, sensory-motor level, the perception that we are within the work.

The intellectual ability to appreciate a medium well enough to construct a robust mental model must be acquired and maintained through learning, play, and practice. On the surface, it might seem that such intellectual articulation is at odds with active, participatory, tacit knowing. Polanyi noted this "peculiar contrast," which he reconciled by demonstrating that articulation is never complete.[30] But under deeper consideration, it should appear more reasonable that the mental model should couple with several other levels of awareness.

Recall Gelertner's spectrum of intellectual focus, wherein focal symbolic reasoning is complemented by diffuse free association, and where creative work moves back and forth along the spectrum of focus. To support such work, an effective mental model should not tie up so much attention that this oscillation between levels of consciousness cannot occur. This requires that once we suspend our disbelief, we should be able to work with those assumptions in the background, and not suffer being dropped out of the model or its representation by anomalies we encounter. Conversely, it demands that the lower-level operations we conduct within the representation should reinforce the assumptions and contribute to building an understanding at a higher, more symbolic level. This is another embodiment of Alan Kay's summary principle about graphical human-computer interfaces, that "doing with images makes symbols."

There may exist correspondences between tacit skill or appreciation and the structure of the mastered medium. Cognitive psychologists may have much to contribute here: even if the mind is assuredly not a sequential symbolic-processing mechanism, specific structures of cognition may yet reflect particular creative states. If so, these might inform our approach toward engagement and appreciation. Holtzman argues this. "One can conclude that approaching expressive media in terms of abstract structure should not limit their ability to be expressive even of the most profound and subtle emotions. To the extent that the emotions themselves are built on a system of structures and relationships, expressive media viewed as systems of relationships can represent profound emotions. The challenge in designing abstract systems of expressive capability is not a limitation of the systems themselves—of dealing with abstract structure. Rather, the challenge is to develop abstract descriptions of sufficient richness, capable of capturing profound emotions and subtle expressive nuances."[31]

Just because a medium is structured does not mean that it has to be confining. The presence of structure does not necessarily reduce the opportunities for improvisation and expression. As we overcome the residual notion that computing is for objective documentation only, we must cultivate expressive sensibilities. These may result in a digital aesthetic or poetics, and they may involve artifacts that convey latent content and reflect active intent. Already we can begin from works that simply involve economy and emphasis. And in the end, chances are that appropriate artifacts and descriptions will engage us through rich and transparent tools, built on newfound densities of symbolic notation and personally experienced as a medium.

8 Play

In almost anything you might do today, you have got to improvise. There is simply too much change for tradition to handle; there are too many possibilities for any methodology to anticipate in advance. So improvisation plays a major role in serious matters with real stakes, from business plans to scientific research. In all kinds of work people take pride in thinking on their feet, inventing solutions when under pressure, and practicing originality in the face of risk. They just don't call it play.

But it is a distinct advantage of computation to introduce play; this is a natural consequence of working in bits. As we have seen, the irreversibility of so many traditional processes is rooted in the physical laws of material—in the atoms. You can only move atoms around so much before material starts to break down. Testing, in particular, is often destructive. Thus you cannot play around indefinitely with a physical medium: you have to get to work. But when rearranging bits, processes may be reversed completely without any loss of quality or affordance. Furthermore, true copies are possible, and these are just as good as the original—indeed every copy is an original. This is important, for it means that tentative processes may be applied without risk to extra, throwaway copies. Finally, the very structure of the medium contains variables, which invite modification along established parameters. You might recall that when spreadsheets popularized personal computing, very much on the basis of these advantages, the exploratory process was simply referred to as "What if?"

Play and Learning

Play is for learning: that is why children do it most. Yet adults play too, for simple relaxation, for learning about one another, and for continued skill development. Play lets us search for some lost sense of wonder. A philosopher might argue that in some higher sense all is play. The cycle of becoming, replete with Sisyphean setbacks, is like a game of fetching the ball. "Some Hilarious God in charge of us," wrote the beat poet Ferlinghetti after a day of whitewater rafting on the Rogue.

Adult play we call recreation. So much work involves so little play that after we work hard, we must also play hard. Although it is more usually physical sport, sometimes recreation still involves making things, and this is the one surviving form of traditional craft. To the artisan this same process was work, but in comparison to the chaotic work of today, and relieved of the tedium of repetition for earning a livelihood, craft becomes recreation. Yet to its proponents, it is no mere frivolity. Recreational craft is more satisfying than mere amusement, precisely because it is merged with work.

If productive play or serendipitous work fill an inner need, then perhaps there is some truth to the axiom that the basic material every craftsman works with is himself. Popular literature is full of books on getting in touch with a medium as an allegory for finding oneself: "what is the craft of being human?"[1] Given that people are becoming involved with creative computing for recreation, it is probably only a matter of time before we see books on *The Tao of Photoshop* or *Zen and the Art of AutoCAD.* Yet the inner component of work is more than indulgence: it, as much as any engagement of the senses, is exactly what so much sterile computer usage lacks. If we are to conduct some sort of personal work amid the one-time military-industrial world of computing, one important way to do so is to play.

Play takes many forms. For example, it can be individual or social. According to one classic taxonomy, individual play includes pursuit of sensations, exercise of motor apparatus, and experimentation with higher mental powers. This mental play includes exercise of attention, emotion, and will. Attention play includes tests of memory, imagination, focus, and reason. On the other hand, social play includes fighting and rivalry, loving and courtship, imitation, and status seeking. Imitative play includes movements, drama, behavioral constructions, and emulation of inner states.[2]

Crafts and craft learning embrace quite a range of these playful forms. Arguably, no other productive process combines so many so well. Sensation, skilled motion, attention, involvement, will—all must be balanced, and this is the basis for craft as recreation. Craft learning is a form of imitative social learning. Movements are physical skills taught directly, whether by demonstration or coaching. Drama is a lesser component here, although it may be understood in the willful suspension of disbelief that allows participation in an abstract medium. Constructions are the artifacts. They are the plastic play, the visual examples, the operational learning. Finally the inner state is the patience, reflectivity, and intent that distinguish the master.

Play serves learning though experimentation without risk. Play often lacks any immediately obvious aim, other than the pursuit of stimulation, but functions almost instinctively to serve the process of development. Learning occurs through quick, imprecise actions, conducted within understood rules of a game, and free from threat or consummation. Play does not use up so much as build. One thing it builds is common sense. Play's endlessly variable series of awkward, exaggerated motions seeks out the approximate arena for later development of true competence.

Fittingly, then, by far the majority of academic literature on play comes from educational psychology, which has increasing crossovers with cognitive psychology and software engineering. The idea of structure is one key to these interdisciplinary associations. It has been a widely shared belief that developmental psychology reveals cognitive structures of the mind. For example, some psychologists refer to the arena established by exploratory play as the "cognitive unconscious," and they hold that mature learning consists of making aspects of this cognitive ground fully conscious later on.[3]

There is also much thought that both cognitive structures and the learning processes by which they are confirmed can inform effective human-computer interface design. In general, software designers model computation according to human cognitive systems of goal setting, task planning, and action. Software tutors emphasize cognitive learning, particularly for the early stages of a beginner assimilating a new piece of software. This is because initial skill acquisition is a particularly active process, and subsequent forms of learning actively employ trial and error as they try to find the right analogies by which to build a mental model of how a particular system behaves.

The usual wisdom on developmental levels follows from the teachings of Jean Piaget, one of the principal originators of structuralist thinking. Piaget saw learning in distinct stages: a sensory-motor stage focused on physical object behavior, such as learning that things have continuity; an iconic stage that introduces representations, such as pictures, albeit as yet unrelated to one another; a concrete-operational stage that develops mental actions on objects (e.g., classifications); and a formal-operational stage that develops symbolic reasoning. The applicability of these stages to skill acquisition should be immediately apparent. You might even be able to imagine these very stages in the mastery of some software medium.

Yet surprisingly, as Howard Gardner has noted, Piaget had relatively little to say about play. Nor did Piaget demonstrate much about affinity or knowledge of a specific medium. A generation of psychologists, having reacted in so many ways to his theories, have found too little in Piaget to account for differences either in creativity or in approaches to learning.[4]

There is much to be said for play in a medium. If a medium is defined by its affordances and constraints, then learning consists of exploring these properties. Experimentation is especially useful for becoming familiar with constraints: we learn from our mistakes. We must accept that beginning work in a new medium will be full of setbacks. There will also be fortuitous discoveries, however, particularly of affordances. Design is not only invention, but also sensitivity to a medium. Craft cannot be merely in service of technique, or of inappropriately conceived ends. The craftsman must begin to feel something about the artifacts, and only certain moves will feel right.

Of course when it comes to computation, we all must learn. In a sense, we're all children—the medium is that new. And of course, the most fluent experts here are often quite young. As all of us learn about this promising new domain, a chain of developments should be clear: play shapes learning; learning shapes the mind; mental structures shape software; and software data structures afford work and play.

Structure and Improvisation

The master at play improvises. Consider the jazz pianist. In *Ways of the Hand—The Organization of Improvised Conduct* (1978), the musician David Sudnow gives us a rare description of otherwise tacit knowledge in action. Improvising on a piece takes much more talent than simply playing from a notation or learning by rote, Sudnow explains. Moreover, improvising begins with a sense of structure, from which it builds a cognitive map. For example, the "way in" to an arpeggio is mentally mapped. The structure of the keyboard presents a physical map of a chord, which may be modified in countless ways by physical moves. One could play the adjacent keys, for example, or one could translate by any arbitrary interval. One could transpose or invert. One could change the order in which the notes were played, or the tempo, or the attack and decay. Of course one could substitute dominant, major, and minor chords.

Sudnow argues that because these variations are sequences of physical positions, they are learned as active skills no longer necessary to be understood at a mental level. Each becomes a *handful.* That the hand gets a hold of a variation on a chord is indicated by observed tendencies to start into particular sequences with certain fingers on certain keys. The maneuver is known by the hand, and the mind only maps the way in. The ability to modify the run note by note—which would require conscious attention—only comes later. Even without attentive intellectual guidance, however, the natural tendency of the hand is not to repeat itself, even in a series of figural repetitions. Thus once a sufficient repertoire of runs is learned, this tendency inherently ensures a richness to the sound. The hand searches its territory for sequences, which process replaces a faithfulness to the score, and that makes jazz. For example:

> The new run could be in various other ways only 'essentially related' to the preceding run. Say the first started slow and went up fast, then doubled back and went fast again, while the second started slowly and came back down through the same pitches as the first, the doubled back and went fast again, but over different pitches . . .
>
> There were innumerable variations possible; looking at 'structure' in this way and corresponding to various continuity practices, ways of the hand were cultivated that were suited to the performance of such maneuvers . . .
>
> Transposition of such a figure to a new segment and correct repetition with respect to pitch, without slowing it down or slowing down parts of it, involved coping with the topography of the terrain by the hand as a negotiative organ with various potentials and limitations.[5]

Although jazz is the obvious case, it is hardly alone. Improvisation plays a role in many contemporary practices, and in many traditional crafts. Few of these worlds employ such a singular instrument as the piano; few are able to turn so much over to the hands, but all involve playful response to a structure.

For example, of industrial design, Herbert Read insisted that "Art implies values more various than those determined by practical necessity."[6] As a modernist and industrialist, he felt admiration for fundamental structural laws, such as the golden section also admired by his contemporary Le Corbusier. He was convinced, however, that metrical irregularities based on a governing structure, rather that slavish adherence to the laws in their precision, was the basis for pleasurable expression. He cited Ruskin's line that "All beautiful lines are drawn under mathematical laws organically transgressed."[7] He held that this was the case even in the useful (industrial) arts. Note the similarity to Pye's argument for sensitive deviations at the level of material microstructure as a basis for workmanship.

Consider the case of processing a digital photograph. The makeup of the raster image file and the various tone scale and filtration operators provides a very clear structure in which to work, but demands no particular order of operation. The complex microstructure of the sampled pixels provides a substance upon which to act. (Compare the more difficult situation of sitting down to a blank screen with a paint system.) Patterns of these pixels may be modified and replicated within the image in all variety of ways. Moreover, the ability to copy and paste particular groups of pixels (which you might understand as figural objects, but to the software are just pixels) between multiple files provides excellent capacity to play with compositions. You might process several separate images separately, for example, to bring them into the same level of contrast and similar color balances, then extract and compose elements from them into one new image or on top of one existing image chosen as a background. The overlay process can be used to experiment not only with the relative scale and position of several elements, but also with masking and degrees of transparency. You might cross-fade between two backgrounds. You might paste a figure into a limited area of a background, with the effect of it appearing behind other parts of the background. You might drag several elements around on different layers and experiment with the order in which they are overlaid. You might flip or stretch some elements to get their foreshortening right or to have the shadows falling in the appropriate direction.

Tone scale adjustments alone provide enough means with which to improvise variations in an image for hours. Components of red, green, and blue can be controlled separately, as can relatively lighter or darker areas.

Intensity distribution graphs (histograms) can be manipulated to control particular thresholds and ranges. Adjustments can be applied to selections of pixels. Potential results of each individual step can be previewed, often quickly enough for the work to feel continuous.

Filters themselves are improvisations by programmers. Aside from a few obvious ones such as sharpening and despeckling, there is no clear repertoire. Rather, they are possibilities: pure affordance. More become available all the time, and from these you might establish and explore your own particular collection.

All of this is to say nothing of the improvisatory nature of finding one's raw material for image processing. Sources abound: direct shots from digital cameras, scanned pieces of traditional prints, 35mm slides, video stills, scanned objects, found images on the internet, commercial clip art. The emphasis is on sampling, but many sources may be the result of pure synthesis: raytraced renderings, charts and graphs, polygonal maps, views of geometric models—indeed anything that appears on your screen.

At the level of devices, skilled people improvise with astonishingly crude instruments. For example, these many image operations are controllable through quick keyboard combinations. All else being equal, one's sensory-motor knowledge of these key combinations can affect one's choice of moves: we tend to do what we know. But what some people get out of a simple keyboard is quite remarkable, and the same is true for an ordinary mouse. For the future, better devices will assure richer improvisation.

Of course the impetus to improvise is deeper than the availability of moves by reflex or the assurance that one can undo any given step. The artifacts themselves invite speculation in the form of moves. Even—perhaps especially—when the goal is a single, studied composition, improvisation plays a role in study. Finished artifacts may go through inchoate stages, and separate study artifacts may be prepared. By nature, study artifacts are always incomplete and contingent. As is commonly understood among designers, the particularities, eccentricities, and implications of intermediate objects influence the outcome of the creative process.

Thus if we could say that improvisation is a manner of inhabiting design worlds, we must note that those worlds are populated by evolving objects. You try things using these elements and operators, and if you like them, you keep the results, and the object of your work evolves. You develop a style based on emphasizing particular processes, but you also try processes in response to the state of the artifact.

As noted in the study of constructions, the ability to navigate a continuum of possibilities is a fundamental advance over the slower iterations of traditional design. We have seen one example in the excursions through a continuum of parametric variations. In this case the mental model of the design world builds a corresponding space of solutions (not necessarily limited to three dimensions), and the physical action consists of moving along design vectors through that space. The eye is engaged in appraising the changing condition of the artifact as the hand modifies one of its design variables in real time. Note that despite its tremendous fluidity, this method is quite structured. The individual parameters shape the kinds of variational excursions that may be made. Moreover, the initial establishment of all parameters frames exactly one design world, and nothing the variational process can do will change that. Thus the design process really occurs in two stages: composing a structure, and then exploring the consequences of that structure.

One could conceivably improvise at a higher level, however, by swapping structures. To continue the case of theme and variations, this means looking for the right theme. When describing an artifact, it means parsing the artifact, or more accurately the formulation of the artifact, in different ways. That is, the same artifact could have many different potential parameterizations. This in turn means understanding the design problem in different ways. Substitution is a normal element of play, and so this fundamental challenge of *seeing as,* so basic to creativity, involves improvisation in its own right.

Converse to swapping structures of the same artifact, we can swap different artifacts having the same structure. This is essentially a matter of syntax. The usual context is the ordering and relation of discrete elements, for example, windows in a facade. Consider that animation software takes the metaphor of actors on a stage: elements with individual character are subject to a structure of moves, blocking relationships, and scene transitions, and this overriding structure, which is represented in a score, can be enacted with different cast members. This same idea applies in many media: instead of modifying individual dimensions or positional relationships, one can quickly substitute elements in a given armature. To do so involves a playful grasp of structural equivalence that is essential to human outlook.

Finally, just as there is play in applying the software tools within a particular medium, there can be play in choosing the medium in which to work. This is different for digital media, which as we have seen share many more concepts and techniques. We have seen how the capacity to realize the affordances presented by a given structure was presented as a means of guiding explorations, or workmanship. Furthermore, each medium is distinguished by particular vocabulary, constructions, and modifiers, and these together establish within it a limited but rich set of possibilities. This has been referred to as a design world. Working in a digital medium consists of experimenting in a design world, and as we have also seen, doing so involves certain suspensions or assumptions that allow one to enter the representation.

Generative Systems

Syntactic structure can serve as a recipe for growing entire formal systems. As is an increasingly common image thanks to contemporary discussions of genetics, the identity and integrity of the system are encoded in the structure. It becomes an interesting proposition, then, to invent generative structures, albeit less marvelous than those found in nature, which incorporate patterns of growth as in the dynamics of natural systems. We see this in the growing interest in fractals and biomorphic form. Growth algorithms, of which fractals are just one example, seem to offer an interesting future for design.

Time factors add a rich source of algorithmic beauty. Form may evolve in uninterrupted time, or in artificial intervals (as in game cycles), or as a frame of the design process (e.g., version history). Note that although craft depends on the impetus of the craftsman, elements of the work may have dynamism of their own, like material spinning on a lathe. Although the choice of what to do when belongs to the craftsman, the rate at which the work occurs has a timeframe of its own, based on the meeting of the craftsman's skill with the workability of the material. Nevertheless, there are dynamic representations where not having to exert control over lower-level operations yields a higher sense of control over a complete process. One can work at the level of derivatives, for example, controlling velocity rather than position. By altering the settings of a dynamic system (e.g., the coefficients of a system of differential equations), one can improvise within the context of a simulation. Probably the most prevalent example of playing style in simulations is the "builder" games such as *SimCity* or *Civilization.*

The popularity of simulations without explicit winning conditions may reflect a constituency that also keeps a playful attitude in productive computing. As a measure of this, consider the proliferation of multimedia animations in applications ranging from product design to education to crime reconstructions. Consider the tremendous success of the art/tech magazine *Wired,* or observe how many software advertisers suggest "going places" or doing "cool stuff."

In this world, generative systems sometimes replace finished artifacts as the tokens of creative arts and entertainment. *Wired* magazine editor Kevin Kelly writes, "If anyone could be said to embody the spirit of the artist in the digital age, it's Brian Eno." In a recent interview, Eno comments:

> In the future, you won't buy artists' works; you'll buy software that makes original pieces of "their" works, or that recreates their way of looking at things . . .
>
> What people are going to be selling in the future is not pieces of music, but systems by which people can customize listening experiences for themselves. Change some of the parameters and see what you get. In that sense, musicians would be offering unfinished pieces

> of music—pieces of raw material, but highly evolved raw material, that has a strong flavor to it already. I can also feel something evolving on the cusp between "music," "game," and "demonstrations"—I imagine a musical experience equivalent to watching John Conway's computer game of *Life* or playing *SimEarth,* for example, in which you are at once thrilled by the patterns and the knowledge of how they are made and the metaphorical resonances of such as system. Such an experience falls in a nice new place—between art and science and playing. This is where I expect artists to be working more and more in the future.[8]

These configurable worlds of generative action need not exactly mimic corresponding physical worlds. In particular, they may allow better crossovers between different media and representations and therefore allow for the practice of higher-level meta-techniques. Alan Kay:

> The protean nature of the computer is such that it can act like a machine or like a language to be shaped and exploited. It is a medium that can dynamically simulate the details of any other medium, including media that cannot exist physically. It is not a tool, although it can act like many tools. It is the first metamedium, and as such it has degrees of freedom for representation and expression never before encountered and as yet barely investigated.[9]

This may mean that one can simultaneously inhabit and redesign a design world, an idea that is especially interesting with regard to generative structures. One can tweak the algorithms as they run.

We have seen the role of structure, particularly generative structure, in several contexts already: the syntax of notation, the design of an interface, the constructions of a type, the essence of a medium. In each of these contexts, structure is revealed in transformation. Notational structure suggests transformations, independent of content. Interface structure invites the application of specifically focused software tools to abstract digital media. Design worlds are structured by distinct repertoires of operations on particular vocabularies. Pushing the stuff of medium, be it bits or atoms, reveals affordances and constraints, and invites workmanship. All of these are forms of exploration, improvisation, and, to use the simplest word, play.

Recognition and Discovery

Recall that both vision and computation are quite prone to abstraction, and that the point is to get them to coincide. Here is where this can happen: the eye, more than the hand, can sense algorithmic beauty, see evolution in action, and recognize desirable states in the dynamic flux of forms.

Computation and vision combine playfully for invention and discovery. Like the hand, the eye is playful. It loves computing, where it comes up with such improbabilities as flying toasters. How else but with the eyes can you tell when you have found something?

In traditional craft, the eye constantly monitors the effect of the hands to guide the work toward some abstract vision. One might argue that the ability to recognize correctly emerging results was intrinsic to traditional crafts. If you had seen enough similar artifacts before and lived with them all your life, it was fairly easy to make another one. Because each piece was slightly different, there was always room for a bit of experimentation. Because the conduct of the work was less mediated, there was a shifting back and forth between work and play.

Now the same may begin to occur in computing, but under slightly different conditions. First, as noted much earlier, the eye is elsewhere than upon the hand itself: hand-eye coordination changes. Second, the effect of the hand is given leverage by generative structures. One might say that the hand need only steer. This acceleration, amplification, or transformation makes the role of the eye all the more important. The hand, even if fully, sensuously engaged, cannot feel its way. The eye is the monitor of abstraction.

What the eye does best, especially in comparison to computers, is to recognize. We come upon configurations. We see more than we can think of. We appraise. We come upon structural equivalencies—through "seeing as." We discover. Here again, craft is more sensitivity than invention.

Hand-eye coordination has its particular ways of learning, play, and discovery. The reversible and proliferating natures of operations on structures of bits enable this coordination to develop. The algorithmic beauty of generative structures gives new meaning to the truism that vision is the innate sense of order.

Playful coordination produces the best single record of craft. The beauty of the object derives from the quality of the work: not only workmanship but also playful vision. Outer beauty reflects inner beauty, and rediscovering aesthetic and intellectual pleasure is part of the design and craft process.[10] The relation of work and play is the source of style and beauty.

Toward the end of a long compilation of scholarly papers on play, the eminent psychologist Jerome Bruner included a short piece of his own entitled "On Craft, Creativity, and Surprise."[11] It tells the story in just five hundred words:

> If the creative product has about it anything unique, it is its quality of surprise. It surprises, yet is familiar, fits the shape of human experience. Whether truth or fiction, it has verisimilitude.
>
> Surprise in the creative takes three forms. One is the surprise of the fitting but unlikely, an empirical or functional surprise. "How clever to use *that* in *that* way!" Psychologists use the principle in a "multiple uses test" to find whether someone uses objects creatively. Empirical surprise is ingenious rather than deep. Consider formal surprise, by contrast. Take a hand of bridge. Any hand is equally unlikely. Some are extremely interesting—all spades, for a case. What makes such a hand interesting is not its improbability but its relevance to a rule structure. That feature is at the heart of formal surprise. Suppose one produces a solution to a mathematical problem that is within the formal constraints of a rule system, yet is shockingly new and yet obvious (once done). Almost inevitably, such a

product will have both power and beauty. The powerful simplicity of the great formulations in physics are a case in point.

Formal surprise is also to be found in music. Music has structure; composers have signatures within that structure. One can simulate Bach-like or Mozart-like music by computer. It is quite banal. Yet both Bach and Mozart used the same sort of "programme" and produced surprises—and not just historical ones. Their nature is harder to characterize since music lacks anything by way of the truth-testability of elegant scientific formulations or the consistency tests of logic.

Finally, there is metaphoric surprise. Its shock value depends upon that structured medium of language and symbols. Metaphoric surprise opens new connections in awareness, relates where relations were not before suspected. Eliot's line "I should have been a pair of ragged claws/Scuttling across the floors of silent seas" bring together furtive darkness beneath the sea with the dark agonies of depression. Why does it illuminate? What does it satisfy? The answer remains obscure.

While our three forms of surprise have creative novelty about them, they are almost always the fruit of disciplined craft. The proverb about poor workmen blaming their tools is relevant. Auden comments that a poet likes to "hang around words". Good painters cannot let go; neither can the good mathematician, though his hanging on (like Lewis Carroll's) may be full of fun. For the production of creative surprise demands a masterful control of the medium. It is not the act of spontaneous seizure, an act of sudden glory. Music and mathematics give gifts to the well-prepared. So, too, poetry, and engineering. How curious that surprise grows in the soil of grinding work. A woman at a dinner party is alleged to have said to Alfred North Whitehead, "We are all philosophers, you know." "Yes," he agreed, "but some of us spend all day at it."

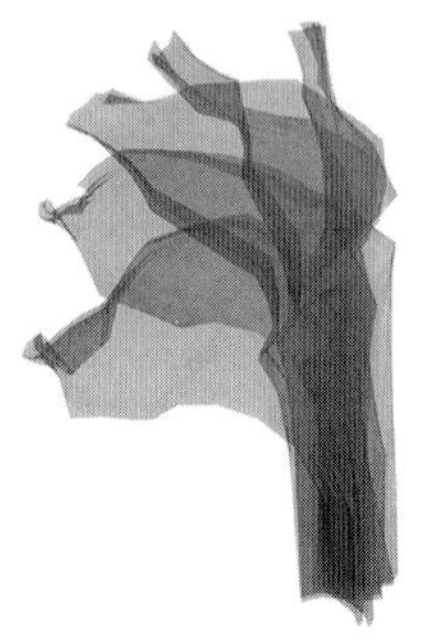

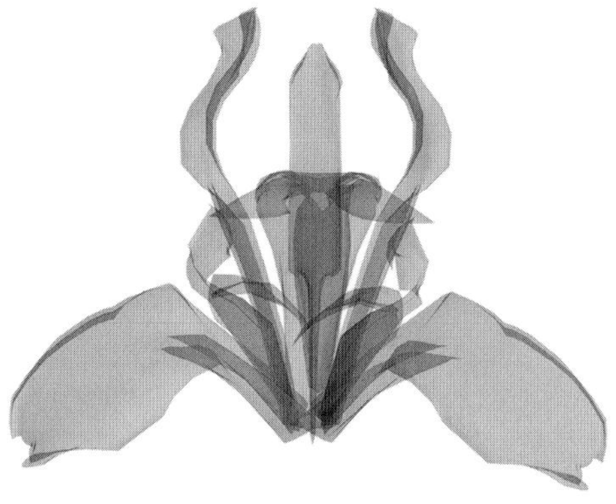

8.1 Freeform modeling using spline surface lofting

8.2 Structured improvisations in reflectivity and transparency

8.3 Improvised refinements of texture: a series of quick (five-minute) studies using ray-tracing techniques

8.4 Improvisations on informal structure: freely inflected blocks in quick sketch models in CAD

8.5 Structured improvisations in diffuse lighting using radiosity-rendering techniques

8.6 Generative worlds in "liquid architectures": navigable form produced by spatialization of genetic algorithms

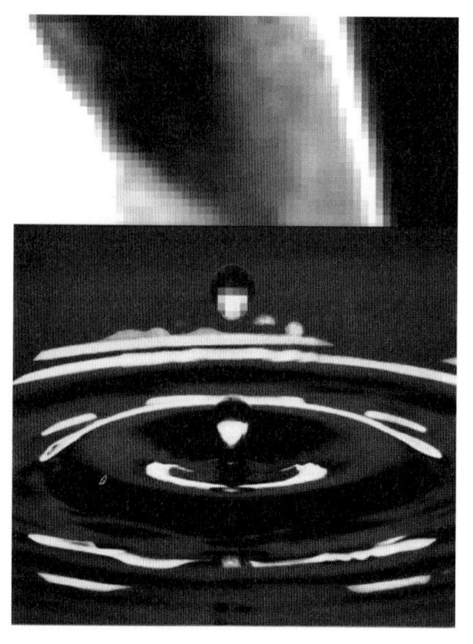

9 Practice

Near the end of the sixteen-year run of *The Craftsman,* the magazine's founding publisher Gustav Stickley ran an editorial entitled "The Truth About Work." Like most of the views published in this magazine, his truth was simple enough: through practice we rediscover intrinsic beauty, the interrelation of work and play, and the folly of separating art from practical production.

> As we have so often said, it is work which creates to meet a need, and creates sincerely and as vitally as possible, that is responsible for practically all permanent beauty outside of that in which nature herself is the craftsman. But there is much to be understood in connection with the word 'work', which most of us have never taken into consideration. Work, especially in America, has come to mean the ignominious, arduous performance of duty, to be accomplished in a state of coma, and to be finished swiftly, to be forgotten. . .

> The plea which *The Craftsman* wishes to make is for intelligent labor which meets a practical need and which is also productive of beauty; which is wiser than play because it includes the element of play and yet leads to results; is more lasting in effect than work unrelated to life because it is the result of enlightened purpose . . .
>
> We have lost the knowledge of what a stupendous force work is and should be in the development of the individual, and we have forgotten the great lessons of restraint, concentration, and discipline which work, and work only, can teach the youth of a land.[1]

Almost from its inception, the Arts and Crafts movement had been criticized as being out of touch with modern thought, yet here in its wish to motivate was its legitimacy. *The Craftsman* argued that, if nothing else, it would elevate popular taste by reacquainting people with the nature of how things are made. "The Arts and Crafts movement ought to bring a better standard to industrial work, and to establish a permanent demand for better things."[2] It sought neither to antagonize the advocates of machinery, nor to achieve its ends by reversion to primitive methods, but only to educate, and to set practices in motion.

> [Even] the work of the genuine amateur holds forth much of promise. From the ranks of amateurs come many who are tempted beyond mere busy work for idle hands, who develop persistence and staying qualities, who come to realize that the study of design is quite as serious and arduous a matter as the study of music or medicine and who learn through their own efforts to appreciate a good thoughtful piece of craftsmanship and thus acquire a real appreciation of relative values of productive work.[3]

The Craftsman restated a commitment to learning and practice for an age where mechanized industry was discouraging personal industry. This ethic was reflected in its motto, "The Lyf so short, the Craft so long to lerne," which it adopted from William Morris, who had revived it from

9.1 ***Als Ik Kan*, Stickley's colophon**

Chaucer. Stickley revived "*Als Ik Kan,*" taken from the Flemish painter Ian van Eyck's shop legend, as his colophon. "If I can" inscribed to each piece of work meant a constant effort toward greater mastery, and that no work was merely competent or executed with indifference.[4]

The movement also absorbed a new dimension of the work ethic from Japan. For in comparison with European practices, the Japanese crafts traditions held a simpler and more sympathetic relation with natural beauty. This was quite an important lesson to Westerners of the time, and many notable designers such as Frank Lloyd Wright were overtly affected. Humble artisans felt its unspoken pull on their amateur works too, and Japanese influence was evident throughout *The Craftsman,* which, for example, often ran reproductions of Hokusai prints.

In *Cha-No-Yu,* the Way of Tea, Japanese tradition demonstrated a clear embodiment of this more respectful attitude toward nature in craft. As one classic English-language book introduced it: "*Cha-No-Yu* might be described as a household sacrament of esthetics, economics, and etiquette." . . . "The ceremony has over thirty specific steps, and a history of masters; yet it is valued for its simplicity."[5] The tea ceremony was a point of view, in which simplicity was not the same as efficiency. Rather than a will to control, it expressed a certain humility, grounded in materiality. This simplicity was evident in the customary utensils such as the *raku* tea bowls, which were the artifacts of most mature craft, and "inexpressibly pleasing to a highly developed touch."[6] Edward Lucie-Smith has observed that "In *raku,* fineness, by a typical zen paradox, meant irregularity, apparent lack of finish, and deliberate absence of technical virtuosity. What the *raku* potters sought to embody was the quality the Japanese call *wabi*—the spirit of restraint and lack of ostentation which is the essence of the tea ceremony itself.[7] Stickley and his contemporaries seemed to understand this moral and practical lesson. The humble sympathy expressed in *wabi* corresponds closely to Stickley's truth about work: "If you understand the truth about beauty and then labor to express it, you have discovered the secret of right, happy living."[8]

Individual Mastery

More than productive daily repetition, craft is a point of view. We have seen its many aspects: tactile play, visual thinking, knowing one's tools, intent with symbols, mental models, software constructions, digital media, generative design worlds. In all these regards, craft is commitment to the worth of personal knowledge. It exists as a form of personal responsibility, unintimidated by institutions, corporations, or science. Yet it is not merely subjective, for its commitment allows us to participate in those same social spheres more effectively.[9]

The philosophical conceptions of *homo faber* and *vita activa* describe work as the making of worlds and goods. Hannah Arendt contrasted this creative impetus with other dimensions of business and labor:

> With the term *vita activa,* I propose to designate three fundamental human activities: labor, work, and action. They are fundamental because each one corresponds to one of the basic conditions under which life on earth has been given to man . . . Labor is the process which corresponds to the biological process of the human body . . .

> Work is the activity which corresponds to the unnaturalness of human existence . . . [It] provides an artificial world of things . . . Action, the only activity that goes on directly between men without the intermediary of things or matter, corresponds to the human condition of plurality.[10]

The things made by work include not only goods, but also ideas and information. Work employs not only tools and machines, but also symbols; it applies not only the hands, or bodily strength, but also the mind. Traits such as patience, inventiveness, attentiveness, even devotion contribute to this kind of work. To practice these traits is the kind of activity we relish. Such practicing gives greater satisfaction than merely laboring (like attending a pushbutton machine) or managing (like being handed the results produced by someone else). This is why more than toil or business, fabrication often becomes an avocation.

Whether it is a high art or a lowly trade, practice can be a calling, or the routine of losing ourselves to that calling. You might practice boatbuilding, or playing the violin, or bending metal. You might become a master, if you have talent, but you will do so only if you practice. You might work alone, or alongside helpful colleagues. You might produce items of value to others or just produce an emotional state of value to yourself. Under the right circumstances, your practice lets you forget troubles, desires, and dislikes, and lose your usual sense of time. Time becomes that of the process; a more subtle focus takes over; and this is the way toward some truth about work or beauty.[11] It is why, in the end, we just want to practice our skills. To live well, we wish to work well.

Working with a computer should be no exception. You might practice laying out images, turning machine parts on a computer numerically controlled lathe, or editing audio sequences. What you do, and how well you do it, will depend at least as much upon the many factors discussed in this book as upon any performance characteristics of technology. If you render images of scenes, for example, that will be because of your ability to see and compose, and your experience with the rendering medium, not simply because you own the right technology and push the right button. Good work reflects attention, and as has been noted, working a digital medium can much more engaging than operating an industrial machine.

To reach a satisfying level of engagement, you must acquire and maintain an expertise: anything really worth doing takes practice. With regard to tools and a medium, you might understand practice as acquiring a working knowledge, or becoming devoted to ever-improving execution. In practice you aspire to transparency, that is, mastering your means to the point where they no longer interfere with attaining your ends. But as a beginner you may have difficulty reaching any subsidiary awareness, not only for lack of sensory-motor reflexes but also for lack of perspective on the process. Habit hones skills, but it also expands sensibility. Even first stages of practice involve more than rote repetition. As any good coach or instructor knows, each iteration of a routine can reinforce a certain skill, test a specific condition, or add a particular new dimension. Through this experience, the neophyte begins to gain a coherent sense of an overall process.[12]

As has been discussed in the context of play, learning a medium consists of exploring its affordances and constraints and developing a basic sense of how things work—what psychologists call a cognitive background. We learn from our exaggerations and mistakes; we accept that beginning work in a new medium will be full of setbacks; but we also look out for discoveries. Often we can discover more easily from demonstration than experimentation: sometimes a few tips or examples from a master are worth more than all the suggestions in an instruction manual. We want to be shown.

Lessons build a faith that a knowingly selected process will lead to effective learning with a minimum of setbacks. Demonstration invites imitation, which encourages a visceral form of identification with the process. This physical empathy seems to make it easier to draw on any cognitive background. For this reason, learning by prolonged contact with a teacher has always been the surest way to master subtle practices. Demonstrative one-on-one teaching is essential to most definitions of craft. Almost everyone who works at a craft has been taught it; almost everyone who works with any proficiency has also taught others.[13]

A teacher learns too because showing is more than simply doing. A teacher deepens his or her own knowledge by understanding what a beginner is ready to learn, knowing how rich but difficult a medium the student is ready to take on, and showing how things are done. Teaching consolidates, expands, and provides an outlet. Crafts teaching is among the most humane activities available to us, and it remains unspoiled by much that has afflicted classroom education today.[14]

As the learning stages of practice mature, you begin "getting it right." Now the frustrations and tedium begin to diminish. It becomes easier to add critical skills by which to guide established instrumental skills. The long road to mastery may have helped you establish idioms, genres, and goals. You now know what to try, or what you want to say. You can shift your focus from your means to these ends. First techniques, then strategies, then mental models all become second nature.

Context and Praxis

With mastery, new level of awareness begins to emerge, and that is of context. If beginners can only follow instructions, and competent individuals solve problems by following rules, then experts are more likely to interpret work in terms of cases. That is, masters respond to context, even when doing so means breaking the rules.[15] As much as any control of tools, a tacit contextual comprehension allows the master to work more quickly and effectively than a merely competent person. This case-based expertise is another usual meaning of the word "practice."

An experienced person often redirects contextual awareness back onto the process itself. It is a good sign of expertise to have a sense of how well one is doing. Imagining process improvements while working also indicates some degree of mastery. But if contextual awareness goes unused, it may be expended peripherally, often in the form of daydreaming or boredom. This is why control of pace and scope of work are so important: workers who have no control over quality have no outlet for leftover contextual awareness except boredom, resentment, and ultimately opposition.

Masters also cultivate contextual awareness in a meditative manner. We all associate feelings with skills, and as discussed in chapter 4, this associative linking complements focalized reasoning. In the case of skilled crafts, the rhythms and sensations of the tools and medium may prompt associations. Practical processes can give rise to independent modes of expression. For example, in Javanese music it is said that the polyrhythms of the mortars for husking rice grew into the percussive orchestral sound of the *gamelan.* In other words, contextual awareness can employ the structure of the process as a framework for meditation. If we work in a way that allows each moment to fall of its own weight, we attain a greater sensitivity, and this state can be come a goal in itself.[16]

In some cases, this meditation on the process can fuse with ongoing intent to improve the immediate result. Considering the nature of a process at a meta-level often suggests where to go with it—what it wants to be. Some great craftsmen go so far as to say the quality of their work primarily reflects the meditative state of their processes.

Contextual awareness also promotes a critical conscientiousness capable of questioning the bias of contexts. This more intellectual mindfulness can be traced to the idealism of Hegel, interpreted by Marx, as *praxis.* Explained as a philosophical fundamental, *praxis* is spirit (*geist*) in action, a way to overcome alienation, a natural approach to the social world that is essentially practical. It remains the best expression of the will to work. It maintains critical subjectivity in a world seen to be losing that trait to externalized knowledge and mediated experiences. So much as any political dualism still exists, this is the oppositional version of the work ethic. For good work there must be intent, for change there must be interaction, and therefore *praxis* cannot be reduced to *tekne.*[17] Much like craft, praxis is subjectivity at work; but praxis remains a more credible tradition among academics, unsullied as was craft by amateurism.

Contextual criticism often operates by reappropriating, that is, by operating in way other than the perceived bias of a situation would suggest. This may occur as a slacker-style deconstruction such as outlined by Michel de Certeau.[18] It may occur environmentally, as in the community actions and appropriate technologies espoused by philosophies of Wendell Berry.[19] It may invest meaning, as in the affirmations of Morris Berman.[20] But in any case the goal remains the same: reshape context to correct bias toward local values.

Few people normally reach such critical or meditative levels of contextual awareness in computing. Personal mental models do shape the experience of a digital medium, and software designs do try to build background contexts conducive to good mental models. But we have encountered only partial successes so far: computing remains very distracting. Part of the problem is that digital tools and media change almost as rapidly as anyone can master them. Fundamental concepts have stabilized in media such as imaging, CAD, and animation, but new features keep appearing, interaction methods evolve, and underlying contexts such as operating systems change. As a result, going back to a feature-laden program like *Photoshop* after, say, a three-year absence is hardly the same as dusting off your trusty old table saw.

Technologists understand that they must build more stable and unobtrusive media. They must establish more coherent contexts into which the technology may disappear. To accomplish this, they must reduce demands for new forms of intuition and make better use of the existing cognitive background that so effectively drives traditional craft learning.[21]

Educators may address this media stability problem too. They must approach digital media at the conceptual level where frameworks are already quite stable—and they must almost expect the circumstances under which these concepts manifest themselves to remain in constant flux.[22] They must counteract the effects of merchandising and chauvinism that surround superficial differences between systems that are fundamentally the same. They cannot simply train as in trade school, nor educate in the abstract as in engineering analysis, but must combine skill and intellect.

The costs and rigors of education have normally placed technology usage in a different organizational context than artisanry, namely the professions. Where the trained craftsperson has always learned mainly through observation and action, the educated professional has first learned a body of rational principles and then applied them to specific cases. In other words, professions have differed from trades mainly by administering bodies of coded knowledge rather than bodies of enactive skills. Now somebody might do both. If the abstraction of craft unites educated knowledge and trained skill, new forms of practice will emerge. Young fields quickly advance their knowledge by informal sharing at conventions, in technical magazines, and in online news groups. New bodies of knowledge cement new kinds of working communities, and these deserve careful attention from would-be artists, managers, and software designers.

Communities of Practice

The relationship of the skilled individual to the working organization has probably received more attention than any other subject in the social sciences. But now as postindustrial conditions intensify, the old labor-management dialectic has given way to newer forms of work sociology. In the process, many previous assumptions about the opposition of craft and technology are simply disappearing. For example, we have noted how with computers the means of production are no longer too expensive for individuals to own and operate. Small businesses and sole proprietorships flourish again, much as before their yielding to centralized factories. Although factories still exist, and continue to disenfranchise the skilled worker, they are no longer the main locus of work. And where technology usage was once delegated to an underclass, now it occupies owners, directors, and entrepreneurs.

Larger issues of postindustrial sociology lie beyond our focus on individual practice here, but must nevertheless influence any study of digital work. For example, the shift from corporate hierarchy to freelance network contributes to the viability of small practice niches. Increasing legitimacy of informal collective knowledge, even within corporations, puts the brakes on procedural deskilling. The rise of social computing suggests that technology has more important uses than automation or information processing. The emergence of more widespread authorship suggests new possibilities for practice.

Although our study has focused on individual, personal-computer-based work, the theme of contextual awareness has resurfaced throughout our examination of tools, media, improvisation, and expertise. Note then that context also includes community. Relationships to clients, coworkers, and other working communities can inform and give value to our work. Networks in particular build context. But before exploring newly networked conditions, consider traditional trades, modern professions, and the procedural organizations of scientific industry for their contributions to our understanding of practice.

Perhaps some ancient artisan practiced completely alone: he who made things just for use by himself or by his immediate community, working with whatever was at hand, may have been completely independent.[23] But for us to argue over who is truly self-sufficient is nearly as useless as to debate about what, if anything, is truly made by hand. It would be better to examine the evolving relation of the artisan and the organization.

Working organizations are built not only on particular technologies, but also shared methods, assumptions, and premises of practice. This is evident in the way that trades have remained a normal working arrangement throughout history. As members of trades, craftsmen have naturally banded together to share a specific training, to learn from one another's talents, and to enable themselves to work in complementary ways. Such communities have inevitably been more capable than lone individuals, for they allow diversification of skills and conversely provide for a sharing of abilities and experiences. Whether around the glassblowers' oven or over the digital color printer, co-workers take part in a heightened sense of productivity. This sense has a philosophical component: shared avocations, reflecting masters' admiration for one another's commitments and achievements. Of course there have been overriding economic and logistical motives as well—commerce in particular. For once people have mastered a way of making things, it is naturally advantageous to band together to make and sell many of them.

Trades that allow some masters to practice a whole process have earned lasting admiration. The important distinction is division at the natural scale of specific practices, and this arrangement reached its apex with the medieval guilds. Notably, unlike an artisan in an earlier age, whose status obtained directly from the wares he produced, the guild member's status obtained from a place in an organization. Nevertheless, the workmanship at the heart of a guild required commitment and risk because irreversible mistakes could be made at any step of the way. As a result, the master artisan was in full control of a whole process.

The steady decline of this arrangement in the face of industrialization was accompanied by the rise of a new organization based on individual expertise: the profession. Because of the generally more scientific thinking of the age—stressing parsimony, technicality, and abstraction—industrial organization grew beyond the point where it could be served by unwritten experience. Industrialization required explicit planning. To survey and develop land, harness engine power, plan factory processes, create manufacturable product designs, and otherwise manage industry in a reliable, predictable way would have been impossible without abstract formulations. The groups that rose to provide these services were professions.

As already mentioned, the foremost distinction between the professional and the craftsman (or laborer) was education. With technology, *tekne* now required *logos*. Science in particular provided a body of knowledge that could form a universal basis of practice as well as a curriculum for aspiring students.[24] Symbolic thinking now become more important than knowledge acquired through observation and action. The aspiring professional learned a body of symbolic knowledge, the intern refined his understanding of this knowledge by application to specific cases, and the expert continually tested and expanded the domain. Practices administered domain knowledge.

Professionals have also been distinguished by their scholastic orientation. While a professional conducted business, he did not exactly engage in commerce, or advertise. There is a historical basis: if the trades grew out of cities, the professions came from the universities, which themselves originally emerged from the church. Individual professional qualification, if not a true priesthood, was at least based on familiarity with classical learning and with gentlemanly status.[25] Professions gave certification a new form, one that only a few gentlemen could afford at first. The liberal arts and the social rank which had traditionally been the locus of general wisdom became precisely the basis for the professional right to use judgment and recommend extent of services, rather than having to deliver on demand like tradesmen.

Professionals today are central players in an information economy. You could say that we conduct much of society's principal business through professions. Donald Schön observed: "There are few occupations that have failed to seek out professional status." "Institutions such as governments, schools, armies, and hospitals are arenas for the exercise of professional activity." "In modern society where almost everyone works, and occupation is a major factor in social rank, most educated individuals aspire to professional status."[26]

Professionalism fits well with the contemporary conception of the knowledge worker. Mere information processing does not suffice: one cannot just amass the most information, but must grasp the best relations. One must move enough data that patterns emerge. In the search for pattern, information technology changes organizations and transforms domain knowledge itself. Much as data become information, so information becomes knowledge—and any of this may build intellectual capital. Knowledge is then produced to be sold and consumed, and even knowledge about consuming knowledge is legitimized: marketing is now a recognized discipline in many universities.[27]

Many disciplinary communities leveraged by information technology reach quasi-professional status by giving overt substance to a shared body of knowledge. Practices based on the union of skill and intellect may often occur as information practices such as publishing, filmmaking, and exhibit design. Creative computing disciplines such as animation, visualization, educational software, and web design spring up more quickly than they can be absorbed into professions or certified as trades. Often they do so in service to the professions, which are less inclined to rush into new areas themselves, and which tend to perpetuate the identity of computers as business machines. Yet rote business automation without organizational change now appears as a version of cultural lag: economic forces are rapidly changing what constitutes practice, and with it the role of the professional.

What ultimately distinguishes productive communities of practice, then, is not so much status as the presence of a shared domain of knowledge. This may be a code of rules, a body of cases, an abstract process model, or a particular configuration of technical specialties. Together such domains form an intellectual capital, ownership and application of which is the basis for livelihood. If a new breed of artisan/professional, using both skill and intellect, is to find a place in the new economy, it must have access to intellectual capital and must recognize and contribute to this traffic in knowledge.

Procedural Organization and Its Limits

Remember that capitalization is essentially organizational. Despite the increasing importance of technological leverage, it is organization, not automation, that adds the most value to production. To illustrate this point, historians like to raise the example of Etruria, Josiah Wedgwood's eighteenth-century proto-industrial pottery factory. Etruria came to dominate its industry without any fundamental changes in technique, but only changes in organizational structure.[28] Wedgwood is most famous for historically inspired pieces, for which Etruria employed celebrated artists to copy motifs from Classical antiquities, which they did largely without regard to the materials or processes in which those would be executed. There was a second component to the work, however: the Queen's Ware, a line of plain, useful fine cast earthenware, produced in volume for what Wedgwood astutely perceived as a newly emerging middle market. Queen's Ware was arguably the first unwitting example of what later became understood as industrial design. For both these businesses, Wedgwood not only manufactured but also marketed, improved distribution, and even influenced taste. In this regard, trading on ideas, he was also unwittingly administrating an information practice. Etruria illustrates the power of an explicit process model. It is a seminal example of intellectual capital.

It is also highly organizational. Within Etruria, Wedgwood rearranged the older piecework model into an essentially modern form: he divided the craftsmen's work into simpler tasks and he recruited and trained semiskilled workers to perform them; he regimented the content and duration of the work, for which he paid by time and not by piece. Upon this model, and without regard to machine technology, Adam Smith built his theories published in *The Wealth of Nations.* Among other things, Smith noted that "parsimony, not industry, is the immediate cause of the increase of capital."[29]

By the twentieth century, parsimony had come to mean scientific management, and scientific process models had acquired a particular notoriety, especially due to Frederick Taylor's management philosophy of disenfranchising the skilled worker. Rather than allowing the discretion of the skilled worker to regulate the process flow, as had been the case in traditional work, Taylorism turned the tables so that process flow now regulated the individual work rate. This was achieved by first reducing the scope of each task to the point where so little skill was required that it could hardly be withheld, conducting time-and-motion studies to establish what was fair to expect, and then enforcing production quotas. In effect, this shifted care from individual pieces to composite processes, and helped establish the assembly line. It transferred control from labor to management, which indicated that if deskilling had already become a reality, now it was made into policy.[30] Perhaps nothing has done more to enforce the stereotypical opposition of craft and technology.

Yet as we are witnessing today, the archetypal assembly line is hardly the final state of industrialization. The historian David Noble has identified it as the third of four successive stages: division of labor, mechanization, continuous process automation, and control systems. The fourth stage, closed-loop feedback command and control, was begun at midcentury, when "war-related developments in electronics, servo-mechanisms, and computers converged in the postwar period to create a powerful new technology and theory of control."[31] Some of these theories formed a very practical basis for a fledgling discipline in numerically controlled machining. Others extended the theory of intellectual capital into a neural version of scientific management, which Norbert Wiener coined the word "cybernetics" to embrace.[32] At MIT, Wiener's work on the theory of messages led him beyond electrical engineering into language, sociology, the structure of nervous systems, and the machine automata that could correspond to all of these. Wiener saw beyond command and control toward a metaphorical equivalence to biological systems, and that within any such cybernetic nervous system, the "brain" would need "hands" too:

> The computing machine represents the center of the factory, but it will never be the whole factory. On the one hand, it receives detailed instructions from elements of the nature of sense organs . . . Besides these, the control system must contain effectors, or components which act on the outer world . . . Of course, we assume that the instruments which act as sense organs record not only the original state of the work, but also the result of all the previous processes. Thus the machine may carry out feedback operations. In other words, the all-over system will correspond to the complete animal with sense organs, effectors, and proprioceptors.[33]

A generation earlier than almost anyone else, Wiener understood that adaptive production would replace the rigid assembly line as the ideal of industrial engineering practice. Cybernetics would involve not only production machinery but also sophisticated process models and self-regulating sensory systems.

Today's flexible-production CAD/CAM shop is a crude embodiment of this vision. Approaches such as computer-aided process planning, group technology, concurrent engineering, rapid prototyping, just-in-time planning, and other such "enterprise workflows" are being adopted by an entire generation of manufacturers.[34] Together these stages comprise an information infrastructure that makes it easier to reconcile business schedules and manufacturing volumes. The direct economic benefits of this flexibility include lower inventory, less waste, less delay, and a larger range of products and sales. We see the abundant and varied results all around us.

But look again. Beyond the coupling of flexible manufacturing systems to management information systems, the leverage of programmed capital trading pushes the abstraction of work toward the point where a global economy becomes largely autonomous. Currently the world's ten biggest corporations make more money than the world's hundred smallest nations, and they do it with the efforts of a twentieth of one percent of the world's people. Some thirty times the value of the gross global product circulates through world financial markets daily. Scientific management has come to means global optimization of capital, and the personal worth of work has come to be fairly incidental. Worldwide, nearly one person in six is unemployed.[35] Many more are underemployed, or employed unsustainably. It is easy to project these developments to the point were we can imagine an economy with no workers, only laborers and owners.

Within the higher echelons of management, procedural rationalism threatens to undermine human judgement until experts become an endangered species. As Hubert and Stuart Dreyfus warned during the furor over artificial intelligence in the mid-1980s, purely procedural competence is less likely to grow into true expertise: "If we fail to put logic machines in their place, as aids to human beings with expert intuition, then we shall end up as servants supplying data to our competent machines. Should calculative rationality triumph, no one will notice that something is missing, but now, while we still know what expert judgement is, let us use that expert judgement to preserve it."[36]

As noted in the discussion of symbols in chapter 4, numerical models cannot represent when they are appropriate. Thus according to its critics, the problems raised by the global mechanism economy are mostly an accounting error.[37] When the operands in the algorithms of the abstract autonomous economy have no human referents; when raw material, both human and planetary, is treated as income, not capital; when downstream or true costs of depleting these resources do not enter the all-powerful numerical simulations; when the incidental benefits of work on the worker are forgotten; then there cannot be *praxis, wabi,* or craft. We are drowning in goods, but lacking in good.

The Place of Participatory Expertise

At the end of the 1980s, just as computer-aided process management was taking hold, industrial historian Shoshana Zuboff published *In the Age of the Smart Machine,* which has become a standard work on the relation of the individual to the automated workplace. Zuboff coined the term "informate" (distinct from "automate") to signify the emergence of an explicit process model—perceptible intellectual capital.

> On the one hand, the technology can be applied to automating operations according to a logic that hardly differs from that of a nineteenth century machine system—replace the human body with a technology that enables the same processes to be performed with more continuity and control. On the other, the same technology simultaneously generates information about the underlying productive and administrative processes through which an organization accomplishes its work . . . In this way information technology supersedes the traditional logic of automation.[38]

Zuboff concluded that in effect intellectual capitalization changes the level at which people work. In support of this theory—which had not yet been generally accepted—she spent years interviewing factory workers. Here is a selection of their remarks:

> "We never got paid to have ideas; we got paid to work."
>
> "Things occur to me now that never would have occurred to me before."
>
> "With all this information in front of me, I begin to think about how to do the job better."
>
> "I think being successful here has a lot to do with imagination. You have to be able to imagine things that you have never seen, to visualize them. For example, when you see a dash on the screen, you need to be able to relate that to a thirty-five-foot-square by twenty-five-foot-high room full of pulp."
>
> "In this environment, the key to influence is not telling people what to do but in helping to shape the way they interpret data."
>
> "It's the process of looking at something from different angles that I find so valuable."[39]

Zuboff also emphasized the limits of hierarchy in "informated" organizations. When skill bases transform to the point where mental agility is required of everyone, the tiers of obedience typical of conventional industry lose effectiveness. "As the work becomes more abstract, the need for positive motivation and internal commitment becomes all the more crucial."[40] What Zuboff found for factory workers bears a striking similarity to what Polanyi had said for scientific researchers. When participation demands trust in an abstract method, and production requires mental models of process, then personal involvement becomes essential.

This is only more obvious for professionals. When things are proceeding normally, experts don't solve problems and don't make decisions; they just do what normally works.[41] Their choice of approach is personally involved. Like craftsmen, professionals practice an art that has an important component of reflectivity. Schön said: "If it is true that there is an irreducible element of art in professional practice, it is also true that gifted engineers, teachers, scientists, architects, and managers sometimes display artistry in their day-to-day practice. If the art is not invariant, known, and teachable, it appears nonetheless, at least for some individuals, to be learnable."[42]

Increasingly, that learnable art involves experience with technological context. We have explored this at length: digital tools serve as metaphors for defining symbolic contexts. A medium is experienced as the structured affordances of context. Better interfaces relieve attention overload by getting computing out of the way, that is, changing it from active task into passive context. Digital production occurs within a highly visual and networked environment, where our primary context is communication.

The social context of postindustrial practice presents limits to procedural policies. For one thing, there is only so far that technologists can instrumentalize and capitalize human interaction without the active participation of domain experts—and experts prefer to intervene only in defense of their judgment and oversight. Thus analysts and ethnographers increasingly contend that instead of being forced to reify and stereotype work practices in service of further automation, members of work communities must be allowed to use social computing as a means of drawing out, enriching, and constantly redefining their tacit expertises.[43]

If there is a unifying theme to the economics of the 1990s, it is the expansion of authorship. Instead of administrating a chain of command, managers create conditions where individuals find and solve problems themselves. This also effects cultural expression: the passivity once associated with both work and entertainment is giving way to something more participatory—"interactive"—which at least means some active response to a dynamic model, or better yet creative contribution to process, and with these a certain reunion of work and play.

Correspondingly, if there is a unifying theme from the personal perspective, it seems to be simply this: *increasingly abstract work takes greater personal commitment.* Perhaps paradoxically, the emergence of intellectual capital increases the emphasis that organizations must place on individual creativity. Deskilling ceases to benefit management, mental agility gets some credit, and informal networks complement deliberate organization. Influence, contingent action, technological structuring, and mutual learning occur primarily, most effectively, and as always, at the level of expert community.

An Ecology of Talents

Not surprisingly, the organizational mantra of the 1990s has become to emulate the dynamics of natural systems. Unlike the detachment and waste of late modern industrial production, natural systems thrive on interconnection, diversification, and self regulation of huge numbers of very small entities. Perhaps the first widely received expression of this principle was the economist E. F. Schumacher's *Small Is Beautiful* (1973):

> For every activity there is a certain appropriate scale, and the more active and intimate the activity, and the smaller the number of people that can take part, the greater is the number of such relationship arrangements that need to be established.
>
> The economics of giantism and automation is a left-over of nineteenth century conditions and nineteenth century thinking and it is totally incapable of solving any of the real problems today. An entirely new system of thought is needed, a system based on attention to people, and not primarily attention to goods—(the goods will look after themselves!).[44]

In an ecology, phenomena occur more at the level of the system than in any of its particular constituents. Systematic stability, sensitivity, transient responses, and long-term adaptability occur at the level of a whole made from a great many parts. Within this dynamic, the majority of energy transmitted is devoted to maintenance and self-regulation. There is minimal waste, and the by-products of one process become the raw material for another. There is no unemployment in nature. Known ecologies exhibit intense diversity of constituents, and moreover, great range of scales and linkages between constituents. Processes often exhibit cyclical patterns, as well as recursive similarities of form between different orders of magnitude of scale.

In *The Ecology of Commerce* (1993), Paul Hawken has applied these principles to sustainable business enterprise. In response to the numerical modeling errors of extractive industry, he explains the need to account true costs and argues that when this is done, small-scale practices that develop rather than exhaust the human being may indeed appear to be the most profitable of all. When social and environmental costs enter the balance sheet, traditional processes emphasizing realtime maintenance and fewer products of higher value may again become competitive.[45] Hawken presents a context for a latter-day artisanry in *restorative* work. If business is about adding value, and the deficit we live under is really because modern business took more than it gave, then there should be value in giving back, in taking care of things continuously, and working in small, incremental ways. The artifacts of this new work include models of material cycles and sustainable systems. Making, keeping, mending, and maintaining, all of which are characteristics of traditional craft with respect to isolated objects, now need to become characteristics of postconsumerist practices with respect to whole systems. Under an economics of true cost, sustainability is the least costly way to work, and thus business and environmental sense become reconciled.[46] But this is anything but a throwback to preindustrial conditions, for there are no low-tech solutions in order.[47] Business ecology consists of using the best of high technology to support diversification, empower small organizations, and model the dynamics of systems. Throughout this work, small businesses have a better chance to sense needs, adapt to new conditions, and respond to local variations. And for individuals, mental agility and contribution of personal values become essential qualifications for work.

Only the internet provides a means to interconnect enough constituents to comprise an ecology. Conversely, the net is a niche-enabler: better

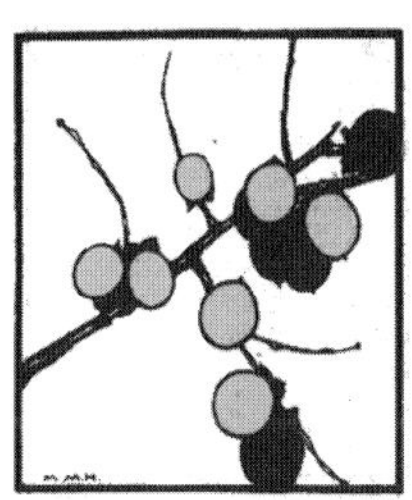

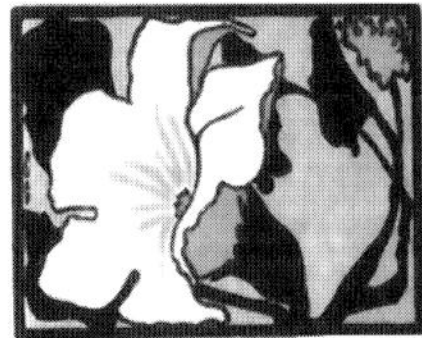

9.2 *The Craftsman* magazine covers used nature motifs

communications allow businesses to occupy very small roles and still be noticed. Broad scope of contact causes small organizations doing similar work in different territories to expand territories, and, rather than go into direct competition, further differentiate their respective services. Larger organizations already in direct competition become more aware of their respective moves, and more prone to match one another, or merge and restructure, or crumble into looser, better-balanced agglomerations. It is not just small is beautiful or bigger is better: increasing scale diversity stabilizes all scales. On the internet, organizations improve relationships with smaller independent practitioners and larger global markets and indicators. One of the chief differences between ecology and late-modern corporate structure is the degree of linkage and similarity of pattern across a greater range of scales.

Furthermore, note that the dynamics of the internet enable more continually adaptive organizational change. As William J. Mitchell observes in *City of Bits* (1995), "We are entering the era of the temporary, recombinant, virtual organization—of business arrangements that demand good computing and telecommunications environments rather than large, permanent home offices." The internet distributes supply and demand for more sophisticated resources—and to more remote locations—with the result that people can often work when, where, and with whom they want. This in turn leads to a more distributed approach to domain knowledge, where the power of the system resides more in adaptable configurations of expert niches, and less in institutionalized territories.

As complexity theorists have demonstrated, such ecological properties as diversity, scale recursion, and self-regulation emerge more effectively in a recombinant realm than under a rigid structure.[48] This phenomenon also corroborates what postmodern theory says about how societies and their technologies continually reconstruct one another. As networks and computing shift emphasis from managing information to mediating relationships, information technology becomes an increasingly powerful means of organizational change.[49] Much like architecture, technological arrangements represent sociopolitical structures, and some do so

Fixed hierarchy	Recombinant network
Task automation	Social computing
Controlled process	Community process
Procedures	Concepts
Deskilling	Mental agility

9.3 Postindustrial management

better than others. As Winston Churchill had so memorably said for the effect of buildings, so now Mitchell restates the matter: "We make our networks, and thereafter our networks make us."[50]

Networked communities are knowledge wells that flow from and sustain highly differentiated participants. These communities find representation in shared workspace technology, such as groupware, liveboards, and virtual studios. Shared space and documents in turn may foster more collaboration, and less contention among individually preconceived agendas, than in conventional business conduct. But at the same time, interconnection builds on noninterchangeable roles, more like a hospital or an orchestra than a command-and-control platoon.[51] It gives the connected specialist an advantage over the conformist or the loner. Even design work, which has long been portrayed as the crusade of the solo artist among philistines, gets recast as negotiation and multidisciplinary exchange. In place of freelancers and power teams emerges a loosely structured community of interests.

Practical digital media are too new, and the internet is changing too rapidly, for there to exist much formally prepared evidence for a new class of postindustrial artisans.[52] But indirect everyday indications abound: proliferating low-cost software, hundreds of social virtual realities (MUDs),

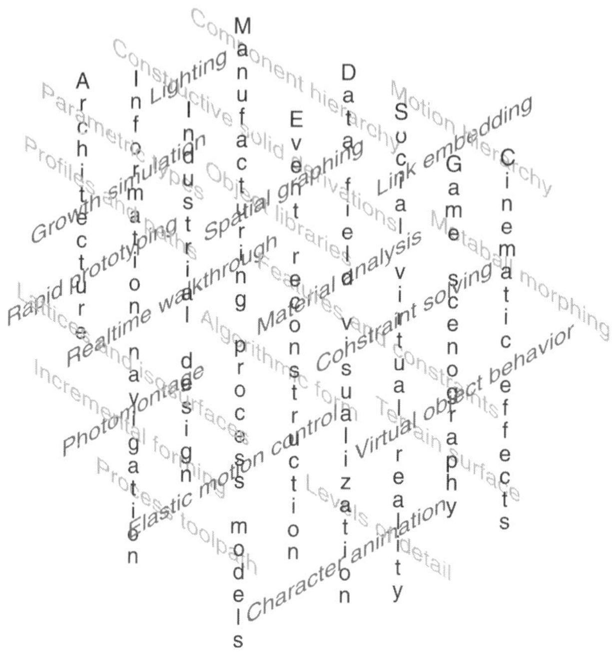

9.4 From techniques to specializations in three-dimensional design

thousands of news groups, tens of thousands of participants at media-related congresses, nearly a million subscriptions to the art-tech magazine *Wired,* a clear shift in business literature toward contingent collaboration rather than structured procedures, and of course the appearance of the word "craft" in so many contexts. Together these phenomena suggest, amid the incomprehensible context of the internet, a healthy future for humanly scaled, personally involved, and knowably talented work.

Plugging In

"Happiness is good activity, not amusement," wrote Aristotle. "It would, indeed, be strange if the end were amusement, and if one were to take trouble and suffer hardship all one's life in order to amuse oneself." The *Nichomachean Ethics* begins its entire discussion of moral virtue on the subject of habit, the very word for which was *ethos* . . .

> Moral virtue comes about as a result of habit. The virtues do not arise by nature, nor [contrary to nature], but rather we are adapted by nature to receive them, and are made perfect by habit . . .
>
> Virtues we get first by exercising them, as also happens in the case of the arts as well. For the things we have to learn before we can do them, we learn by doing them, e.g., men become builders by building and lyre-players by playing the lyre; so too we become just by doing just acts, temperate by doing temperate acts, brave by doing brave acts.[54]

And so should it be with digital craft. As the Arts and Crafts movement contended, merely putting in time at a job is insufficient, and a vestige of industrialism. There is little satisfaction among salary men working only for what their pay can obtain: work itself must provide some satisfaction. "To live well is to work well," the theologist Matthew Fox says, echoing Stickley's position, and that of Aquinas before him, as a creed for the postindustrial world: to work for good, not goods, to work on the human beings themselves—these are the components of a restorative economy.[55]

Such ideals seem far from the hard realities of digital production. We seem to work more for our machines than they for us, or us for each other. As we have reviewed in detail here, computer operations remain quite crude and especially lack enough touch. Like the industrial production protested by the proponents of Arts and Crafts movement, computers' incontestable practicality gives rise to an astonishing amount of banal and cheaply executed work. Their programmatic requirements necessarily stereotype, proceduralize, and level-down subtle aspects of work and practice. Their tool structures and media genres, which are among their more appealing properties, remain without the stability and duration to support cultivated lifelong practice. Moreover, their association with residual assumptions about the opposition of craft and technology keeps many potential enthusiasts and accomplished artisans away.

Writ large, the technology economy seems little better. We build an ever more intractable technical edifice, as if that is what is expected of us. The computer industry's intense impetus to come up with solutions in search of problems, and then to oversell them, invites a backlash of skepticism. The obvious power of postmodern marketing to wedge goods into any fissure in society, thereby driving people further apart and thus multiplying demand for still more goods, both through redundancy and as a substitute for civic life, is especially pernicious in computing. Shall we all end up fortified alone in our home offices, glued to our monitors?

And yet there is room for optimism based on something more than critical resistance. For example, some favorable aspects of modernity remain viable in the webs of postmodernity. As Habermas stated it, "The goal is to relink modern culture with an everyday praxis that still depends on vital heritages, but that would be impoverished through mere traditionalism."[56] Today when cultural production with digital technology claims aspects of nontraditional craft, it is pursuing that same goal. Even amid the premodern Arts and Crafts movement, Stickley had implied a similar orientation: "The modern trouble lies not in the use of machinery, but with the abuse of it, and the hope of reform would seem to be in the direction of a return to the spirit which animated the workers of a more primitive age, and not merely to an imitation of their method of working."[57]

Whatever the likelihood of a virtual Arts and Crafts movement to go with a second Industrial Revolution, creative computing has long since escaped the glassed-in worlds of authoritarian control. And while many people still suffer at back-office data entry, at least somewhere, somehow, others are making the leap from rote computer operations to satisfying practices. We have explored several components of this leap. Networks make artifacts more transmissible, and provide more settings for comparisons and discussions of practice, than to do their grassroots traditional craft counterparts. Genuine collaborations need not interfere so much with individual aspirations as they did in the format of corporate teams. We understand better how the value and meaning of work are socially constructed.

New practices develop critical discourses more rapidly, and communities based on a shared appreciation find venues more easily.

And whatever the timeframe for developing better sensory engagement, computers are already a lot more enjoyable than they used to be. As interaction design matures, software can occasionally stir our imagination with its invitation to build and inhabit mental models. Computers let us improvise better, with more notational density, with more variations possible in realtime, and with that particular merger of continuity and notation so difficult to achieve in material media. Fascinating possibilities emerge to work algorithmically, to experiment with variables of premise and process, in a manner that at the same time involves practices and skillful action. The cultures and critical conventions of an established medium emerge, even if outside the academy at first, much as they once did with film. Probably there is no better approach to what is positive about computing than to explore it as a medium. Already such explorations have shown properties of economy, emphasis, and execution that we normally associate with arts and crafts.

Working with a personal level of motivation and commitment, we have a renewed opportunity for restoring value to the working knowledge of a medium. We have no choice but to respond to the computer, but we are well advised to see that the impetus for work remains with ourselves. The medium is still quite new, and its unforeseen uses have only begun to be imagined. But even if better technologies may be a long time coming, already the needs for sensory balance, habitual practice, and personal knowledge are being acknowledged. Already too, and even with today's technology, we can acknowledge the role of the individual as someone more than a "user." We can suggest that the most important aspect about how to use a computer is how to *be* when using a computer.

You might find that it takes a lifetime to master, or that your workplace discourages its pursuit, but already there is some possibility of craft in the electronic realm. Visual thinking, tacit knowledge of tools, experience in the affordances of media, and intelligent practices all may yet combine to make these devices worthwhile. The quality of the outcome will depend less on the technology than on those of us who master it. The possibility of craft lies not so much in the technology as in the outlook you bring to it. The great paradox of computing is that the better this thinking apparatus becomes, the more we appreciate the value of a conscious human being.

Notes

Chapter 1: Hands

1. Diane Ackerman, *A Natural History of the Senses,* provides the style, although not these words.

2. Christine MacKenzie and Thea Iberall, *The Grasping Hand,* at least admits this incompletion, and summons an interesting breadth of literature to describe what is known.

3. Michael Polanyi, *Personal Knowledge—Towards a Post-Critical Philosophy,* 50. One of the main references here. A rigorous case for participation and tacit understanding in scientific research.

4. For a standard survey on MIDI, see Curtis Roads and John Strawn, *Foundations of Computer Music.*

5. Polanyi, *Personal Knowledge,* 56.

6. Henri Bergson, *Creative Evolution,* 193.

7. Henri Focillon, *The Life of Forms in Art,* 34. A revived classic on the phenomenology of creativity.

8. Ibid., 174.

9. Ibid., 162.

10. Ibid., 180.

11. Octavio Paz, "Use and Contemplation," in World Arts Council catalogue, *In Praise of Hands.*

12. Edward Lucie-Smith, *The Story of Craft,* is an excellent, concise history from which many of the following anecdotes have been taken.

13. Fernand Braudel, *Wheels of Commerce,* 314.

14. Maria Hirszowicz, *Industrial Sociology,* 28.

15. Braudel, *Wheels of Commerce.*

16. Lucie-Smith, *The Story of Craft,* 11. See also Roger Coleman, *The Art of Work—An Epitaph to Skill,* 7.

17. Denis Diderot, *Encyclopédie,* cited in Henri Petroski, *The Pencil,* 76.

18. John Ruskin, "The Lamp of Truth," *The Seven Lamps of Architecture,* 53, 55.

19. Ralph Waldo Emerson, "The Young American," cited in John Kasson, *Civilizing the Machine—Technology and Republican Values in America, 1776–1900,* 123.

20. Kasson, *Civilizing the Machine.*

21. Hirszowicz, *Industrial Sociology,* 29.

22. Sigfried Giedion, *Mechanization Takes Command,* 482.

23. V. A. Howard, *Artistry—The Work of Artists.*

24. David Nye, *Electrifying America.*

25. Herbert Read, *Art and Industry—The Principles of Industrial Design,* xi. A first, best proclamation of industrial design as a discipline.

26. Ibid., 4.

27. Giedion, *Mechanization Takes Command,* 46–47.

28. E. F. Schumacher, *Small Is Beautiful—Economics as if People Mattered,* 141.

29. Nicholas Negroponte, *Being Digital,* 204.

30. Ben Shneiderman, "Direct Manipulation: A Step beyond Programming Languages," in *IEEE computer*16:(8), and cited in interview in Jenny Preece, Yvonne Rogers, Helen Sharp, David Benyon, Simon Holland, and Tom Cary, *Human-Computer Interaction,* 207.

31. These ideas have been well voiced by Bill Buxton, of Alias/Wavefront Research, among others.

32. Mark Weiser, "The Computer for the 21st Century."

33. Nicholas Negroponte, *Being Digital,* 204.

34. Ben Shneiderman, "Direct manipulation: a step beyond programming languages," in *IEEE computer* 16:(8), and cited in interview in Jenny Preece, et. al., *Human-Computer Interaction,* 207.

35. These ideas have been well voiced by Bill Buxton, of Alias/Wavefront Research, among others.

36. Mark Weiser, "The Computer in the 21st Century."

Chapter 2: Eyes

1. Again, a debt to the style, and in some places the very words, of Ackerman's *A Natural History of the Senses.*

2. John Walker, "Through the Looking Glass," in Brenda Laurel, ed., *The Art of Human-Computer Interface Design.*

3. Rudolf Arnheim, *Visual Thinking,* 153, 161.

4. Ibid., 153–174.

5. David Gelertner. *The Muse in the Machine.*

6. The reason-imagery schism has preoccupied Lacan, in particular.

7. Conversation with Floyd Wray.

8. Ken Wilber, *Eye to Eye—The Quest for the New Paradigm,* 201.

9. Ernst Gombrich, *The Image and the Eye,* 12, 178–179.

10. Eugene Ferguson, *Engineering and the Mind's Eye.*

11. Standard MIT Media Lab dictum. Source and accuracy unknown.

12. Marvin Heiferman, Lisa Phillips, and John Hanhardt, eds., *Image World* catalogue.

13. Ibid., 174–183.

14. For example, Jean-Francois Lyotard, *The Postmodern Condition—A Report on Knowledge,* Susan Sontag, *On Photography,* and especially Fredric Jameson, *Postmodernism, or, The Cultural Logic of Late Capitalism.*

15. New York Times story on Champion shirts, 1992.

16. Walter Benjamin, "The Work of Art in the Age of Mechanical Reproduction," in *Illuminations,* 220- 221.

17. Consult the vast literature on deskilling, or just spend a day around the local high school.

18. Oliver Wendell Holmes, "The Stereoscope and the Stereograph," cited in William J. Mitchell, *The Reconfigured Eye.*

19. Mitchell, *The Reconfigured Eye.*

20. Susan Sontag, *Against Interpretation.*

21. Mitchell, *The Reconfigured Eye.*

22. See for example Jameson, *Postmodernism, or, The Cultural Logic of Late Capitalism.* "People don't think so much as they are thought."

23. Ferguson, *Engineering and the Mind's Eye.*

24. Benjamin, "The Work of Art in the Age of Mechanical Reproduction."

Chapter 3: Tools

1. Cited in Matthew Fox, *The Reinvention of Work.*

2. Warren Wake, *TIGRIS—A Tool-Structured Interface and Graphic Interaction System for Computer-aided Design.* This is an excellent exploration of the tool metaphor and direct manipulation. It is one of many initial inspirations for this book.

3. Lewis Mumford, *Technics and Civilization,* 326.

4. Polanyi, *Personal Knowledge,* 54.

5. David Pye, *The Nature and Art of Workmanship.*

6. Thorstein Veblen, *The Instinct of Workmanship and the State of the Industrial Arts,* 304, 307.

7. Gustav Stickley, "The Uses and Abuses of Machinery," in Barry Sanders, ed., *The Craftsman—An Anthology.*

8. Jacques Ellul, *The Technological Society,* 4, 306. Along with Theodor Roszak's *The Cult of Information,* this may rank as the leading antitechnological rant of our time.

9. David Rothenberg, *Hand's End—Technology and the Limits of Nature,* provides an excellent new take on the place of technology.

10. Although this definition differs somewhat from his own, this follows from to Warren Wake.

11. Francis Klingender, *Art and the Industrial Revolution,* 89–90. Klingender and Tom Stonier, *The Wealth of Information,* offer heady views of the two respective industrial revolutions.

12. Karl Marx, cited in Kasson, *Civilizing the Machine.*

13. Veblen, *The Instinct of Workmanship,* 352.

14. Klingender, *Art and the Industrial Revolution,* 42.

15. Ruskin, *The Seven Lamps of Architecture.*

16. Peter Mathias and John A. Davis, eds., *The First Industrial Revolutions,* provides an interesting collection of revisionist papers.

17. Norbert Wiener, *Cybernetics,* 1948.

18. Ibid.

19. Gregory Bateson, *Mind and Nature.*

20. Norbert Wiener, *The Human Use of Human Beings—Cybernetics and Society,* 159. The cyberprophet's recasting of cybernetics for the general reader could be a technology management manual fifty years later.

21. See those Frankfurt School writers on "loss of the subject," or just go to the mall.

22. Teilhard de Chardin, *The Phenomenon of Man.* The post-Darwinian masterpiece is rediscovered by the web generation.

23. Warren Chappell, *A Short History of the Printed Word.*

24. Mathias and Davis, eds., *The First Industrial Revolutions.*

25. Tom Forester, ed., *Computers in the Human Context,* is the best representative collection here.

26. Joseph Weizenbaum, *Computer Power and Human Reason,* 27, 38.

27. Kranzberg, "The Information Age," in Forester, ed., *Computers in the Human Context,* 29.

28. Adam Smith, cited in Klingender, *Art and the Industrial Revolution,* 26.

29. Arno Penzias, *Ideas and Information,* began with ten aphorisms on the fallacies of computation. Literacy was number one.

30. Wake, *TIGRIS.*

31. The main forum is *SIG-CHI: Proceedings of ACM Siggraph Symposium on Computer-Human Interaction.* See also *UIST: Proceedings of ACM Siggraph Symposium on User Interface Software and Technology.*

Chapter 4: Symbols

1. This example is taken from a classic book on the history of mathematics, Tobias Dantzig, *Number—The Language of Science,* 80–85.

2. Ibid.

3. Closure on the operations of basic arithmetic, that is, with the one exception of division by zero.

4. Michael Heim, *The Metaphysics of Virtual Reality.*

5. W. T. Stace, *The Philosophy of Hegel,* 463. Before psychology, there was Hegel on symbols.

6. Hugh Kenner, *The Mechanic Muse,* 117.

7. Steven Holtzman, *Digital Mantras,* 128–129. A significant near-neighbor to this book. Holtzman renews the call for generative, structuralist digital aesthetics.

8. Nelson Goodman, *Languages of Art,* 131–150.

9. Ibid., 114.

10. Ibid., 197–198.

11. Ibid., 221.

12. Ibid., 113.

13. Modern sensibilities that place individual art in opposition to mass production may miss the point here. One piece being as good as the next does not mean they lack unique value, but that they are all good.

14. Jean Piaget, *Structuralism,* 5.

15. Holtzman, *Digital Mantras,* 97–112.

16. Setrag Khoshafian and Razmik Abnous, *Object Orientation—Concepts, Languages, Databases, User Interfaces.* Among so many instruction books, this one is a good representative conceptual summary.

17. Piaget, *Structuralism,* 5.

18. Holtzman, *Digital Mantras,* 18–20.

19. Ibid., 27.

20. Ibid., 51.

21. Howard Gardner, *Art, Mind, and Brain,* 39. Gardner's later work on multiple intelligences, alas not pursued enough here, may serve further arguments on diversifying digital media, in digital craft for example.

22. Penzias, *Ideas and Information,* 46.

23. Ibid., 39.

24. John Searle, *The Rediscovery of the Mind,* 1. Spectators describe a Searle-Minsky axis, in reference to Minsky's countervailing disclaimers about the "meat machine."

25. Ibid., chapter 1.

26. Ibid., chapter 8.

27. Ibid., 195.

28. Gelertner, *The Muse in the Machine,* 7–16.

29. Ibid.

30. Searle, *The Rediscovery of the Mind.*

Chapter 5: Interfaces

1. The best review and discusssion appears in *SIG-CHI: Proceedings of ACM Siggraph Symposium on Computer-Human Interaction.*

2. Alan Kay, "User Interface, a Personal View," in Laurel, ed., *The Art of Human-Computer Interface Design,* 194–197. The word "enactive," has been attributed to the psychologist Jerome Bruner.

3. James Foley, Andries van Dam, Steve Feiner, and John Hughes, *Computer Graphics—Principals and Practice,* chapters 8–10 give an extended treatment.

4. John Walker, "Through the Looking Glass," in Laurel, ed., *The Art of Human-Computer Interface Design,* 441–443.

5. Stuart Card, *Radical Interfaces,* ACM video.

6. Foley, et al., 402.

7. Preece, et al., *Human-Computer Interaction,* chapter 5.

8. Steve Aukstakalnis and David Blattner, *Silicon Mirage,* 29–33, provides a survey of 3D pointing and tracking devices.

9. Diane Ackerman, *A Natural History of the Senses,* 77.

10. Preece, et al., *Human-Computer Interaction,* 337.

11. Aukstakalnis and Blattner, *Silicon Mirage,* 146.

12. See "online references" in this book.

13. "*Fuhlmouse,*" Web reference, University of Vienna.

14. Only practical at a few thousand polygons per second, which is not enough yet for creating convincing virtual spaces.

15. Ben Shneiderman, *Designing the User Interface: Strategies for Effective Human-Computer Interaction,* 286–290.

16. This subliminal rate is not to be confused with the very-high-frequency cycles at which computers in their very essence are interrupt driven; but it is something which some true craftspeople, themselves being the reverse, take as an excuse for staying with nondigital tools.

17. Shneiderman, *Designing the User Interface.*

18. David Mandelkern, ed., *Next Generation Interfaces.* Special focus issue of *Communications of the ACM 36:(4).* One extra degree of summary beyond the more elaborate *CHI* proceedings.

19. Agents are an increasingly prominent research topic, for example at the MIT Media Lab.

20. For example, Morris Berman, *The Reenchantment of the World.*

21. The examplar of this approach is Don Norman, whose books *The Design of Everyday Things* and *Things That Make Us Smart* are standards. See also his Voyager CD-ROM.

22. William James, cited in Preece, et al., *Human-Computer Interaction,* 100.

23. Shneiderman, *Designing the User Interface,* 24, 72.

24. Ibid., 72.

25. Richard Bolt, "Put-That-There."

26. Shneiderman, *Designing the User Interface,* 24

27. Xerox PARC philosophy explains this well. See *The PARC Story,* CD-ROM.

28. Observation by Richard Dodge.

29. Frances Yates, *The Art of Memory.*

30. George Robertson, "Information Visualization using 3D Interactive Animation," in Mandelkern, ed., "Graphical User Interfaces."

31. One of the first and most convincing proponents of semantic spaces was the late Muriel Cooper.

32. Wake, *TIGRIS.*

33. Ibid., 13, 52. Maybe his central idea.

34. Ibid., 23.

35. Brenda Laurel, *Computers as Theater,* notably shifts the balance from computer to human, and from simulation to participation.

36. Jakob Neilsen, "Non-Command Interfaces," in Mandelkern, ed., "Graphical User Interfaces."

37. Polanyi, *Personal Knowledge,* 59.

Chapter 6: Constructions

1. William J. Mitchell, *The Logic of Architecture.* Among Mitchell's several very good studies of constructive design computing, the theory of design worlds is described best here.

2. Gelertner, *The Muse in the Machine,* 118–120.

3. William J. Mitchell and Malcolm McCullough, *Digital Design Media.*

4. In Stewart Brand, *The Media Lab.*

5. The *Pro-Engineer* software has set the standard here.

6. Jami Shah and Martti Mantyla, *Parametric and Feature-based CAD/CAM.*

7. For example the *Max* software works with diagrams of transfer functional hierarchies to create audio works through graphics.

8. Two thorough overviews are Glenn Graham, *Encyclopedia of Industrial Automation,* and Mikell Groover, *Automation, Production Systems, and Computer-Integrated Manufacturing.*

9. David Noble, *Forces of Production,* chapter 8.

10. Sylvia Lavin, *Quatrèmere de Quincy and the Invention of a Modern Language of Architecture.*

11. Mitchell, *The Logic of Architecture.*

12. Ibid.

13. Edward Lucie-Smith, *A History of Industrial Design,* meshes well with his book on the history of craft.

14. Noble, *Forces of Production.*

15. Read, *Art and Industry,* 41.

Chapter 7: Medium

1. Carla Needleman, *The Work of Craft,* 4, 139.

2. The term "affordances" is attributed to the psychologist J. J. Gibson, and was popularized by the industrial designer Don Norman.

3. David Rothenberg, *Hand's End—Technology and the Limits of Nature.*

4. Needleman, *The Work of Craft,* 88–92.

5. Laurel, *Computers as Theater,* 101.

6. Ernst Gombrich, *Art and Illusion,* 376. Still the classic on the nature of representation and the relation of form and content.

7. Veblen, *The Instinct of Workmanship,* 28.

8. Ibid., 318.

9. Ibid., 32.

10. David Pye, *The Nature and Art of Workmanship,* 2.

11. Ibid., 4.

12. Henri Focillon, *The Life of Forms in Art,* 33.

13. Gombrich, *Art and Illusion,* 370.

14. Ibid., 389.

15. Polanyi, *Personal Knowledge,* 54.

16. Octavio Paz, "Use and Contemplation," in World Arts Council, *In Praise of Hands.*

17. Read, *Art and Industry,* 12.

18. Ibid., xvi.

19. Sontag, *Against Interpretation,* 10.

20. Paz, "Use and Contemplation."

21. Sontag, *Against Interpretation,* 11.

22. Marshall McLuhan, *Understanding Media—The Extensions of Man,* 24.

23. Jameson, *Postmodernism, or, The Cultural Logic of Late Capitalism,* 48.

24. Negroponte, *Being Digital,* 18.

25. Ibid., 71.

26. Kenner, *The Mechanic Muse,* 37–61.

27. Ibid., 54.

28. See Mitchell and McCullough, *Digital Design Media.*

29. Laurel, *Computers as Theater,* 113.

30. Polanyi, *Personal Knowledge,* 103, 131.

31. Holtzman, *Digital Mantras,* 276.

Chapter 8: Play

1. Needleman, *The Work of Craft.* Without sampling great numbers of books by craftspeople, it is clear that this book is a standard with much to say to the academic researcher as well as to the folk practitioner. Needleman speaks largely as a teacher and is able to present the reflective aspects of her work in straightforward terms.

2. Karl Groos, *The Play of Man.*

3. Berman, *The Reenchantment of the World,* 136.

4. Gardner, *Art, Mind and Brain.*

5. David Sudnow, *Ways of the Hand—The Organization of Improvised Conduct,* 7.

6. Read, *Art and Industry.*

7. Ibid.

8. Brian Eno, interview with Kevin Kelly, in *Wired* 3.05.

9. Alan Kay, "Computer Software," in *Scientific American* 251:(3),1984, cited in Laurel, *Computers as Theater,* 32.

10. Needleman, *The Work of Craft.*

11. Jerome Bruner, "On Craft, Creativity, and Surprise," in Jerome Bruner, Alison Jolly, and Kathy Silva, eds., *Play.*

Chapter 9: Practice

1. Gustav Stickley, "The Truth About Work," in Sanders, ed., *The Craftsman—An Anthology.*

2. Ernest Batchelder, "The Arts and Crafts Movement in America: Work or Play," in Sanders, ed., *The Craftsman—An Anthology.*

3. Ibid.

4. Gustav Stickley, "Als Ich Kanne," in Sanders, ed., *The Craftsman—An Anthology.*

5. Sadler, A. L., *Cha-No-Yu, The Japanese Tea Ceremony,* 1, xix. Amusingly, Sadler saw parallels in the efficiency movements of modern America, which were spreading from industry into domestic life of the time, much as the tea ceremony had spread from the monastic world into the domestic routines of Japan.

6. Ibid., 1.

7. Lucie-Smith, *The Story of Craft,* 84.

8. Stickley, "The Truth About Work."

9. Polanyi, *Personal Knowledge.*

10. Hannah Arendt, *The Human Condition.*

11. Needleman, *The Work of Craft,* 9.

12. V.A. Howard, *Artistry—the Work of Artists,* 157–177.

13. Needleman, *The Work of Craft,* 112.

14. Ibid.

15. Hubert Dreyfus and Stuart Dreyfus, *Mind over Machine.*

16. Needleman, *The Work of Craft,* 9.

17. Richard Bernstein, *Praxis and Action.*

18. Michel de Certeau, *The Practice of Everyday Life.* The ubiquitous manual on privileging the reader. How to sift, incriminatingly, through the detritus of the junk tribe.

19. Wendell Berry, *The Unsettling of America.* Something of the Buckminster Fuller tradition here too.

20. Morris Berman, *The Reenchantment of the World.* Some might argue that this work is uncritical. Is affirmative praxis an oxymoron?

21. Xerox PARC philosophy. Cf. Brown, Buxton, Card, Weiser.

22. Mitchell and McCullough, *Digital Design Media.*

23. Douglas Harper, *Working Knowledge,* 19.

24. Philip Elliot, *Sociology of the Professions,* 40.

25. Ibid., 27.

26. Donald Schön, *The Reflective Practitioner,* 3–4.

27. Jean-Francois Lyotard, *The Postmodern Condition—A Report on Knowledge,* 4. See also Daniel Bell, *The Coming of Post-Industrial Society.*

28. Lucie-Smith, *The Story of Craft,* 194. Lucie-Smith, *A History of Industrial Design,* 35–37. Mathias and Davis, eds., *First Industrial Revolutions,* 162.

29. Adam Smith, cited in Stonier, *Wealth of Information.*

30. Noble, *Forces of Production,* 33.

31. Ibid., 36, 52.

32. Wiener, *The Human Use of Human Beings—Cybernetics and Society,* 1. The word "cybernetics" derived from the Greek *kubernetes,* or "steersman," which is also the root word for "governor." *Cyber-* may not be the right descriptor for today's ungovernable online spaces.

33. Ibid., 157.

34. New developments occur rapidly here. Try using any of these terms as web search criteria: flexible manufacturing systems, computer-aided process planning, group technology, concurrent engineering, rapid prototyping, just-in-time planning.

35. Paul Hawken, *The Ecology of Commerce,* 92.

36. Dreyfus and Dreyfus, *Mind over Machine.*

37. See for example the Global Business Network web site, including the industrial ecology definiton by Hardin Tibbs.

38. Shoshana Zuboff, *In the Age of the Smart Machine,* 9.

39. Ibid., 74, 75, 86, 290, 368, 380.

40. Ibid., 291.

41. Dreyfus and Dreyfus, *Mind over Machine.*

42. Schön, *The Reflective Practitioner,* 18.

43. Lucy Suchman, ed., "Representations of Work," issue focus of *Communications of the ACM.* 38(9).

44. Schumacher, *Small Is Beautiful,* 62, 70.

45. Hawken, *The Ecology of Commerce.*

46. Ibid.

47. Conversation with Paul Hawken.

48. See chaos and complexity theory, for example Stuart Kauffman, *Origins of Order: Self-Organization and Selection in Evolution.*

49. Michael Schrage, *Shared Minds—The New Technologies of Collaboration.*

50. William J. Mitchell, *City of Bits,* 97.

51. Schrage, *Shared Minds,* 126, 140.

52. Putting such empirical study in the foreground would make another good book, but the choice was made here to gather diverse elements into a synthesized craft theory first.

53. Aristotle, *Nichomachean Ethics,* X.6.

54. Ibid., II.1.

55. Matthew Fox, *The Reinvention of Work,* 6, 21, 34, 56. The radical priest, never likely to be honored by either academics or business experts, makes a postindustrial, postjob case for the moral value of work.

56. Jurgen Habermas, "Modernism, an Incomplete Project," in Hal Foster, ed., *The Anti-Aesthetic,* 13.

57. Stickley, "The Uses and Abuses of Machinery."

References

Ackerman, Diane. 1990. *A Natural History of the Senses.* New York: Vintage.

Arendt, Hannah. 1958. *The Human Condition.* Chicago: University of Chicago Press.

Aristotle. *The Nichomachean Ethics.* 1925. Tr. David Ross. New York: Oxford University Press.

Arnheim, Rudolf. 1969. *Visual Thinking.* Berkeley: University of California Press.

Aukstakalnis, Steve, and David Blattner. 1992. *Silicon Mirage.* Berkeley: Peachpit Press.

Bateson, Gregory. 1979. *Mind and Nature.* New York: E. P. Dutton.

Beggs, Joseph. 1955. *Mechanism.* New York: McGraw-Hill.

Bell, Daniel. 1973. *The Coming of Post-Industrial Society—A Venture in Social Forecasting.* New York: Basic Books.

Benjamin, Walter. *Illuminations.* 1955. Tr. Harry Zohn. New York: Schoken.

Bergson, Henri. 1911. *Creative Evolution.* New York: Holt.

Berman, Marshall. 1981. *All That Is Solid Melts into Air—The Experience of Modernity.* New York: Viking.

Berman, Morris. 1981. *The Reenchantment of the World.* Ithaca, NY: Cornell University Press.

Bernstein, Richard. 1972. *Praxis and Action.* Philadelphia: University of Pennsylvania Press.

Brand, Stewart. 1986. *The Media Lab.* New York: Viking.

Braudel, Fernand. 1981. Tr. Sian Reynolds. *Structures of Everyday Life: Limits of the Possible.* New York: Harper & Row.

Braudel, Fernand. 1982. Tr. Sian Reynolds. *Wheels of Commerce.* New York: Harper & Row.

Bruner, Jerome, Alison Jolly, and Kathy Silva, eds., 1976. *Play.* Harmondsworth: Penguin.

CAAD Futures. *Proceedings on Computer-Aided Architectural Design Futures.*

Certeau, Michel de. 1984. *The Practice of Everyday Life.* Berkeley: University of California Press.

Chappell, Warren. 1970. *A Short History of the Printed Word.* New York: Knopf.

Chardin, Pierre Teilhard de. 1955. Tr. Bernard Wall. *The Phenomenon of Man.* New York: Harper and Row.

Chomsky, Noam. 1957. *Syntactic Structures.* 's-Gravenage: Mouton.

Coleman, Roger. 1988. *The Art of Work—An Epitaph to Skill.* London: Pluto Press.

Dantzig, Tobias. 1930. *Number—The Language of Science.* New York: Free Press.

Davis, Philip, and Reuben Hersh. 1986. *Descartes' Dream—The World According to Mathematics.* Boston: Houghton Mifflin.

Diderot, Denis. 1780. *Encylopedia.* Text selections. 1967. Stephen Gendzier, tr., ed. New York: Harper and Row. Graphical selections published as *Pictorial Encyclopedia of Trades and Industry.* 1959. Charles Gillespie, ed. New York: Dover Press.

Dreyfus, Hubert, and Stuart Dreyfus. 1986. *Mind over Machine.* New York: Free Press.

Elliott, Philip. 1972. *Sociology of the Professions.* London: Macmillan.

Ellul, Jacques. 1964. *The Technological Society (La Technique).* Tr. John Wilkenson. New York: Knopf.

Ferguson, Eugene. 1992. *Engineering and the Mind's Eye.* Cambridge, MA: MIT Press.

Focillon, Henri. 1934. *The Life of Forms in Art.* (1992 edition) New York: Zone.

Foley, James, Andries van Dam, Steve Feiner, and John Hughes. 1989. *Computer Graphics—Principles and Practice* (2d ed.). Reading MA: Addison-Wesley.

Forester, Tom, ed., 1987. *Computers in the Human Context.* Cambridge, MA: MIT Press.

Foster, Hal, ed., 1991. *The Anti-Aesthetic.* Seattle: Bay Press.

Fox, Matthew. 1994. *The Reinvention of Work—A New Vision of Livelihood in Our Time.* New York: Harper Collins.

Gardner, Howard. 1982. *Art, Mind, and Brain—A Cognitive Approach to Creativity.* New York: Basic Books.

Gelertner, David. 1994. *The Muse in the Machine.* New York: Free Press.

Gibson, J. J. 1979. *The Ecological Approach to Visual Perception.* Boston: Houghton Mifflin.

Gibson, William. 1984. *Neuromancer.* New York: Ace.

Giedion, Sigfried. 1948. *Mechanization Takes Command.* New York: Oxford University Press.

Gombrich, Ernst H. 1960. *Art and Illusion.* Princeton: Pantheon.

Gombrich, Ernst H. 1982. *The Image and the Eye.* Ithaca, NY: Cornell University Press.

Goodman, Nelson. 1976. *Languages of Art.* Indianapolis: Hackett.

Graham, Glenn. 1988. *Encyclopedia of Industrial Automation.* Dearborn, MI: Society of Manufacturing Engineers.

Groos, Karl. 1901. *The Play of Man.* New York: Appleton and Co.

Groover, Mikell. 1987. *Automation, Production Systems, and Computer-Integrated Manufacturing.* Englewood Cliffs, NJ: Prentice-Hall.

Harper, Douglas. 1987. *Working Knowledge.* Chicago: University of Chicago Press.

Hartson, H. Rex, ed., 1994. *Advances in Human Computer Interaction.* Vols 1–4. Norwood, NJ: Ablex.

Hawken, Paul. 1993. *The Ecology of Commerce: A Declaration of Sustainability.* New York: Harper Collins.

Heiferman, Marvin, Lisa Phillips, and John Hanhardt. 1989. *Image World* (catalogue). New York: Whitney Musuem of Art.

Heim, Michael. 1993. *The Metaphysics of Virtual Reality.* New York: Oxford University Press.

Hirszowicz, Maria. 1981. *Industrial Sociology.* Oxford: Martin Robertson.

Hodges, Matthew, and Russell Sasnett. 1993. *Multimedia Computing—Case Studies from MIT Project Athena.* Reading, MA: Addison-Wesley.

Holtzman, Steven. 1994. *Digital Mantras.* Cambridge, MA: MIT Press.

Howard, V. A. 1982. *Artistry—The Work of Artists.* Indianapolis: Hackett.

Jameson, Fredric. 1991. *Postmodernism, or, The Cultural Logic of Late Capitalism.* Durham, NC: Duke University Press.

Jung, Carl. 1928. *Civilization in Transition.* Princeton: Bollingen.

Kauffman, Stuart A. 1993. *Origins of Order: Self-Organization and Selection in Evolution.* Oxford: Oxford University Press.

Kasson, John. 1976. *Civilizing the Machine—Technology and Republican Values in America, 1776–1900.* New York: Penguin.

Kenner, Hugh. 1987. *The Mechanic Muse.* Oxford: Oxford University Press

Kepes, Gyorgy. 1944. *Language of Vision.* Chicago: Theobald.

Khoshafian, Setrag, and Razmik Abnous. 1986. *Object Orientation—Concepts, Languages, Databases, User Interfaces.* New York: John Wiley.

Klingender, Francis. 1947. *Art and the Industrial Revolution.* London: Noel Carrington.

Lakoff, George, and M. Johnson. 1980. *Metaphors We Live By.* Chicago: University of Chicago Press.

Laurel, Brenda, ed., 1990. *The Art of Human-Computer Interface Design.* Reading, MA: Addison-Wesley.

Laurel, Brenda. 1991. *Computers as Theater.* Reading, MA: Addison-Wesley.

Lavin, Sylvia. 1992. *Quatrèmere de Quincy and the Invention of a Modern Language of Architecture.* Cambridge, MA: MIT Press.

Lovejoy, Margot. 1989. *Postmodern Currents: Art and Artists in the Age of Electronic Media.* Ann Arbor: UMI Research Press.

Lucie-Smith, Edward. 1981. *The Story of Craft—the Craftsman's Role in Society.* Ithaca, NY: Cornell University Press.

Lucie-Smith, Edward. 1983. *A History of Industrial Design.* Oxford: Phaedon.

Lyotard, Jean-Francois. 1974. *The Postmodern Condition—A Report on Knowledge.* Minneapolis: University of Minnesota Press.

MacKenzie, Christine L., and Thea Iberall. 1994. *The Grasping Hand.* Amsterdam: Elsevier.

Mandelkern, David, ed., 1993. "Graphical User Interfaces—The Next Generation." Focus issue, *Communications of the ACM* 36:(4).

Marx, Leo. 1964. *The Machine in the Garden—Technology and the Pastoral Ideal in America.* New York: Oxford University Press.

Mathias, Peter, and John A. Davis, eds., 1989. *The First Industrial Revolutions.* Cambridge: Basil Blackwell.

McCullough, Malcolm, William J. Mitchell, and Patrick Purcell eds., 1990. *The Electronic Design Studio.* Cambridge, MA: MIT Press.

McLuhan, Marshall. 1964. *Understanding Media—The Extensions of Man.* New York: McGraw-Hill.

Mitchell, William J. 1990. *The Logic of Architecture.* Cambridge, MA: MIT Press.

Mitchell, William J. 1992. *The Reconfigured Eye.* Cambridge, MA: MIT Press.

Mitchell, William J. 1995. *City of Bits.* Cambridge, MA: MIT Press.

Mitchell, William J., and Malcolm McCullough. 1994 [1991]. *Digital Design Media,* 2d. ed. New York: Van Nostrand Reinhold.

Mumford, Lewis. 1934. *Technics and Civilization,* New York: Harcourt, Brace.

Needleman, Carla. 1979. *The Work of Craft.* New York: Knopf.

Negroponte, Nicholas. 1995. *Being Digital.* New York: Knopf.

Noble, David. 1984. *Forces of Production.* New York: Knopf.

Norman, Don. 1988. *The Design of Everyday Things.* New York: Norton.

Norman, Don. 1992. *Things That Make Us Smart.* New York: Norton.

Nye, David E. 1990. *Electrifying America: Social Meanings of a New Technology.* Cambridge, MA: MIT Press.

Paz, Octavio, and the World Arts Council. 1974. *In Praise of Hands.* Greenwich, CT: New York Graphic Society.

Penzias, Arno. 1989. *Ideas and Information.* New York: Touchstone.

Petroski, Henry. 1992. *The Pencil.* New York: Knopf.

Piaget, Jean. *Structuralism.* (1968, tr. 1970 C. Machsler.) New York: Basic Books.

Polanyi, Michael. 1958. *Personal Knowledge—Towards a Post-Critical Philosophy.* Chicago: University of Chicago Press.

Polanyi, Michael. 1967. *The Tacit Dimension.* New York: Doubleday.

Porat, Marc. 1977. *The Information Economy.* Washington, DC: US Department of Commerce.

Preece, Jenny, Yvonne Rogers, Helen Sharp, David Benyon, Simon Holland, and Tom Cary. 1994. *Human-Computer Interaction.* Reading, MA: Addison-Wesley.

Pulos, Arthur. 1983. *The American Design Ethic: A History of Industrial Design to 1940.* Cambridge, MA: MIT Press.

Pye, David. 1968. *The Nature and Art of Workmanship.* Cambridge: Cambridge University Press.

Read, Herbert. 1954 [1934]. *Art and Industry—The Principles of Industrial Design.* New York: Horizon Press.

Roads, Curtis, and John Strawn, eds., 1985. *Foundations of Computer Music.* Cambridge: MIT Press.

Rogers, James, ed., 1995 "The Computer in the 21st Century." Special issue of *Scientific American.*

Rose, Margaret. 1991. *The Post-modern and the Post-industrial.* Cambridge: Cambridge University Press.

Roszak, Theodor. 1986. *The Cult of Information.* New York: Pantheon.

Rothenberg, David. 1993. *Hand's End—Technology and the Limits of Nature.* Berkeley: University of California Press.

Rowe, Peter. 1990. *Design Thinking.* Cambridge, MA: MIT Press.

Ruskin, John. 1849. *The Seven Lamps of Architecture.* 1989 edition, New York: Dover.

Sadler, A. L. 1933. *Cha-No-Yu—The Japanese Tea Ceremony.* Rutland, VT: Charles E. Tuttle.

Sanders, Barry, ed., 1978. *The Craftsman—An Anthology.* Santa Barbara: Peregrine Smith.

Saussure, Ferdinand de [1959]1916. *Course in General Linguistics.* New York: McGraw-Hill.

Schön, Donald. 1982. *The Reflective Practitioner.* New York: Basic Books.

Schrage, Michael. 1990. *Shared Minds: The New Technologies of Collaboration.* New York: Random House.

Schumacher, E. F. 1973. *Small Is Beautiful—Economics as if People Mattered.* New York: Harper.

Searle, John. 1992. *The Rediscovery of the Mind.* Cambridge, MA: MIT Press.

Shah, Jami, and Martti Mantyla. 1995. *Parametric and Feature-based CAD/CAM.* New York: John Wiley.

Shneiderman, Ben. 1987. *Designing the User Interface: Strategies for Effective Human-Computer Interaction.* Reading, MA: Addison-Wesley.

SIG-CHI. *Association for Computing Machinery, Special Interest Group on Computer-Human Interaction.* Proceedings.

Sontag, Susan. 1966. *Against Interpretation.* New York: Anchor.

Sontag, Susan. 1977. *On Photography.* New York: Farrar, Strauss, and Giroux.

Stace, W. T. 1924. *The Philosophy of Hegel.* New York: Macmillan

Stonier, Tom. 1983. *The Wealth of Information—A Profile of the Post-industrial Economy.* London: Thames Methuen.

Suchman, Lucy (ed.) 1995. "Representations of Work." Issue focus of *Communications of the ACM.* 38(9).

Sudnow, David. 1978. *Ways of the Hand—The Organization of Improvised Conduct.* Cambridge, MA: Harvard University Press.

Swenarton. Mark. 1989. *Artisans and Architects— The Ruskinian Tradition in Architectural Thought.* New York: St. Martin's Press.

Tufte, Edward. 1983. *The Visual Display of Quantitative Information.* Cheshire, CT: Graphics Press.

Tufte, Edward. 1990. *Envisioning Information.* Cheshire, CT: Graphics Press.

UIST. *Proceedings of ACM Siggraph Symposium on User Interface Software and Technology.* New York: Association for Computing Machinery.

Veblen, Thorstein. 1914. *The Instinct of Workmanship and the State of the Industrial Arts.* New York: Macmillan.

Wake, Warren. 1992. *TIGRIS—A Tool-Structured Interface and Graphic Interaction System for Computer-aided Design.* Dissertation, Harvard University.

Weiser, Mark. 1995. "The Computer for the 21st Century." In *Scientific American,* special issue, "The Computer for the 21st Century."

Weizenbaum, Joseph. 1976. *Computer Power and Human Reason.* New York: Freeman.

Wiener, Norbert. 1948. *Cybernetics, or, Control and Communication in the Animal and the Machine.* Cambridge, MA: Technology Press.

Wiener, Norbert. 1950. *The Human Use of Human Beings—Cybernetics and Society.* Boston: Houghton Mifflin.

Wilber, Ken. 1990. *Eye to Eye—The Quest for the New Paradigm.* Boston: Shambhala.

Williams, Michael R. 1985. *A History of Computing Technology.* Englewood Cliffs, NJ: Prentice-Hall.

Winograd, Terry, and Fernando Flores. 1986. *Understanding Computers and Cognition—A New Foundation for Design.* Reading, MA.: Addison-Wesley.

Yates, Frances. 1964. *The Art of Memory.* Chicago: University of Chicago Press.

Zuboff, Shoshana. 1988. *In the Age of the Smart Machine.* New York: Basic Books.

Online References

Link rot sets in before books get through press, and the internet citation style changes almost as rapidly as the items, so there is not much use in printing a set of bookmarks (as they were called for one period). However, keyword search is here to stay, and in order to reflect the role of the World Wide Web as a reference for the book, here is a list of general launching spots, search suggestions, and interesting sites. Find them in the latest, most effective manner: the whole idea of the web is that you should not have to know where things are stored.

Arts and Crafts Bibliography

ArtServe

CHI: ACM special interest group in Computer-Human Interaction

Electronic Smithsonian

Harvard University Graduate School of Design

HCI Launching Pad

History of Science and Technology Program, Stanford University

Image Soup magazine

MIT Media Lab

MIT Press

Ragtime: Online Arts and Crafts Resource Directory

Smithsonian Computer History

The HCI Bibliography

Virtual Library: Design

Virtual Museum of Computing

Illustration Credits

Chapter frontispieces by Noam Maitless.

1.1 Hands on clay. Still from *In Praise of Hands*. National Film Board of Canada.

2.1 Early exhibition of television. RCA.

2.2 National Film Board of Canada.

2.3 "Cow with Subtile Nose." Museum of Modern Art, New York.

2.4 "Image Duplicator." Roy Lichtenstein. Roy Lichtenstein Studios.

2.5 "TV Buddha." Nam June Paik Stedelijk Museum.

3.2 Skills chart, after a diagram by Dennis Holding.

3.3 Aldine Virgil. Photo courtesy of Lydia Chappell.

5.6 *Phantom* fingertip interface. SensAble Devices.

5.10 *Myst* still. Broderbund, Inc.

5.11 *Web Forager.* Courtesy of Stuart Card, Xerox PARC.

6.2 Compass. David Mann.

6.3 *Cone Tree.* Courtesy of Stuart Card, Xerox PARC.

6.5 Borromini sketch. George Liaropoulos.

6.8 Relational drawing. Branko Kolarevic.

6.10 Recursive joinery. SungAh Kim.

7.1 Glassblower. Photos by Sidney Waugh, courtesy Corning Glass Museum.

8.2 Reflectivity studies. Wade Hokoda.

8.5 Radiosity studies. Myong Sue Kim.

8.6 Generative worlds. Marcos Novak.

9.4 From covers of *The Craftsman.*

All other illustrations by the author.

Index